The Radical Attitude and Modern Political Theory

The Radical Attitude and Modern Political Theory

Jason Edwards
School of Politics and Sociology
Birkbeck, London

First published in 2007 by
PALGRAVE MACMILLAN
Houndmills, Basingstoke, Hampshire RG21 6XS and
175 Fifth Avenue, New York, N.Y. 10010
Companies and representatives throughout the world.

PALGRAVE MACMILLAN is the global academic imprint of the Palgrave
Macmillan division of St. Martin's Press, LLC and of Palgrave Macmillan Ltd.
Macmillan® is a registered trademark in the United States, United Kingdom
and other countries. Palgrave is a registered trademark in the European
Union and other countries.

ISBN-13: 978–1–4039–9488–2 hardback
ISBN-10: 1–4039–9488–9 hardback

This book is printed on paper suitable for recycling and made from fully
managed and sustained forest sources.

A catalogue record for this book is available from the British Library.

Library of Congress Cataloging-in-Publication Data

Edwards, Jason, 1971 Oct. 3–
    The radical attitude and modern political theory / Jason Edwards.
        p. cm.
    Includes bibliographical references and index.
    ISBN 1–4039–9488–9 (cloth)
      1. Political science – Philosophy. 2. Radicalism. I. Title.

JA71.E37 2007
320.01—dc22   2006044837

10 9 8 7 6 5 4 3 2 1
16 15 14 13 12 11 10 09 08 07

Printed and bound in Great Britain by
Antony Rowe Ltd, Chippenham and Eastbourne

Contents

Acknowledgements

I'd like to thank Diana Coole and Alejandro Colàs for reading versions of the early chapters. My thanks also to Charles Peyton who helped with proof reading the manuscripts. Around half the text was written in the summer of 2005 when I was on sabbatical leave at the Department of the History and Philosophy of Science at the University of Melbourne. My thanks go to the staff there, and to my friends in Melbourne for accommodating me, especially, John, Abigail and Esther Waller.

Jason Edwards,
Birbeck, London
August 2006

Introduction

This book has three main aims. The first is to provide an introduction to some of the principal radical texts in modern Western political theory. This task is more complicated than it might at first sight seem because it requires criteria for what constitutes a 'radical text'. What I have tried to avoid is treating the texts in question as if they belonged to a 'tradition' or 'ideology' that can be described as 'radical'. In fact, a glance at the principal authors under consideration in this book – Luther, Müntzer, Calvin, the Levellers, Hobbes, Montesquieu, Rousseau, Burke, Paine, Tocqueville, Marx, Lenin and Schmitt – should be enough to establish the foolhardiness of any effort to weave together substantive principles of social and political organisation from such disparate material. The primary criterion of a radical text I have adopted, then, is that it be radical in its context: that it provide a fundamental challenge to established ways of thinking, talking about and acting in politics.

Given the importance that has been attached in intellectual history in recent times to social and political context for the recovery of meaning, I have presented the main authors and texts as addressing certain problems in particular historical circumstances. The chapters are accordingly organised around specific periods and events: the early European Reformation; the English civil wars; the Continental European Enlightenment; the French Revolution; the European revolutions of the mid-nineteenth century; and finally the crisis of social and political life prior to and in the wake of the First World War. The texts examined in the chapters are both a product of and an intervention in these particular contexts. However, the character of the texts and the solutions they provide to the problems they address in these periods differ substantially. In each chapter, I have quite deliberately chosen to contrast the texts of authors, writing simultaneously or in close succession, who are usually

1

regarded as political and intellectual foes. More precisely, we traditionally tend to think of these texts in relation to each other as adopting 'radical' and 'conservative' positions. 'Radicalism' and 'conservatism', in this respect, conventionally stand for support for fundamental and rapid change on the one hand and support for established or the recovery of past authority on the other. For example, we might interpret Montesquieu's *Spirit of the Laws* as a 'conservative' text in so far as it calls for a re-entrenchment of the position of the nobility in French social and political life, whereas Rousseau's *The Social Contract* can be seen as a radical text in the sense that it challenges established authority and provides a prescription for popular legislative democracy.

By contrasting 'radical' and 'conservative' texts in this way, however, I want to contest the idea that they somehow subscribe to different worldviews, traditions or at least in any substantive sense, political ideologies. To be sure, it is the case, for example, that Burke's *Reflections on the Revolution in France* largely supports established political authority and social relations whereas Paine's *The Rights of Man* presents a sustained challenge to them. But I claim that it is misleading to see them as originating, respectively, a modern conservative and radical tradition or articulating distinctly conservative or radical ideologies. Of course, later authors in 'traditions' of political thought have appropriated these texts as their own, but that they have done so tells us more about their intentions and the conceptual and ideological world they operate in than it does about the texts in question. It is also possible to read into these texts concepts that may form part of current political ideologies conceived of as complex conceptual structures,[1] but they cannot be considered as subscribing in any systematic way to 'conservatism' or 'radical liberalism' as ideologies.

The importance of context for the radicalism of the texts considered in the book is that it establishes the vocabulary and conceptual resources with which they are constructed. At one level, then, I have attempted to follow the kind of approach to the history of political thought pioneered in recent times by J. G. A. Pocock and Quentin Skinner,[2] one that prioritises political languages and concepts in their historical context. Accordingly, my claim is that both 'conservative' and 'radical' texts in the periods under investigation operate with political vocabularies and concepts that are radical in the sense that they mark a departure from established ways of talking and thinking about politics. It is in this respect that the texts of 'conservative' authors like Luther, Hobbes or Burke, are as much an index of shifting patterns of social and political life as the texts of 'radical' authors such as Müntzer, the

Levellers or Paine. At the same time, in their contexts both the 'radical' and 'conservative' texts contest political concepts and ideologies and present a challenge to established political and social life.

My second aim in the book, however, involves a departure from this emphasis on establishing the radical credentials of the texts in their particular context. It is my contention that we can discern in these various texts written over a relatively long span (around 400 years) a distinct kind of attitude toward political power that is limited to and characteristic of modern Western political thought. More precisely, this attitude – the 'radical attitude' – holds an ambivalent perspective on the nature and function of political power. On the one hand, it recognises and understands political power as a distinct domain of human life and action that can be seen in isolation from others domains: the religious, the moral, the social, the cultural, the technological and the economic. Political power performs a central, if not the central, role in the consti- tution of these other domains. At the same time, political power may be wielded to fundamentally change the character of the modern world. This recognition of the specificity and transformative potential of political power is one to be found at work in these texts, whether 'radical' or 'conservative'.

On the other hand, these texts also disclose a view of political power as inherently dangerous. They are anti-political in so far as they seek a means of subordinating the domain of the political to the religious, the moral, the social, the technological, the economic and so on. The view of the manner in which this subordination of the political should occur and the imperative that drives it, differs across texts and contexts. But what remains constant is the attitude that political power is a menace. It must be overcome and, at least from the Enlightenment into the nine- teenth century, it became widely accepted that it would be overcome given philosophies of history that posited the moral, social, cultural, economic and technological progress of man. But even prior to the Enlightenment, this understanding of the historical waning of political power had been prepared for by the anti-political aspect of the radical attitude that emerged around the time of the European Reformation.

In Chapter 1, I will explore how this conception of the specificity, power and danger of the political domain emerges in the texts of Protestant reformers – namely Luther, Müntzer and Calvin – in the six- teenth century. The 'magisterial' reformation of Luther largely supported worldly princes, who were needed in order to transform the character of the church, whereas 'radicals' like Müntzer directly challenged the secular authorities. However, Luther and Müntzer (and Calvin) were at one in recognising that secular political power was needed to protect the universal Christian community from sin, but that it was a temporary and divinely ordained necessity that was ultimately subject to the kingdom of heaven and which, at the end of days, would be overcome. In secularised form, it is this ambivalent attitude toward political power that characterises the radical attitude in Western political theory.

Of course, the understanding of the specificity and reach of modern political power could only take place with the transformation of social and political institutions and relations in early modern Europe. In medieval Europe, political authority was diffused through a complex and often contradictory structure of overlapping authorities: religious (the Roman Catholic Church); economic (feudal landowners, guilds, merchant leagues); imperial (the Holy Roman Empire); civic (self-governing city states); and sovereign territories under the control of kings and princes. The success of the Protestant reformation was in part due to the support it received from powerful territorial rulers who, during the sixteenth and seventeenth centuries, were increasingly able to assert their claims to sovereignty over local and supraterritorial forms of political organisation, such as city states on the one hand and the Catholic Church and Holy Roman Empire on the other.[3]

The emergence of the sovereign territorial state as a distinct form of the organisation of political power is one of the principal historical preconditions of the modern radical attitude. The texts examined in this book are all concerned, at some level, to conceptualise the form of political organisation represented by the modern state as it appeared from around the sixteenth century. By the time of the French Revolution, organised political power is largely equated with the state. Like political power itself, then, that state comes to be seen as both a vital agent of transformation and also as a great danger to those domains of life in which human freedom is expressed: moral, cultural, social and economic. Organised political power in the form of the state comes to be seen as necessary for freedom at the same time that it represents the greatest threat to its practice. Again, this is the case whether the particular text under consideration is, in its context, 'radical' or 'conservative', or whether it can be seen (appropriately or not) as subscribing to a particular substantive political ideology.

The third aim of the book, which is perhaps less obvious than the first two, is to think about the relationship between political knowledge and political action as a problem for contemporary political theory. The texts that are examined in the chapters below are not, by and large, exercises in pure abstraction. Each of them was written as a distinct intervention into an ongoing political problem. In doing so, they employed a language and a conceptual field provided for in a given context in order to talk and think about the political problem presented to them. Yet what results out of these texts is often a transformation of political vocabulary and concepts and at the same time a radical shift in perspective on the 'problem'. However, as my use of the notion of the radical attitude suggests, there are certain limits on the way in which we think, talk about and act in politics that have been in place over a prolonged period of time. Part of the challenge that political theory faces in the present is to think how we might overcome the constraints imposed for too long on contemporary forms of political organisation and action by the anti-political or depoliticising tendencies exhibited in the radical attitude. We need to recognise what is most important in the texts considered in this book – their recognition and analysis of the specificity and efficacy of the political domain – while rejecting the notion inherited from the Protestant reformation of its subjection and ultimate overcoming. If we accept from the outset that political power is always with us, we will be more likely to concentrate our efforts on how it is best organised to meet specific goals. There is unlikely ever to be universal human agreement over values. A genuinely radical attitude in the present would recognise that our values are largely and inescapably shaped by and realised through political power. As Carl Schmitt saw, such an understanding of the political is more likely to preserve peace when different values collide than the Utopian belief in the end of politics and the achievement of universal agreement.

1
The Reformation and the Radical Attitude: Luther, Müntzer and Calvin

In the introduction we mentioned the role played by theological discourse in the formation of some of the central concepts of modern political theory. In this regard, the intellectual and political landscape crafted in the European Reformation of the sixteenth and seventeenth centuries is crucial. The challenge posed to the Roman Catholic Church by the various Protestant reform movements was not simply theological in character. In the early sixteenth century the Catholic Church still played a central role in Europe, acting as the main force for unity and pacification among the diverse and competing forms of political authority that characterised the late medieval and early modern period. Historically, however, the Church had also promoted division, most famously in the Great Schism of 1054 between the Roman and Eastern Orthodox churches and on a number of occasions in medieval Europe when kings and princes contested the papacy's claims to secular authority. The challenge that was mounted to the Roman Church in the early sixteenth century, then, was not of itself remarkable. The consequences of the Protestant challenge were, however, of incalculable importance for the formation of the modern political system in the West and for the character of modern political theory.

The Reformation oversaw the consolidation and eventual triumph of a form of political organisation that in 1500 was only barely discernible in certain parts of the West: the sovereign territorial state. The Reformation empowered princes, allowing them to contest the authority of the pope while defeating internal enemies in order to establish unquestioned sovereignty over their territories. At the same time, Reformation theology and political theory increasingly looked to the state as the means by which the 'true' Christian faith could be protected.

From the outset, then, Protestant political theory had a radical character. It sought to fundamentally change the world through a reformation of the church. But in the Reformation we can see at work the ambiguous conceptualisation of public power that is characteristic of the modern radical attitude. On the one hand, the reformers acknowledged the specificity and necessity of secular authority, of the 'sword' placed in the hand of the prince by God to punish the sinful and defend the faithful. On the other hand, the Protestant reformers recognised the superiority of the kingdom of heaven over the kingdom of earth. God's will must be done before that of any prince. There was much agonising in both the theology and political theory of the Reformation (though the two are not by any means distinct) about the role played by secular authority in the reform of the church and the extent to which the Christian owed it his obedience. It is often thought that Reformation thinkers can be divided between 'conservatives' like Martin Luther and Jean Calvin, who claimed that secular authority must always be obeyed, and 'radicals', such as the Anabaptists and Thomas Müntzer, who rejected any form of worldly power over men. This distinction between a conservative or 'magisterial' and a radical reformation is misleading, at least with respect to the political theory that emerged out of the period. As we will see in this chapter, Luther, Müntzer and Calvin are all 'radicals', not least in the sense that their texts reveal a deep ambivalence about public power and politics.

Luther

Chronologically and intellectually, Martin Luther (1483–1546) is the figure most distant from us and from modern political theory in this study. Luther sought a transformation of worldly life principally through the reform of the Catholic Church (originally Luther had no intention of breaking with Rome), and not through the reordering of everyday life. What is radical in Luther's texts, then, is his attitude towards the Catholic Church and the view of Christian freedom developed in them. Luther's notion of freedom, when it is announced in a secular form in the seventeenth century, acts as the conceptual foundation for the distinction between state and society. It is worth stressing, however, that this distinction in its modern form would have been, on the whole, unrecognisable to Luther. As we will see, he does indeed draw a line between two realms of authority, the spiritual and the temporal, but these are seen as two aspects of a single order, that created by God to his own design.

Luther's texts are best seen as the product of an absolutely committed Christian scholar working in the intellectual context of late medieval theology. Of course, this does not mean that the social and political role of the Catholic Church in Luther's day did not have a major bearing on the character and reception of his writing. It was the corruption of the church, and in particular the sale of indulgences, that provided Luther with his primary target. Yet Luther was entirely consistent across his works in attributing the failings of the contemporary church not to the character flaws of its prelates (though he was far from slow in pointing these out) but to its misconception of the nature of Christianity. Luther's particular understanding of Christian life was formed some time before he famously posted his Ninety-Five Theses in Wittenberg in 1517.[1] In the face of massive anxiety about the failure of his miserable works, or indeed those of any Christian, to atone for inherent sin, Luther turned toward the idea that was to be at the centre of all his theology and by extension all his political pronouncements: justification cannot be achieved through good works but by faith alone (*sola fide*).

While Luther was not the first to support this doctrine, with its lineage traceable back to St. Augustine of Hippo in the fourth century and more latterly to William of Ockham and the *via moderne*,[2] a school of thought Luther was familiar with through his early theological studies, his articulation of it in the context of the Holy Roman Empire in the early sixteenth century would act as an important intellectual moment in the foundation of a European-wide reformation of the church. The notion that salvation was to be obtained through faith alone was a rebuff not only to the teachings of the Roman Church, but to the practices of simony and the sale of indulgences in which it was engaged; in Luther's eyes these amounted to mortal sins. The repudiation of the administrative financial practices of the Catholic Church, which imposed heavy *annates* on German bishoprics thus taxing princes and nobility alike, was a political boon to those who had come to resent the authority of the papacy. In the early sixteenth century, the Holy Roman Empire was a patchwork of contending sovereignties with the power of the Emperor on the wane as its constituent kingdoms, principalities and free cities became increasingly powerful. Luther's challenge to the Roman Church was thus supported, in what has come to be known as the 'magisterial Reformation', by various princes and nobles as a means of challenging the authority of both pope and emperor. It is in this respect, that Luther's ideas take on the character of active contributory causes of the Reformation as a social and political transformation in which the power of the sovereign territorial state would be significantly enhanced. But we must be careful not to see this strengthening of princely sovereignty as in itself one of Luther's goals, or consider it as a necessary outcome of the assertion of the doctrine of justification by faith alone. In so far as the rise of the modern state as an organisation and set of practices is concerned, what was important the manner in which Luther's ideas were interpreted and used as a means of legitimisation of particular forms of political and then military action.

Luther's aim in condemning the Roman Church's practices against the standard of justification by faith alone was to assert the 'freedom' of the Christian faithful. This is most apparent in a tract written in 1520, 'On the Freedom of a Christian'. The text was written after Luther had been condemned by papal bull, by which point his criticisms of the Catholic Church and the papacy in particular had attracted widespread support both in Wittenberg, the site of the university at which Luther lectured, and further afield. It is a slightly unusual text for this (early) period in Luther's writing: it is not filled with the usual invective aimed against the Pope's agents that had much to do with Luther's initial noto-riety. Indeed it is a conciliatory piece that, at least from Luther's point of view, was a sincere and open account of his beliefs. In it Luther outlines his understanding, based on the scriptures, of the character of Christian freedom. He starts out with an apparent paradox, claiming both that 'a Christian is a perfectly free lord of all, subject to none' and that 'a Christian is a perfectly dutiful servant of all, subject to all'.[3] The solution to this paradox is to understand man as having a 'twofold nature', being divided into soul and flesh, the 'inner' and 'outer' man. Freedom is something possessed by the inner man alone and therefore 'it is evident that no external thing has any influence in producing Christian right-eousness or freedom, or in producing unrighteousness or servitude'. In other words, whatever effects the world has on the external man of flesh, whatever he does with his body, this has no impact on his free-dom. 'One thing, and only one thing is necessary for Christian life, righteousness, and freedom. That one thing is the most holy Word of God, the gospel of Christ.'[4] From this it follows that:

> The Word of God cannot be received and cherished by any works whatever but only by faith. Therefore it is clear that, as the soul needs only the Word of God for its life and righteousness, so it is justified by faith alone and not any works; for if it could be justified by anything else, it would not need the Word, and consequently it would not need faith.[5]

This did not mean that for Luther works had no part to play in salvation. But the point of good works is that they constrain the external or fleshly man and thus instruct men to be faithful to the Word of God. The commandments of the Old Testament remind us that we are born sinners and no matter how much we may endeavour we can never be free from sin. It is for Luther 'impossible' for us to keep the commandments. It is thus that we despair, as did Luther in his youth, at salvation. Such despair is, however, unwarranted. The New Testament provides us with God's promise that if we lead a life in faith and belief, that if we glorify God and have no other before him as in the first commandment, salvation is at hand. Despair over good works is eliminated when we recognise that:

> a Christian has all that he needs in faith and needs no work to justify him; and if he has no need of works, he has no need of the law; and if he has no need of the law, surely he is free from the law ... This is that Christian liberty, our faith, which does not induce us to live in idleness or wickedness but makes the law and works unnecessary for any man's righteousness and salvation.[6]

Luther's claim does not, as we will see, suggest that a Christian need not obey the law of either God or temporal authority. He must strive to keep the commandments as this is God's will and a faithful man must not question the necessity of obeying God's commands, even if his sinful imperfections mean that it is impossible for him never to breach divine laws. But such breaches, in so far as they are minor and do not amount to mortal sin, God is prepared to forgive so long as the sinner is faithful. This is God's promise to the faithful: it is trust in God and not obedience to his laws alone that leads to righteousness and secures salvation.

Clearly, what Luther was not arguing here was that freedom *per se* is freedom from secular or civil law. That would be an unjustifiable secularisation of his thought. Nonetheless, Luther's distinction does serve to place freedom within an 'inner realm' that obtains in the absence of coercion. No one can be coerced, even by God's commandments, to be a Christian. Belief is a voluntary act of faith that one can only achieve when one has separated himself from his worldly attachments, when one has accepted the mortality and evanescence of the flesh. The true Christian is free in so far as he is separate from other men and places God above all else. This view did not lead Luther to adopt a narrow asceticism because of his acceptance that the external, fleshly man is the necessary vehicle in which we must achieve righteousness through faith. God's creation of man in his twofold nature has a purpose. It is only on the 'last day when the dead are resurrected' that men are 'wholly inner'; until then 'he remains in this mortal life on earth' and must work to subject his body 'to the Spirit so that it will obey and conform to the inner man and faith and not revolt against faith and hinder the inner man, as it is in the nature of the body to do if it is not held in check'.[7]

Part of the subjection of the external to the inner man involves belonging to a community of men and acting in accordance with the precepts of Christian charity, 'taking upon himself the form of a servant'.[8] This service extends to placing oneself under and obeying temporal authority:

> Of the same nature are the precepts which Paul gives in Rom. 13 [:1–7], namely that Christians should be subject to the governing authorities and be ready to do every good work, not that they shall in this way be justified, since they are already righteous through faith, but that in the liberty of the Spirit they shall by so doing serve others and the authorities themselves and obey their will freely and out of love.[9]

Fleshly men are subject to the kingdom of the world, a kingdom that in turn is subject to the kingdom of God. The separation of these two kingdoms is itself something that was ordained by God for purposes that are mysterious to men, but even at this early stage in his writings, on the cusp of the Reformation, Luther limits freedom to the realm of the kingdom of God, that is the realm of faith and belief.

Indeed, so clear is Luther about the disjunction between faith and the world that in writings which follow immediately after 'On the Freedom of a Christian', and which are considerably less conciliatory in tone, he claims the church itself should be subordinate to temporal authority. The 'Treatise on Good Works' (1520) was dedicated by Luther to John, brother of Elector Frederick the Wise of Saxony who had acted to protect Luther after the papal bull against him. Luther again affirms the priority of the first commandment, that faith alone justifies and that the other commandments and worldly laws are necessary 'simply because we do not all have or heed faith. If every man had faith we would need no more laws'.[10] In his consideration of the fourth commandment – 'Thou shalt honour they father and mother' – Luther claims, 'after the excellent works of the first three commandments there are no better works than to obey and serve all those who are set in authority over us'.[11]

Significantly, Luther argued that *all* men must be subject to authority, and this applied equally to the pope and Catholic Church, all the more so given their corruption:

> Now if such unbearable abuses are committed in the name of God and St. Peter, as if God's name and spiritual authorities were instituted to blaspheme God's honour and destroy the life and soul of Christendom, then we are certainly duty bound to offer appropriate resistance as far as we are able.
>
> Now these are the real Turks whom the kings, princes and nobles ought to attack first, not in their own interest, but for the benefit of Christendom and to prevent blasphemy and the disgrace of the divine name. The nobility should deal with the spiritual estate as they would with a father who had lost his sense, who, if he were not restrained and resisted, might destroy child, heir and everybody (yet with due respect and regard). Thus we are to honour Roman authority highly as our father superior. Yet at the same time, because the authorities at Rome had gone mad and lost their senses, we must not allow them to do what they want to do, lest Christendom be destroyed by their conduct.[12]

While it is acceptable to resist the authority of a corrupt church and its clergy, Luther demanded the submission of men to secular authority. Men sin if they disobey temporal authority or even if 'they speak evil of the government and curse it'. Temporal authority is ultimately 'but a very small matter in the sight of God'. It is no more than a means for punishing wrong doing, but even where it is run by corrupt men a Christian should obey it for 'my faith in God still pursues its own course and does its job, for I do not have to believe what the temporal power believes'. However, Luther did allow for passive resistance to temporal authority where it 'would compel a subject to do something contrary to the command of God, or hinder him from doing what God commands ... In such cases we should indeed give up our property and honour, our life and limb, so that God's commandments remain'.[13] As we will see, later in his life Luther argues that active armed resistance can in circumstances be justified. But in these early works resistance appears only in the last instance as a response to authority's attempts to commission sinful acts.

The subordination of spiritual to temporal authority is also pressed by Luther in his letter 'To the Christian Nobility of the German Nation', a text that has been seen as announcing a proto-German nationalism. But the claim overlooks Luther's intentions, which were concerned with repudiating what he describes as the 'three walls' of the Romanists. The first of these, that there is a distinct realm of spiritual authority on earth constituted and exercised by the clergy, is rejected on the grounds that it has no scriptural authority. Luther asserted instead the doctrine of the priesthood of all believers, that all baptised Christians are part of the spiritual estate and that 'no one dare take upon himself what is common to all without the authority and consent of the community ... The authority of the office-holding priest is ultimately grounded in the consent of the Christian community: it follows from this argument that there is no true, basic difference between laymen and priests, princes and bishops, between religious and secular, except for the sake of office and work, but not for the sake of status'.[14] In his strongest statement of the priority of temporal over spiritual authority, Luther wrote: 'I say therefore that since the temporal power is ordained of God to punish the wicked and protect the good, it should be left free to perform its office in the whole body of Christendom without restriction and without respect to persons, whether it affects pope, bishops, priests, monks, nuns, or anyone else.'[15] The second and third walls of the Romanists, that only the pope may interpret the scriptures and call a council of the church, are also dismissed as popish inventions with no foundation in scripture.

Luther's account of the character of temporal authority was, then, crafted by his understanding of the misconception of Christian life that had been propagated by the Roman Church to meet its worldly ends. The denial of Christian freedom and equality were the preconditions of the abuse of spiritual office. Despite his florid invective against individuals, such as his main theological opponent at this time, Johann von Eck, and the Pope himself, Luther saw the perilous state of the church as the outcome of centuries of doctrinal error rather than the wilful misconduct of this and that individual. Luther understood history as the necessary manifestation of God's will, ultimately pointing toward the day of judgement which he thought to be imminent. The correct understanding of the Christian life as part of a wider and coherent nature ordained by God was for him an entirely necessary labour in the face of the final judgement where only the righteous faithful would find salvation. The reformation of Christendom was an urgent task, one that could only be fulfilled by an appeal to all Christians and not just by the will of the 'spiritual estate'. Here, then, Luther was clearly a radical. His challenge to the authority of the Catholic Church was, once any chance of reconciliation had been lost, complete. The reorganisation of the church must proceed from the understanding that it was not a form of spiritual estate comparable to temporal authority, nor the manifestation of spirit in houses of worship and the rituals of the sacraments, but rather a community of the faithful that looked only to scripture, the Word of God, as its means of salvation.

This identification of the Christian life with faith in the Word rather than worldly practices required that the Christian had access to the Word in the form of the gospel. The material effects of this belief were evident in the changes that Luther and other reformers such as Zwignli, Melancthon and later Calvin, prompted in the liturgy which was, in part at least, to be conducted in the vernacular. Perhaps Luther's most enduring work, in this respect, was his translation of the New Testament into a form of written German that was comprehensible to speakers of different and often mutually incomprehensible dialects. This act was not designed to have worldly effects, but of course it was a crucial moment in the formation of the social and political identity of modern Germany. The principal political effect of the production of a common written language inscribed in increasingly widely circulated printed literature was, in concert with the Lutheran denunciation of the Romanists, a greater identification between the temporal authorities and the German-speaking populations over which they ruled. It would be teleological to argue that the Lutheran Reformation acted as the origin of the creation of Germany as a distinct political and social space, but as we have seen the Reformation can certainly be taken as a central moment in the consolidation of the authority of the sovereign territorial state, even if this was not the intention of Luther and other reformers.

In the following section, we will consider how this identification of temporal authority with particular religious and linguistic communities was mobilised by other radical reformers to press for widespread changes to social relations by very worldly means. While these reformers had interpreted Luther's works as legitimating such radical action, Luther was mainly consistent in his denunciation of any attempts to use temporal authority to affect changes to social relations. As was suggested in his letter 'To the Christian Nobility of the German Nation', such authority should be strictly limited. This view is reinforced by his most famous text on human politics, 'Temporal Authority: To What Extent it Should be Obeyed' (1523). Again, Luther draws a distinction between those who belong to the kingdom of God and those who belong to the kingdom of the world. The former 'need no temporal law or sword. If all the world were composed of real Christians, that is, true believers, there would be no need for or benefits from the prince, king, lord, sword, or law'.[16] Luther repeats Paul's maxim in I Timothy 1 [:9]: 'The law is not laid down for the just but for the lawless.' Yet the restriction of law and the sword of authority to the faithless is, for Luther, more than a temporary expedient. As no one is by nature without sin, all, including Christians, are subject to the authority of temporal leaders:

> There are few true believers and still fewer who live a Christian life, who do not resist evil, and indeed themselves do no evil. For this reason God has provided for them a different government beyond the Christian estate and kingdom of God. He has subjected them to the sword so that, even though they would like to, they are unable to practise their wickedness, and if they do practice it they cannot do so without fear or with success and impunity. In the same way a savage wild beast is bound with chains and ropes so that it cannot bite and tear as it would normally do, even though it would like to; whereas a tame and gentle animal needs no restraint, but is harmless despite the lack of chains and ropes.[17]

For Luther, the inherent sinfulness of man and the permanent necessity of temporal authority meant that it was 'out of the question that there should be a common Christian government over the whole world, or indeed over a single country or any considerable body of people'.[18] What Luther means here is that there can be no spiritual government in the absence of temporal government. By punishing the wicked and keeping temptation out of reach of the good, temporal government fulfils spiritual government in so far as it provides the space in which faith and righteousness may be fostered.

Again, Luther emphasises the requirement of the willing submission of Christians to temporal authority. The Christian 'pays his taxes, honours those in authority, serves, helps and does all he can to assist the governing authority'. He does these things not for his own sake but because 'he concerns himself about what is serviceable and of benefit to others'. This duty extends to more than passive acceptance of the law: 'if you see that there is a lack of hangmen, constables, judges, lords, or princes, and you find that you are qualified, you should offer your services and seek that position, that the essential governmental authority may not be despised and become enfeebled or perish. The world cannot and dare not dispense with it'.[19] The faithful are called on therefore not simply to obey but actively support temporal authority.

Despite this apparent call to total obedience to all forms of law and temporal authority, Luther's concern in the second half of the treatise was to outline the limitations of temporal authority and to indicate under what circumstances disobedience might be justified. Luther's argument turned around the restricted role he attributed to temporal authority as a component part of God's creation, not as something entirely distinct from spiritual authority but one of its means of satisfaction. Ultimately man must obey God and not other men. Consequently: 'A human ordinance cannot possibly extend its authority to heaven and over souls; it is limited to earth, to external dealings men have with one another, where they can see, know, judge, evaluate, punish and acquit.' Temporal government, therefore, has no authority over matters of faith and righteousness, it 'cannot command or compel anyone by force to believe this or that'.[20] Matters of belief do not confine themselves in a simple way to the inner man but are instantiated in the kinds of action and manner of living he adopts. For Luther, this meant that no ruler could compel a subject to side with the pope or 'to get ride of certain books'.[21] The reference is telling as the rulers of a number of German states had prohibited Luther's translation of the New Testament. To such 'tyrants' Luther suggested that the true Christian respond: 'Gracious sir, I owe you obedience in body and property; command me within the limits of your authority on earth, and I will obey. But if you command me to believe or to get rid of certain books, I will not obey; for then you are a tyrant and overreach yourself, commanding where you have neither right nor authority.'[22] Disobedience in a passive form here is more than acceptable: it is required by a Christian's faith.

It has been argued that Luther vacillated between the complete subordination of all to temporal authority and claiming that in certain circumstances a Christian has a duty to disobey or even, as we will see in the next section, actively resist. Thus in writings that follow 'Temporal Authority', Luther appeared to argue once again that there were no grounds of resistance to secular power. The particular circumstance that informed these writings was the growing popularity of reform among the peasantry in southern Germany. Peasant leaders saw Luther's teachings as a means to attack not just the Catholic Church but the feudal lords who gave it support. This growing movement, under the leadership of Thomas Müntzer, was to launch attacks on the Catholic Church and nobility during 1525 in what came to be called the Great Peasant's War. As this movement arose, Luther rejected its calls for resistance to temporal authority while at the same time castigating the nobility for its harsh treatment of the peasants.[23] In the midst of the peasant uprising, however, Luther penned his 'Against the Robbing and Murdering Hordes of Peasants' (1525), an exhortation to princes and nobles to use ruthless violence to suppress the rebels. The temporal authorities could here act with a clear conscience. Even if a leader 'does not tolerate the gospel' this is no bar to him employing whatever means at his disposal to punish the revolting peasants. Christian rulers should be more circumspect in their employment of force, but if attempts at reasoning with the peasants fail he must 'swiftly take to the sword'. If he fails to do so this is to commit 'as great a sin before God as when someone who has not been given the sword commits murder'.[24] This is a consistently reasoned argument if Luther's distinction between the two kingdoms is maintained. Order in the worldly kingdom protects righteousness in the kingdom of heaven. Thus in his consideration of 'Whether Soldiers Too Can be Saved' in the year following the crushing of the peasant uprising, Luther compared the murder involved in soldiery to the practice of amputation:

> In the same way, when I think of a soldier fulfilling his duty of office by punishing the wicked, and creating so much misery, it seems an un-Christian work completely contrary to Christian love. But when I think of how it protects the good and keeps and preserves wife and child, house and farm, property, and honour and peace, then I see how precious and godly this work is; and I observe that it amputates a leg or a hand, so that the whole body may not perish.[25]

While it may be the case, then, that Luther in 'Temporal Authority' was 'at his most hostile to secular authority',[26] there is no inconsistency between his argument in that work and his call for repression of disobedience and resistance shortly afterwards. It is best to understand Luther's texts not as the justification of a narrow 'political' agenda, but rather as the application of a consistent theological framework to worldly events, events which Luther and others around him interpreted as indicating the coming of the end of the world. The three central concepts that Luther delivered from theological discourse – *sola fide*, the primacy of the gospel, and the priesthood of all believers – are married together in his texts to answer the question of the nature of Christian life, that is what it means to be a true Christian. Temporal authority is justified in so far as it is compatible with the leading of a Christian life, which means that so long as it does not actively interfere with a Christian's faith thus committing itself to the work of the devil, in which case it is to be resisted, it is to be presumed part of God's order. Luther's theological and political thought is, in this respect, continuous.

To the modern secular mind Luther's view of the world seems strange. In that world evil is immediately manifest and poses a constant threat.

The devil physically possesses souls, speaks through human mouths, and appears to people in physical form. Evil casts itself against a natural order that has been ordained by God. Luther's texts are replete with comparisons between this natural order and the Christian life. Thus in arguing that the righteous need no law Luther declares that 'a good tree needs no instruction or law to bear good fruit; its nature causes it to bear according to its kind without any law or instruction'.[27] As we saw above the sinful and lawless are compared to 'savage wild beasts' whereas a Christian is a 'gentle and tame animal'. These comparisons act as metonyms rather than metaphors because for Luther God's natural order is seamless. This understanding of the natural order has given rise to the argument that there is a conception of 'natural law' at work in Luther's texts.[28] Yet it would be far too hasty to see any continuity on this front between Luther and later theorists of natural law such as Grotius and Hobbes. These later authors, adopting a much more explicit conception of the modern state, see secular authority as the necessary product of human nature as this is governed by natural law while at the same time recognising the artificial character of the state. For Luther, the state is not an artifice, a product of human contrivance, but is rather part of God's order in the wake of the fall of man into sin. Luther could not countenance the idea of the possibility of a state of nature in the absence of temporal authority for the reason that he saw sin as an irrevocable aspect of the character of the fleshly man. Government is divinely ordained, a central component of the natural order and not a product of human reason working upon nature.

It might seem, then, that there is little in Luther's texts that resembles modern political thought. This is the case both in terms of his concrete assertions about temporal authority to which, for the most part and with one important exception that we will turn to presently, he gave his full support. Luther's view of the world is strange to the modern secular radical. It is premised upon an understanding of the natural order as everywhere suffused with the mystery of God's purpose, and sees worldly conflict as a manifestation of the struggle between God and the Devil. Moreover, Luther's conception of temporal authority is in a number of important respects not the same as that of modern thinkers, and thus his texts do not even provide us with an understanding of the modern state as an obstacle or means to the radical transformation of social life. What Luther's text do contain, however, are a number of concepts that act as the conditions of possibility for the articulation of the modern political theory. Again, this is not to say that Luther's thought leads either to the modern concept of the state or to radical challenges to its authority, but rather that it contains conceptual resources that are worked on by later thinkers in coming to such conceptualisations. These conceptual resources are produced by the application of his theological framework to a certain understanding of the relationship between church, temporal authority and the Christian life that was widespread among educated Christians in the context of the Holy Roman Empire in the early sixteenth century.

The most important concept that Luther's texts articulate with respect to modern political theory is the notion of Christian freedom. This is not liberal freedom in the modern sense of 'negative liberty'. A Christian has attachments to a way of life that are binding and shape his conduct as the 'external' man, the man of flesh who must obey laws and commandments and devote himself to the well-being of his neighbour. Freedom resides in the 'inner man', in the realm of private conscience, the sole basis for faith and belief. Coercion, for Luther, cannot shape belief. It is beyond this world. The importance of this understanding of freedom is that it introduces a distinction between the private realm of conscience and the public realm of conduct. It is a distinction that it necessary for the concept of the modern state, which is defined by what it excludes: this private realm writ large into the relation between free individuals, which constitutes society, civil society and so on. It is also a distinction that is necessary for radical conceptions of the overcoming of the state and of politics. It involves the depoliticisation of a significant part of social life and at the same time offers a promise of a future free of political power and social conflict.

True Christians, for Luther, constitute a community of equals, not in the sense of worldly wealth or status but of freedom. They were united by their membership of the 'priesthood of all believers'. In Luther's context, it was this idea that was at the core of his radicalism, a radicalism which opposed the Catholic Church and proposed its utter reformation. While Luther had hoped this reformation would occur without violence, at least against fellow Christians,[29] the proximity of the Catholic Church to the politics of the Holy Roman Empire and its constituent states meant that were reformation to succeed this was never a likely prospect. In practice the Reformation took place within states with the community of equals identifying ever more closely with their sovereign. As we have noted, the effect of the Reformation was, therefore, to consolidate the power of the sovereign territorial state. At least this was the effect of the 'magisterial' Reformation. Aside from Luther, the Reformation threw up figures whose conception of the priesthood of all believers led to the belief in the legitimacy of challenges not just to the spiritual authority of the Catholic Church but to the temporal authorities that acted as its defender.

Müntzer and Calvin

The 'Radical Reformation' is a term that has been employed to describe the variety of Protestant movements that, from the 1520s onwards, posed a serious threat to both temporal and spiritual authority.[30] The best known of these were the Anabaptists who, under John of Leiden, introduced a short-lived revolutionary and communist form of government in the city of Münster in 1534–5.[31] Anabaptism as a theology originated in the positions set out by a number of the early reformers who, while broadly accepting Luther's central doctrine of justification by faith alone, were displeased with his compromises with secular authority and his belief that the reformation of the church could occur incrementally. There were also points of theological difference, most notably Luther's acceptance of childhood baptism. These dissenting reformers fell into two main groups: those in Zurich, mainly Conrad Grebel, Felix Mantz and Balthasar Hubmaier, who challenged the main 'magisterial' reformer in the city, Ulrich Zwingli; and in Zwickau, the Luther-dubbed 'Zwickau prophets' and Thomas Müntzer.[32] Müntzer (c. 1489–1526) is often considered to be the most radical of all the reformers.

An important figure in early opposition to Lutheran reform and in the Great Peasants' War of 1525, Müntzer articulated a theory of resistance and of Christian community that has been interpreted, particularly by some Marxists, as revolutionary.[33] There are, however, a number of difficulties that arise from attempting to place such modern labels on essentially pre-modern thinkers. It is problematic to call Müntzer a 'revolutionary', or indeed a 'radical', in anything other than a loose sense. What can be seen at work in his writing, however, is an attempt to articulate concepts that are reliant on a certain understanding of the social and political world as this had been constituted in the discourse of the early sixteenth-century German Reformation. While Müntzer arrives at different prescriptions for action than Luther, like him his theology addresses the question of the legitimacy of the temporal realm. As for Luther, this was not simply a question that could be laid to one side. A 'true' theology and soteriology were, for Müntzer like Luther, dependent on the answer to the question of how a Christian's freedom is expressed in the realm of secular conduct. Müntzer's argument, broadly speaking, was that such freedom can be realised only with the total subordination of the secular realm to the Word of God. While Luther had argued that the confession of the prince was of no consequence so long as the temporal sword was wielded to punish sin, Müntzer insisted that the prince must be a (true) Christian as his authority was based on the trust placed in him by the community of the faithful.

Müntzer's first pastoral duties came in Zwickau in 1520, where his attacks on the Franciscan colony in the city and attempts at reformation were initially supported by Luther.[34] Müntzer's polemics against the Franciscans and against the clergy in general bore the influence of the so-called 'Zwickau prophets', the most prominent of whom were Nicholas Storch and Markus Stübner. The prophets were laymen who believed in the necessity of establishing heaven on earth through a theocratic form of government and were an important influence on later Anabaptism. They rejected infant baptism and claimed that their actions were a result of the Holy Spirit working through them.[35] Luther's would later repudiate the prophets, but in 1520 their influence on Müntzer's preaching was left unchecked. Müntzer, therefore, developed a theological position that departed in important respects from Luther and which led him to different conclusions about the character of worldly authority and its duties. What was most distinctive about Müntzer's position was his belief, like the Zwickau prophets, in the importance of revelation given by the Holy Spirit in the form of dreams and visions. Revelation in this sense takes priority over the interpretation of the written word of the gospel. Thus in his 'manifesto', 'The Prague Protest', he asserts that 'Thomas Müntzer will not pray to a dumb God but rather to one who speaks.' And:

> For the new apostolic church will arise first in your land, and afterward everywhere. I want to be prepared, if in church the people question me in the pulpit, to do enough to satisfy each and everyone. If I cannot demonstrate such a skilful mastery of the truth, then may I be a child of both temporal and eternal death. I have no greater pledge. Whoever despises such warnings as these is already, now, in the hands of the Turks. After this raging conflagration, the true Anti-christ will personally reign, the radical opposite of Christ. And shortly after this, Christ will give his elect the kingdom of this world for all eternity.[36]

This apocalyptic vision of the last days, presaged by the rise of the Ottoman Turks in Europe, is one that Müntzer shared with Luther. But while Luther's premonition of the apocalypse led him only to the search for inner proof of faith, for Müntzer the elect are, by the revelation of the end of the world, called to defend the gospel and the Christian community. As part of God's creation and purpose, temporal authority, the 'sword', must do his will. Its failure to do so is a sin, and those who wield the sword against God's revelation are sinners who must be punished. Unlike Luther, the arbiters of punishment for Müntzer were not princes; certainly not the godless and heathen princes that Luther felt could still fulfil God's purpose by wielding the sword. For Müntzer, then, the line that Luther tended to draw between the two kingdoms was one that only legitimately obtained if, beyond it, those given the trust of the sword acted as members of the community of the faithful.

Müntzer's preaching in Zwickau, mainly to the poor, was regarded by the city's council as inflammatory and he was expelled from his position and from the city in 1521. This event radicalised him all the more. After two itinerant years, Müntzer was appointed as pastor by the reform-minded town of Allstedt. It was in this role that he came under fire from Luther for pressing the temporal authorities to play a more forceful hand in the process of reformation. While Luther continued to maintain the distinction between the two kingdoms, for Müntzer temporal authority should serve the revealed purpose of God. He asserted this claim most forcefully in his 'Sermon to the Princes' of 1524, given his audience a somewhat audacious criticism of the temporal authorities.[37] In the sermon Müntzer defended his understanding of the role of prevision by citing Daniel's interpretation of King Nebuchadnezzar's dream in Babylon. Daniel had foreseen the fall of Babylon and the eventual fall of all worldly kingdoms and their replacement by the kingdom of heaven. Müntzer claimed that the last days were upon them and it was the duty of temporal rulers to take up the sword to ensure the hastening of the kingdom of heaven on earth.

The temporal rulers had to 'learn your knowledge directly from the mouth of God and do no let yourselves be seduced by your flattering priests and restrained by false patience and indulgence'. The role of the temporal authorities was to wield the sword 'as a means to destroy the godless'.[38] Unlike Luther, for whom the failure of temporal authority to use its power appropriately would be punished by God alone and not by man, Müntzer insisted that the failure of the temporal lords would lead to them loosing their authority over men. Müntzer makes this argument more forcefully in his response to Luther's criticisms of him: 'I proclaimed before the princes [in "Sermon to the Princes"] that the entire community has the power of the sword ... I said that the princes are not lords but servants of the sword'.[39] Moreover, Müntzer made it clear that in his view it was the duty of princes to prevent insurrection from occurring by removing its causes:

> Behold, the basic source of usury, theft, and robbery is our lords and princes, who take all creatures for their private property. The fish in the water, the birds in the air, the animals of the earth must all be their property ... The lords themselves are responsible for making the poor people their enemy. They do not want to remove the cause of insurrection, so how, in the long run, can things improve?[40]

It is impossible, on this point of view, to define any realm of things that is not at every moment a matter of spiritual concern. While Luther had separated the form and content of temporal authority, so that it was only the form which, from the perspective of the Word, is spiritually essential, Müntzer was convinced that no such distinction was possible. Godless rulers could not be legitimate ones. The power of the sword is only legitimated when the community of the faithful consent to the manner in which it is wielded. Hence temporal and spiritual government cannot be divorced; it is spiritual government that gives temporal government its meaning.

In practice Müntzer was not arguing for the kind of radically egalitarian measures of the later Anabaptists. In effect he was rather arguing in support of a theocracy in which those to whom the Word had been revealed (not the clergy as an estate separate from the rest of society) would be the guiding hand of the sword. Where temporal authority failed to act in such a manner, then the community was entitled to take up arms in order to wrest the sword from godless leaders and subject the wicked to punishment. The most developed account of this theory of resistance is given in an address, 'To The Assembly of the Common Peasantry' (1525), written at the height of the Great Peasants War. Müntzer had by this time become a leading figure in the rebellion. While the authorship of the address remains uncertain, in style and content it bears Müntzer's mark.[41] It begins by noting God's hatred of disobedience but asserts that there are conditions in which disobedience is the only mode of action available to the Christian. Holders of temporal office act 'as a steward of God', such office having been created 'only to tend to God's lambs'. The only justification for office holders raising taxes is 'out of brotherly love, and in order to use them in the interests of their subjects'.[42] More strikingly, it argued for the preferability of elective over hereditary office holding; examining the scriptures 'one finds in truth that immeasurable, unspeakable and terrible misery and grief have arisen from the hereditary authorities'.[43] This argument is fleshed out by reference to history, with the origins of Roman decline being located in their fall from 'communal government [the republic] to emperors', and God and Samuel's displeasure with the Israelites' yearning for a king, being given as evidence for the unchristian character of hereditary rule. 'In sum, [hereditary rule] is not Christian. The fundamental and true root of all idolatry is the unlimited power of hereditary rulers, which had its origins in Babylon under the first established king, Ninus or Nimrod.'[44]

The central chapter of the address asks the question 'whether a community may depose its authorities or not?' The answer begins with the assertion that a lord's power to act can only be legitimately derived from divine law and not from his own will. If a lord does not act according to divine law, 'simply get rid of him and leave him far behind'.[45] Like Luther, the author of the address portrays the function of temporal authority as part of the seamless order of nature that has been created according to God's law. For him, however, rebellion is justified against authority just as we are justified in destroying trees that bear only rotten fruit, or cutting off a limb to save the rest of the body. Also like Luther, the distinction between the inner and outer, spiritual and fleshly realm is taken up, but only as a means of denouncing his support for corrupt temporal authority:

> Their [princes and lords'] power derives ultimately either from the spirit or from the flesh. If it derives from the spirit, it is just and most pleasing to God, says Paul to the Romans in chapter 8[:1–8]. But if their authority is derived from the flesh, it is devilish and a most openly declared enemy of God. May God pity us that such fleshly authority should rule over Christian people. And unceasingly they may talk about two kinds of commandments, namely the divine, which concerns the salvation of the soul, and the political, which concerns the common good. Oh God, these commandments cannot be separated from each other. For the political commandments are also divine: truly to further the common good is nothing except truly to maintain brotherly love, which is of the highest merit for blessedness.[46]

Quite directly, then, the author denounces any attempt to divorce a domain of political commandments or laws from the divine. The common good, the good of the Christian community, is not a matter for the secular rulers independently of God's laws. Temporal authority is an instrument of the community of the faithful, not something that can rule over it.

The general character of Müntzer's thought and that of other early Reformation radicals was, then, geared toward a rejection of the distinction between spiritual and worldly authority as that had been set out in Luther's writings. The political community was the spiritual community. While a good deal of scholarship on Müntzer and the radicals has tended to portray them either as revolutionaries whose main concerns were secular, or as mystics with worldly concerns, it follows from the character of their thought that neither designation is appropriate. As Müntzer's recent biographer, Hans-Jürgen Goertz argues, Müntzer's theological and worldy goals cannot be neatly separated. In their symbiosis, he was a 'revolutionary'.[47] Yet at the same time, Müntzer's identification of spiritual and temporal government appears profoundly pre-modern while Luther's distinction between these two domains seems to bear more in common with modern thought. Müntzer and the rebels clearly looked back to what they understood as the historical foundation of Christianity in the creation of the apostolic church. For them Reformation was concerned with the rediscovery of this church as a precondition of the coming of the kingdom of heaven on earth. What is striking, however, is that Müntzer and the rebels had, in recognising by opposing the very terms of the distinction between spiritual and political authority, grasped something important about the character of the power relations within which their struggle was embedded. The achievement of the kingdom of heaven on earth could not be brought about simply by a reformation of the church, but required the power of the temporal authorities and, if they were not prepared to commit themselves to Reformation, their dissolution.

Luther himself was to adopt this line of thinking with respect to the position of the Holy Roman Emperor. While his works of the 1520s had only permitted passive resistance to temporal authority, in the 1530s he moved toward the justification of active resistance. This can be seen in his 'Dr. Martin Luther's Warning to his Dear German People' (1531), written in the wake of the Diet of Augsburg of 1530 where some of the reformers, including Melancthon, had attempted a degree of reconciliation with the Roman Church. The Diet broke up with the denunciation of the Protestants by the Holy Roman Emperor, Charles V, and his affirmation that he would take up Rome's part in purging the Empire of heresy by force if the Protestants did not cease to publish and proselytise within six months. Luther sought to anticipate such action and to set out the correct response of the faithful:

> This is my sincere advice: If the emperor should issue a call to arms against us on behalf of the pope or because of our teachings, as the papists at present horribly gloat and boast – though I do not yet

expect this of the emperor – no one should lend himself to it or obey the emperor in this event. All may rest assured that God has strictly forbidden compliance with such a command of the emperor.[48]

This is consistent with his earlier argument in 'On Temporal Authority' that passive resistance is legitimated where a ruler attempts to force the believer to act in a manner contrary to his faith. However, Luther goes further arguing that active resistance against a godless ruler employing force to persecute the faithful is legitimate. Insurrection is not acceptable, but 'if the papists – our devil – refuse to keep the peace and, impenitently raging against the holy spirit with their persistent abominations, insist on war, and thereby get their heads bloodied or even perish, I want to witness publicly here that this was not my doing, nor did I give any cause for it'.[49]

The position that Luther took on the question of resistance to temporal authority remained consistent throughout his writings, with the emphasis mainly on the duty to obey regardless of the godliness of the ruler or his laws. The only time when resistance was ever justified was when the faith of the believer was under threat, in which circumstances the Pauline maxim that obedience to God takes priority over obedience to man comes into play. Even in these circumstances, resistance should largely take a passive form, with the faithful refusing to abide by the offending laws or to take up the offending roles of temporal authority. The injunction to active resistance in the 'Warning' is clearly made with some hesitation, and comes again only after Luther has restated his doctrine of obedience and the justification of passive resistance alone. It is clear that the variation that occurs in Luther's texts on the question of obedience and the character of resistance is related to the balance of political forces in the context in which he was writing, and the effects of that balance on the ongoing reformation of the church. Thus in the early years of the Reformation, when Luther realised the importance of magisterial support, he emphasised the duty to obey. After the Diet of Worms, his excommunication, and exile in the Wartburg Castle, he provides the strongest statement of this duty. It was at this time that his authority was being challenged by Müntzer and the radicals. Yet there are other points at which Luther is prepared to advocate forms of resistance in given political contexts, such as in 1523 in 'On Temporal Authority' when the authorities were burning his translation of the New Testament, and after Charles V's statement of his intention to crush heresy at the Diet of Worms.

Similar shifts in emphasis on obedience and resistance according to the balance of political forces and the prospects for future reformation are also apparent in the texts of Jean Calvin (1509–64), alongside Luther the most important reformer of the period. Indeed, it might be said that Calvin is of greater significance in the sense that the movement he founded was to have more far-reaching effects than did the Lutherans. After Luther's death and Charles V's defeat of the Protestant reformers of the Schmalkaldic League at Mühlberg in 1547, it was Calvin and Calvinism that were at the forefront of the more powerful second-wave of the Reformation. By the end of the sixteenth century Calvinism had become established in France, the Netherlands and Scotland, and its effects on those countries and their near neighbours were to be felt throughout the seventeenth and eighteenth centuries. During Calvin's life, however, his influence was mainly confined to the city of Geneva. While Calvin originally saw his task as the reformation of the church in Geneva in line with the reforms that had taken place under the auspices of Luther and Zwingli, that is a break with Rome and changes to the practices of religious life to affirm the brotherhood of the Christian community, he eventually came to see the church as having a role in the social and political life of Geneva.[50] Calvin would develop what Sheldon Wolin has described as 'a political theory of church government'.[51]

This theory was by necessity shaped by the political conditions of Geneva during the early Reformation. Geneva fell into the broader pattern: an autonomous city state (which had recently gained its independence from Savoy) whose city council invited a reformist theologian to reshape the church within the city, the aim being to stave off the anarchy threatened by radicals like Müntzer and the Anabaptists who followed him, while at the same time maintaining political independence by preventing a return to the Catholic fold.[52] Calvin, who was educated in Paris before turning to the cause of reformation in the early 1530s and being forced into itinerancy, arrived in Geneva in 1536, where his reputation as a reformer had already been established by the publication of the first edition of *Institutes of the Christian Religion* in the previous year.[53] He was invited by Guillaume Farel, who had already begun the reform of the church in the city with the council's mandate, to join him. Farel and Calvin's reforms were initially unpopular: they insisted that all citizens subscribe to articles of their Confession of Faith and that the church have the authority to discipline those who failed so to do. This was seen as interference in political affairs by many citizens and magistrates.[54] Early reformation anti-clericism was strong, and this measure seemed to be designed to re-establish clerical authority over the free citizen. Subsequently, Calvin was forced to leave the city in 1538.

Calvin would return to Geneva in 1541. He would never achieve the status of a free citizen, but after his return his reforms proved more popular and he came to exert significant influence over the council and the secular affairs of the city.[55] Unlike Luther, Calvin was concerned to put into practice a doctrine that insisted on the central importance of the organisation of the church for the Christian community. The success of the church required constructing durable institutions which would underpin the faith of believers. Here lies the central difference between Luther and Calvin. It is not, as often thought, Calvin's subscription to the doctrine of predestination that is the real point of difference between the two, but rather his argument that the survival of the Christian religion required more than the faith of the individual believer. The believer had to be part of a community of the faithful that was capable of defending itself without relying on the fickle fortunes of princes and lords. As Wolin argues, the contrast between Luther and Calvin's conception of the role of the church 'was not produced simply by Calvin's willingness to restore a three-term relationship of God-church-believer for the simpler notion of Luther. The real contrast took shape from Calvin's effort to recapture an older conception of the community as a school of virtue and the vital agency for the realization of individual perfection'.[56] The establishment of this community required the rejection of the Lutheran understanding of temporal authority as 'the sword', that is as mere coercive power. Temporal authority was the civil polity, as much concerned with religious virtue as the church. This 'emphasis on a strong church and on the dignity of political society was designed for a double purpose: to make the church safe in the world and the world safe for the church'.[57] In practical terms, this doctrine of church government was reflected in Calvin's Genevese reforms. At the heart of church government lay the Consistory, composed of elders chosen by the city's magistrates and the pastors of the church. It was responsible for ecclesiastical discipline, and was thus to all intents and purposes a church court. But while it could impose ecclesiastical penalties, including excommunication, it held no civil jurisdiction.[58] Thus at an important level, Calvin maintained the distinction between secular and ecclesiastical authority.

Several commentators have argued that Calvin's conception of church government paves the way for the tightly organised radical political movements of the seventeenth century. Indeed, in a famous argument Michael Walzer goes further, arguing that Calvinism acted as a blueprint for modern radical revolutionary movements: thus the Jacobins and Bolsheviks in essence recapitulated the Calvinist marrying of fervent ideological belief with the specifically modern understanding of the world as a product of relations of power that could only be transformed through the constant labour of the elect organised in the communion of saints (or, in other words, the revolutionary party).[59] As Quentin Skinner points out, this kind of interpretation glosses over the fact that there is little in Calvin's writings that supports revolutionary challenges to secular authority. Calvin's followers had to turn to other, Lutheran and Catholic sources in order to construct a justification for active resistance to temporal authority.[60]

Calvin's most developed considerations of the character of political authority, obedience, and resistance can be found in chapter 20 of Book 4 of the *Institutes of the Christian Religion*, headed 'Civil Government'. Calvin opens the chapter by denouncing both those 'insane and barbarous men' who 'furiously strive to overturn ... divinely established order' (such as Müntzer and the Anabaptists) and 'the flatterers of princes' who 'set them against the rule of God himself' (presumably Machiavelli). In contrast to them, Calvin asserts that 'man is under a twofold government', 'the kind that resides in the soul or inner man and pertains to eternal life' and the 'other kind, which pertains only to the establishment of civil justice and outward morality'.[61] It is an error to believe that Christian freedom resides in the abolition of all power over men and that 'nothing will be safe unless the whole world is reshaped to a new form, where there are neither courts, nor laws, nor magistrates, nor anything which in their opinion restricts their freedom'. Like Luther, Calvin draws from the distinction between the inner and outer man the conclusion that 'Christ's spiritual Kingdom and the civil jurisdiction are things completely distinct.' Thus 'it makes no difference what your condition among men may be or under what nation's laws you live, since the Kingdom of Christ does not at all consist in these things'.[62]

Civil government is compatible with spiritual government because it serves its ends:

> For spiritual government, indeed, is already initiating in us upon earth certain beginnings of the Heavenly Kingdom, and in this mortal and fleeting life affords a certain forecast of an immortal and incorruptible blessedness. Yet civil government has as its appointed end, so long as we live among men, to cherish and protect the outward worship of God, to defend the sound doctrine of piety and the position of the church, to adjust our life to the society of men, to form our social behaviour to civil righteousness, to reconcile us with

one another, and to promote general peace and tranquillity. All of this I admit to be superfluous, if God's kingdom, such as it is now among us, wipes out the present life. But if it is God's will that we go as pilgrims upon the earth while we aspire to the true fatherland, and if the pilgrimage requires such helps, those who take these from man deprive him of his very humanity.[63]

The spiritual necessity of civil government in this world means that to think of doing away with it constitutes 'outrageous barbarity'. Without it public peace and property would be constantly disturbed. Civil government 'provides that a public manifestation of religion may exist among Christians, and that humanity may be maintained among men'.[64]

Calvin, then, does not depart from the Lutheran understanding of temporal authority as a spiritual necessity. Temporal authority exists so that the wicked can be punished and in order that the Christian community of the faithful can flourish. There is an element of difference, as we have seen, in the sense that Calvin does not consider temporal authority as merely coercive in character. The role of the magistrate, 'the protector and guardian of the laws', is given by 'divine providence and holy ordinance'. The burden of the magistrate is great, but the magistrate who governs well and in so doing protects the Christian community, does so by virtue of a gift of grace: 'no one ought to doubt that civil authority is a calling, not only holy and lawful before God, but also the most sacred and by far the most honourable of all callings in the whole life of mortal men'. There is no sense in which the magistracy is a human invention; it has not come about due to 'human perversity'.[65] It should be clear, then, that Calvin's understanding of the legitimacy of temporal authority is not founded on an understanding of natural right. While later Calvinists turned to the discourse of natural right to found a theory of resistance, this option was not open to Calvin who saw government as the product of divine, not human, will. He makes it clear that there are no grounds on which disobedience to those in temporal authority can be accepted:

> Let no man deceive himself here. For since the magistrate cannot be resisted without God being resisted at the same time, even though it seems that an unarmed magistrate can be despised with impunity, still God is armed to avenge mightily this contempt towards himself.[66]

Obedience must be given, even to a magistrate who is regarded as unjust. Calvin takes it that where people labour under unjust and tyrannical authority, they have only themselves to blame: 'a wicked king is the lord's wrath upon the earth'.[67]

In providing this seemingly uncompromising defence of the principle of obedience, however, Calvin did not argue that disobedience is necessarily an evil where it arises in the appropriate manner. Thus though it is always the case that it is a sin for an individual to disobey, it may be God's will for a rebellion of sinful men to occur and for them to replace those in authority. These 'unwitting agents' may have 'executed his work unwittingly' as when 'the ungratefulness of the kings of Judah and Israel and their impious obstinacy towards his many benefits, he sometimes by the Assyrians, sometimes by the Babylonians, crushed and afflicted'.[68] The chapter finishes with a reminder of Peter's injunction that 'we must obey God rather than men'. While this does not in itself justify disobedience – 'let us comfort ourselves with the thought that we are rendering that obedience which the Lord requires when we suffer anything rather than turn aside from piety'[69] – as with Luther and the Lutherans who followed him, this maxim was to play an important role in the formulation of a theory of rebellion in late seventeenth and eighteenth century Calvinism.

Perhaps the most striking feature of Calvin's consideration of disobedience, however, is that while he denies any right of disobedience and only provides a vague account of the duty of individuals to disobey, toward the end of 'Civil Government' he seems to argue for the role of the magistrates as the people's guardian in resisting tyrannical princes:

> For if there are now any magistrates of the people appointed to restrain the wilfulness of kings ... I am so far from forbidding them to withstand, in accordance with their duty, the fierce licentiousness of kings, that, if they wink at kings who violently fall upon and assault the lowly common folk, I declare that their dissimulation involves nefarious perfidy, because they dishonestly betray the freedom of the people, of which they know that they have been appointed protectors by God's ordinance.[70]

As Skinner points out, this argument is present in the very first edition of the *Institutes*, so even before he became an active reformer in Geneva Calvin had to an extent accepted the role of the magistrates in siding with citizens in resisting unjust princes. Furthermore, 'there is no doubt that, in the definitive edition of the *Institutes* in 1559, Calvin begins to change his mind. This never prompts him to state a clear and unequivocal theory of revolution, but it certainly results in a tendency, as Filmer shrewdly observes in *Patriarcha*, for Calvin to "look asquint" at the possibility of justifying active resistance to lawful magistrates'.[71]

When this account of the grounds of just disobedience is seen in combination with Calvin's belief in an organised yet egalitarian community of the faithful, his political thought may indeed appear radical. It is not just that the Calvinist ethic, derived from the theological apparatus of the communion of saints and doctrine of predestination, operates indirectly to permit a sustained engagement with the world in order to transform it through political action. This ethic is often understood to be definitive of Calvinism and has been seen, most famously by Max Weber, as a central contribution to the character of Western modernity.[72] But it is usually understood as emerging only after Calvin, when Calvinism as an international movement dedicated to transforming the world had arisen. In Calvin's texts, however, we can already see a promotion of the public power, in the form of the magistracy, as an active agent in the protection and furtherance of men's worldly interests. At the same time, this recognition of the character and purpose of public power is tied to a religious eschatology that regards its transcendence as the final act of world history, in the coming of the kingdom of heaven on earth. While Calvin, more than Luther, recognised the distinctiveness and permanence of political power, its dissolution was still seen as a requirement for the achievement of true freedom: the pure spiritual freedom of the elect in communion with God.

What we witness in the Reformation is the recognition that the public power is in an important sense separate from the Christian community, a separation that acts as a necessary condition for the formation of political theories that subordinate the former to the latter. To the extent that the Christian reformers understood the indispensability of the political domain for spiritual transformation, they also viewed it as something that was to be overcome. What divided the radical from the magisterial reformers was the extent to which they believed existing political authority to be compatible with the aim of spiritual regeneration. However, for Luther, Müntzer, and Calvin what was not in question was that reformation of the Christian community was a political as well as a spiritual act. While the Reformation saw the creation of some sects that believed that spiritual purity required disengagement from the wider world and its forms of authority, its more significant effect was to bind secular authority to the task of worldly transformation. At the same time, the limit of the public power was set by the sanctity of the inner man of faith. This conception of the relationship between secular and divine authority that emerges in Reformation Protestantism thus politicises the community of the faithful by demanding a struggle with the world against the works of the Devil: the papacy, the Turks, Jews, wicked landlords, and so on. At the same time, however, any expression of public power is either a work of the devil or an instrument of right-eousness. Politics is thus subordinate to religious belief. As we will see in the next chapter, by the mid-seventeenth century the bloodletting of the Wars of Religion led radical thinkers to inquire how religious belief might be made subordinate to, or at least safe for the orderly exercise of public power.

2
The Politicisation of Man in the Seventeenth Century: The Levellers and Hobbes

We have seen that in the Reformation, Protestantism provides the conceptual resources for distinguishing between an inner realm of consciousness in which the faith of the individual is inviolable, and the vicarious power of the sovereign, as God's agent, to constrain and punish the outer or fleshly man when his actions harm the peace of the Christian community. This does not equate to the modern liberal opposition between the private and public spheres, nor is there any straightforward way in which this distinction evolves out of that between the inner and outer man. Nevertheless, seventeenth century political thinkers employed the concepts that had been bequeathed to them by the Reformation, and in applying them to contemporary problems of authority they transformed these concepts and the entire field of political discourse. What we see, both in 'radical' thought and action as these are represented by groups such as the Levellers, and in 'conservative' defences of the authority of the absolute sovereign, most famously that provided by Thomas Hobbes, is the construction of one of the central conceptual features of the modern radical attitude. In short, in the seventeenth century we witness the politicisation of man. This conceptual transformation takes place in a fairly short time frame, roughly that encompassing the civil wars in England during the 1640s, and the Commonwealth interregnum between 1649 and 1660. By the end of that period there had emerged, most strikingly in Hobbes's *Leviathan*, a secular account of the way in which men are the authors of public power. At the same time, however, in the texts of this period we see the articulation of the aspiration for men to be emancipated from politics in a fashion that secularises Reformation political thought and acts as an important conceptual resource for the expression of the radical political discourses in the Enlightenment.

The Levellers

In the twentieth century, many on the left saw the Levellers as the founders of a modern radical tradition, centred around popular sovereignty, political liberty and social egalitarianism.[1] While others have been more circumspect about the place of the Levellers in a radical 'tradition', they have nonetheless considered them to mark a transformation in both political thought and organisation. David Wootton writes of them that they 'are the first modern political movement organised around the idea of popular sovereignty. They are the first democrats who think in terms, not of participatory self-government within a city-state, but of representative government within a nation-state'.[2] Others still have questioned whether the Levellers can be seen as genuinely modern because of the influence of religion on their political thought and practice[3] or because they subscribed to an ancient doctrine of natural law.[4] And the very notion that the Levellers were radical egalitarians and democrats was famously brought into question by C. B. Macpherson.[5]

Our concerns here will not in the main be with the kind of questions addressed above: that is the extent to which the Levellers form part of or even originate a radical tradition of left-wing English politics; whether they were genuinely 'radical' in their context in a way which transcended boundaries of class or religious belief; or how 'modern' they were as a political movement. For what it is worth, it is clear from the documents available to us that there is no obvious sense in which they 'anticipate' later radical and left-wing movements; that they were in their context 'radical', at least in the sense that they posed a clear and consistent challenge to existing political authority and social relations; and that the question of how 'modern' they were is largely incoherent, unless we first understand what is meant by that term and what is intended by including or excluding them from the category. Our concern with the Levellers will be focused on the fashion in which they challenged and reshaped the vocabulary of politics in their context. The Levellers are important not because they mark the beginning of political modernity or modern political movements, but because in their texts we see the employment of concepts that, in concert, constitute a shift in the conception of political order and political action. What emerges out of their texts is a particular notion of the political character of men. The political domain is seen by the Levellers as a sphere of action that is contingent on and constituted by social life, which properly understood is the sum of associations created by free men. At the same time, however, this political sphere is considered to be inherently dangerous and corruptible and in this regard needs to be constrained by society.

The Levellers emerged as a movement during the civil wars in England of the 1640s, and more precisely in the years 1644–46. It was in this period that the Long Parliament, at war with Charles I, introduced a number of measures that were to raise concerns amongst more radical supporters of the Parliamentary forces.[6] In general, Parliament fell under criticism on two grounds: first, that it was protecting the interests of its own members by seeking accommodation with the King; second, that it had fallen under the control of the Presbyterians, who wished to create a national Presbyterian church-state that would prohibit and suppress dissenting Protestant sects. These criticisms were articulated most forcefully amongst the independent congregations of London, out of which emerged three leading figures: John Lilburne (c. 1615–57), Richard Overton (c. 1599–1664), and William Walwyn (1600–81).[7] These three came to be identified as the leadership of the Leveller movement, which fairly rapidly came to gather substantial support among the ordinary ranks of the New Model Army.

None of the Leveller leaders wrote texts that were designed as statements of political philosophy. Their work mainly appears in the form of political pamphlets addressing grievances specific to the context of the Long Parliament and the aftermath of the defeat of Charles I in the First Civil War. The Levellers are interesting, then, not because they set themselves the task of propounding a systematic science of politics, as did a contemporary like Hobbes. Rather, the Levellers were concerned with political knowledge in so far as it could address the question presented to them in the 1640s: that is, what constituted an acceptable political settlement for England after the removal of Charles I as sovereign? Nonetheless, in the course of writing pamphlets designed for the purpose of informing and mobilising a popular audience, we can see challenges being presented to the existing vocabulary of politics and the emergence of distinctively novel ways of conceiving of the character of public power. In an important sense, the nature of Leveller writing makes it more interesting than the systematic political treatises of the seventeenth century, since it both registers and marks an intervention in the kind of general, rather than specialised political knowledge, that was the currency of conduct for actors on the ground during the civil wars and in the Commonwealth. The Leveller texts thus provide us with an indication of the kind of changes in political concepts and knowledge that took place in the period 1640–60, which more generally can be seen as crucial in the transformation of social and political relations in Europe in the early modern period.

Many of the Levellers' texts raised concerns that were religious in character. A good example of this is the pamphlet written by Walwyn in 1646 titled 'Toleration Justified and Persecution Condemned'.[8] Walwyn's target was the Presbyterian grouping in parliament, and particularly those in the Westminster Assembly of Divines who argued that the Solemn League and Covenant of 1643 required the abandonment of the Thirty-Nine Articles of the Anglican Church, and reformation along the lines of the Church of Scotland.[9] Walwyn argued against the creation of any national church in favour of the Independents' call for the autonomy of individual congregations to control their own affairs, 'because *every man* ought to be free in the worship and service of God'.[10] It was not in the compass of the state to determine the religion of men, even though the Presbyterians in Parliament had argued that the absence of toleration from any Christian state demonstrated that it was so:

> But that the ministers have been used to speak what they please for a reason in their pulpits without contradiction, they would never sure have let so slight a one as this have passed for them. It seems by this reason, that *if in any* Christian state a toleration by the magistrate had been allowed, it would not have been unreasonable for *our* state to allow it – the practice of states being here supposed to be the rule of what's reasonable. Whereas *I* had thought that the practice of Christian states is to be judged by the rule of reason and God's word, and not reason by them. That which is just and reasonable is constant and perpetually so; the practice of states, though Christian, is variable we see – different one from another and changing according to the prevalency of particular parties – and therefore a most uncertain rule of what is reasonable. Besides, the state of *Holland* doth tolerate; and therefore the ministers' argument, even in that part where it seems to be most strong for them, makes against them. Again, if the practice of a Christian state be a sufficient argument of the reasonableness of a toleration, *our* state may justly tolerate because Christian, and because they are free to do whatever any other state might formerly have done.[11]

It is reason and God's word that dictate a policy of toleration for states. The scriptural injunctions to love one's neighbour and to eschew the domination of others are made imperative by the lesson of history, which shows that 'the cause and reason of subversion and devastation of states and countries' is no other than 'the tyranny of princes and persecution of priests'. Non-believers cannot be coerced into belief, but can only be shown the way to it through 'sound reason and argument'. The 'most violent for persecution' are the weak, 'whereas those whose minds are established and whose opinions are built on firm and demonstrable grounds care not what wind blows, fear not to grapple with error, because they are confident they can overthrow it'.[12]

Walwyn's argument is certainly couched in religious terms, but in contrast to earlier Reformation texts there is little direct reference to scripture and his claim for toleration and the autonomy of Christian communities seems to be as much concerned with social peace and order as individual salvation. Thus, 'there can be no greater argument to the people to venture their estates and lives in defence of their country and that government under which they enjoy not only a liberty of estate and person but a freedom likewise of serving God according to their consciences, which religious men account the greatest blessing on earth'.[13] Nonetheless, it would be an error to see the Leveller texts as embodying any clear or unambiguous distinction between a theological and a secular discourse. The principles of political organisation they come to are consistently derived from considerations of the nature of God and his purpose in the creation of man and the world. There are numerous references throughout Leveller writing to the natural equity that was woven into the creation. In 'The Freeman's Freedom Vindicated', for example, Lilburne wrote that Adam and Eve are:

> The earthly, original fountain, as begetters and bringers-forth of all and every particular individual man and woman that ever breathed in the world since; who are, and were by nature all equal and alike in power, dignity, authority, and majesty – none of them having (by nature) any authority, dominion or magisterial power, one over or above another. Neither have they or can they exercise any but merely by institution or donation, that is to say by mutual agreement or consent – given, derived or assumed by mutual consent and agreement – for the good benefit and comfort of each other, and not for the mischief, hurt, or damage of any ... [14]

It is misleading to suggest, then, that the Levellers were 'strikingly secular'.[15] The problem that informs their thinking and writing is one that lay at the heart of the Reformation: what it meant to be a Christian and to lead a Christian life. Wootton claims that Overton's distinction between a sin, which is for God to judge, and a crime, which is for the laws of the Commonwealth to determine, means that while he 'is not a secular thinker, his argument can be translated without distortion into secular terms. Once one has separated private and public as he does, it is only a short step to Mandeville's claim that private vices, properly regulated, are the securest foundation for public benefits'.[16] However, this misses the fact that for Overton, as for the other Levellers, sinful behaviour and the good ordering of the Commonwealth were not compatible, because there could be no doubt that were people generally wicked this would not be to the benefit of the whole. The Levellers were arguing from a theological principle when they claimed that each Christian should be allowed to find their own path to salvation; they placed the same order of importance on the 'inner' man as did Luther. It does not follow that they believed that worldly sin should not go unpunished if it violates the order of equity manifest in God's creation. Tyranny and treason were clear cases of such worldly sin, and leading Levellers at various points between 1647 and 1649 advocated the execution of Charles I on these grounds.[17] The idea that worldly punishment should be reserved for those sins that threatened the peace of the Christian Commonwealth was quite consistent with the mainstream of the magisterial Reformation. Moreover, as J. C. Davis points out, the Levellers never drew a clear distinction between natural and divine law.[18]

The Levellers departed from the kind of Lutheran and Calvinist political thought explored in the previous chapter not because they were asking different questions. Rather, for them, the question of what it meant to be a Christian and the nature of the Christian life had different answers, even starting from the premise of the distinction between the inner and outer man. Where Protestant theories of resistance had emerged in the late sixteenth century, these had focused on the extent to which the actions of princes forced individuals to violate their Christian duties as revealed in scripture. The Levellers theory of resistance, though it is perhaps misleading to say that this existed in any systematic form, had a similar character, even if its textual expression drew less heavily on biblical exegesis (though this is not surprising given that none of the leading Levellers were theologians). Where the Levellers departed from these earlier Protestant theorists of resistance was in their insistence that temporal authority was not a gift of God, but was rather in the gift of men. In man's original, natural and prelapsarian state, no government or laws had existed. Man was not born to dominate other men and domination could only be justified when the dominated submitted by consent for the sake of the common good. Government ceased to be legitimate where it was no longer based on mutual consent and agreement, in which circumstances it could be removed, if necessary, by force of arms. Thus in 'The Remonstrance of Many Thousand Citizens', written by Overton and Walwyn in 1646, the power given over to 'parliament-men' 'was to deliver us from bondage and to preserve the commonwealth in peace and happiness'. But: 'ye are to remember that this was only of us but a power of trust – which is ever revocable, and cannot be otherwise – and to be employed to no other end than our own well-being'. Any power exercised by Parliament other than that granted expressly by the people is 'a usurpation and oppression from which we expect to be freed'.[19]

It is from the grounds of this theory of resistance and the legitimate basis for the exercise of power by a Commonwealth that the Levellers built their specific proposals for the character of legal and political institutions in the post-civil war polity, and it is these constitutional proposals for which they are perhaps most famous. In this respect, they are quite widely referred to as 'democrats', mainly because they argued for a considerable increase in the franchise for elections to the House of Commons. C. B. Macpherson argues that the Leveller franchise was in fact much less extensive than is suggested by the notion that they supported the vote for all free-born Englishmen. What this category excluded was the large numbers of servants and alms-takers who the Levellers explicitly omitted in pressing their argument for the extension of the franchise, particularly at the famous Putney Debates with Cromwell and other leading members of the New Model Army in 1647.[20] On Macpherson's calculations, the non-servant franchise would have nearly doubled the voting population from 212,100 to 416,700, whereas the manhood franchise would have extended the vote to 1,170,400 men.[21] But Macpherson's interpretation has been contested: the Levellers may have been excluding only live-in servants and beggars with no fixed abode, who together would have constituted a much smaller proportion of the population than all servants and alms-takers.[22] Regardless of the precise figures involved, it is clear from the texts that the Levellers wished to enfranchise all male heads of household, including the very poorest.[23] This would have lead to a considerable increase in the franchise and was in its context a very radical proposal.

Nevertheless, to call the Levellers 'democrats' is an anachronism. In mid-seventeenth century England, the term 'democracy', on the infrequent occasions so it was employed in political discourse, was used mainly in a pejorative sense.[24] The Levellers were certainly not arguing for the organisation of the polity along the lines of ancient democracy, for that system was widely regarded as effectively amounting either to oligarchy or anarchy in the sense of mob-rule. Nor were they arguing for a system of representative democracy on the grounds of prudence, which was to become the main justification for democratic government in liberal political theory after the American Revolution. The 'democracy' of the Levellers can be best understood not so much as a system of government, but as one of a suite of powers and rights that free Englishmen possessed at birth. It was the birthright of free Englishmen to choose their legislators and to have the regular opportunity to remove them if they were no longer making law with the people's consent. Again, and as Hanson remarks, it is important to see that such powers and rights were conceived of by the Levellers as being divinely ordained and that it was a Christian duty to exercise them.[25] While it has been argued that the Levellers anticipate the liberal account of rights provided by John Locke,[26] in this respect alone there is much distance between the two: Locke derived rights and civil society from the state of nature, not from divine law.[27]

There are moments in the Leveller texts where they do indeed seem to anticipate Locke's account of rights and in particular his conception of self-ownership. In his pamphlet, 'An Arrow Against All Tyrants', Overton wrote:

> To every individual in nature is given an individual property by nature not to be invaded or usurped by any. For every one, as he his himself, so he has a self-propriety, else could he not *be* himself; and of this no second may presume to deprive any of without manifest violation and affront to the very principles of nature and of the rules of equity and justice between man and man. Mine and thine cannot be, except this be. No man has power over my rights and liberties, and I over no man's. I may but be an individual, enjoy myself and my self-propriety and may right myself no more than myself, or presume any further ... For by natural birth all men are equally and alike born to propriety, liberty and freedom.[28]

But in the very next paragraph Overton makes it clear that God has 'implanted' such powers in men, which is to say that God has endowed all men equally with the right and power of self-propriety. Moreover, 'by nature we are the sons of Adam, and from him have legitimately derived a natural propriety, right and freedom, which only we require'.[29]

Macpherson, along with other authors who adopt a Marxist perspective,[30] claim that this commitment to self-propriety, or what he labelled 'possessive individualism', enables us to understand Leveller thought principally in terms of economic class. The Leveller's supporters were, overwhelmingly, artisans and small masters whose livelihood was threatened by the taxes and monopolies sanctioned by a Parliament of predominantly large land-owners. The right to self-propriety established ownership of one's own labour and the products thereof. In effect, then, the main thrust of the Leveller claims was to support a capitalist economy in which small producers could trade freely on markets. This argument, however, has to set aside a good deal of the available evidence to be rendered plausible. It is indeed the case that the Levellers argued against arbitrary taxation (that is taxation raised without the consent of the people) and called for an end to monopolies. As we will see presently, these are very important aspects of their texts with respect to the idea of the protection of the common (rather than individual and material) interests. But whatever the 'elective affinity', to use Weber's terminology, between the kind of Protestantism practiced by the Levellers and capitalism, they did not operate in a conceptual universe where individual material interests were primary, nor where their appeal to the protection of the common good necessarily coincided with such interests. To be sure, they supported the right of individuals to ownership of property, but every time they submitted their demands for reform to Parliament such rights were presented, both in lexical and conceptual order, as subordinate to the right to freedom of religion and conscience.

The 'liberty' that the Levellers pursued was not of the same order as that of other radical contemporaries, nor of modern liberalism. Various radicals, such as the Diggers or 'True Levellers' led by Gerrard Winstanley,[31] held a vision of a future without laws or a law-making power in which men lived and cooperated in small agrarian communities. James Harrington, perhaps next to Hobbes the most celebrated political thinker of the period, argued for a form of republican government that was more concerned with the stability and virtue of the polity than with individual liberty of conscience and action.[32] The liberty that the Levellers conceived of was a *political* liberty in a specific sense: that it depended on the constitution of a political community which gathered to itself and exercised all the power of the Commonwealth. The kind of liberty that the Levellers desired could only be achieved given a public power that represented all free-born Englishmen, but which at the same time protected the common interest. This is a 'modern', and one of the earliest, articulations of the concept of popular sovereignty:

> Whereas all power is originally and essentially in the whole body of the people of this Nation, and whereas their free choice or consent by their Representors is the only originall or foundation of all just government; and the reason and end of the choice of all just Governors

whatsoever is their apprehension of safety and good by them, that it be insisted upon positively.[33]

The notion that political sovereignty is constituted by the consent of individual, free men, is perhaps the central conceptual transformation in political thought during the seventeenth century. In the late sixteenth century the concept of the sovereign as *solutus legibus* within a specific territory could be found in the writing of Jean Bodin.[34] Bodin, however, saw such sovereignty primarily in terms of a divine donation to particular sovereigns. In the early seventeenth century, the Dutch jurist Hugo Grotius constructed an account of the laws of nations on the understanding that the rightful sovereignty of each was a product of the implied consent of its members.[35] As we will see in the next section, the most complexly articulated conception of the nature of sovereignty by consent was to be provided by Thomas Hobbes. While the Levellers did not construct a systematic theory of sovereignty, it is nonetheless clear from their texts that they considered the legitimate form of the public power to rest on the consent of the people. Sovereignty was not a gift from God to the sovereign, but rather a 'trust' given over to the lawmakers by those subject to the law.

In the Leveller texts, then, men appear as having permanent political interests in the sense that the public power is ultimately derived from their desire to protect themselves and each other. The sovereign political body is a protective agency that is constantly charged with the duty of safeguarding men's freedom. It should be clear that, unlike in later liberal conceptions, there is no clear distinction here between the public and private interests of man. Certainly, the Levellers argued that there were things that individuals did and believed that the sovereign body should have no power over, most prominently religious beliefs and practices. At the same time, the effect of the Leveller claims was to radically politicise individual men in so far as they were conceived of having a claim by birth over the public power. Why should men be considered to have such a claim? It is clear that the texts do not provide any single answer to this question. In large part, as we have seen, the notion is consistent with the Leveller belief in the natural and divine equality of man. To ensure that no man is subject to law without his consent becomes, in this respect, a duty of all Christians. Yet there are at least two other sources for the Leveller's politicisation of men. The first, which we will turn to presently, is that the public power tends toward corruption and that, consequently, we should not trust individual officers of the sovereign body to always act in ways beneficial to the common good. The second is that man's claim over the public power is his birthright as free-born a Englishman, and that this right had been established prior to the Norman Conquest.

The Leveller belief in an original state of English liberty prior to a Norman yoke is one of the most interesting aspects of their thought. Numerous examples of its expression can be found throughout the texts. For example, Overton and Walwyn wrote:

> If kings would prove themselves lawful magistrates they must prove themselves to be so by a lawful derivation of their authority, which must be from the voluntary trust of the people; and then the case is the same with them as between the people and you – they (as you) being possessed of no more power than what is *in* the people justly to entrust. And then all implications in the writs of the establishment of religion show that in that particular, as many other, we remain under the Norman yoke of an unlawful power, from which we ought to free ourselves, and which ye ought not to maintain upon us, but to abrogate.[36]

As J. G. A. Pocock has written:

> The Leveller attitude to history is a strange hybrid. Their anti-Normanism, as it is sometimes called, amounts in the end to a rejection of history and existing law; there has been a fatal breech in the continuity of the law, six centuries of usurpation during which we have had only fragments of our natural liberties, and now we are free either to reconstruct our society according to reason and equity, or to await the next operation of the Spirit that works in us all. But so inescapable by this time was the clutch of history on English political thought, that this fundamentally anti-historical theory could only be expressed in historical language; the past could only be rejected through a reinterpretation of the past.[37]

R. B. Seaberg has argued that the Levellers may be best thought of not as having rejected the common law in its entirety since the Conquest, but rather its 'procedures' as opposed to its 'substance'. Anglo-Saxon liberty outlived the Norman Conquest, as was witnessed by the claims made in the Magna Carta. For the Levellers, the substance of English law rested on principles of reason and fairness that were articulated at various points after 1066; it was just that Norman procedures of justice acted as an obstacle to the satisfaction of such substantive principles.[38] It may be somewhat misleading, then, to suggest as Pocock does that the Levellers constructed 'a fundamentally anti-historical theory'.

Nonetheless, Pocock at the same time points to the importance in Leveller thought, and indeed in seventeenth century English political discourse more broadly, of historical argument. The appeal to a past tradition of English liberty was as important for establishing the claim of free-born Englishmen over the public power as the Levellers' arguments from divine order or natural equity and reason. This tradition had to be fabricated, since the belief that in Anglo-Saxon England men had enjoyed more liberty than under the post-Conquest kings was largely apocryphal. It nonetheless played an important role in the political discourse of the radicals between 1640–60, and it would do so again toward the end of the eighteenth century.[39] It might be thought that this call to tradition, to a mythical golden age, marks out Leveller thought as pre-modern, since from the time of the French Revolution we have come to expect modern radicals and revolutionaries to repudiate the past rather than call for its return. In reality, the understanding of history that modern radicals and revolutionaries possess tends to be far more complex, and at some level the idea of continuity and return plays an important role in the thought of even the seemingly most rationalist and anti-historical movements. The Jacobins looked to ancient Rome to name, and to an extent model the political institutions of the post-revolutionary republic, and the Bolsheviks were keen to garb themselves in the paraphernalia of the French Revolution. In fact, the invention of tradition, the reinterpretation of the past in order to forge connections of continuity, is a defining feature of modern radical and revolutionary thought and movements. The Levellers, in this respect, were indeed 'modern'. In their texts, the call to tradition acts as a means of forming the political identity of the Leveller movement as an association of free-born Englishmen against the privileged interests that had inherited the mantle of Norman tyranny.

The fashion of the Levellers' appeal to religion and tradition does not render them necessarily 'modern' or 'pre-modern'. Nevertheless, the Leveller texts do represent an important transformation in the character of political discourse in the seventeenth century. What accounts for the peculiarity of their thought is the way in which its religious and traditional elements meld with a particular account of the nature of the common good and the purpose of political power. The real significance of the Levellers' calls for individual rights is not, as Macpherson argues, that these were designed to protect and forward individual property rights. As Alan Houston rightly claims: 'While others pursued private and exclusive interests, the Levellers stood for public and inclusive interests.'[40] This is a more illuminating way in which to approach the Levellers' arguments against arbitrary taxation and monopoly than to see them as a mere manifestation of class interests. Attacks on monopolies are to be found throughout the Leveller texts, and they are made in each of the 'Agreements' submitted to Parliament (though as we have seen, they come after the claim to rights to freedom of religion and conscience). The three 'Agreements' of 1647–49 proposed various reforms, as well as the protection of freedom of worship, including annual (or biannual parliaments), the effective abolition of the House of Lords, trial by jury and voluntary military service. They also call for an end to monopolies, tithes and so on. Thus the petition of 11th September 1648 contains the following articles:

> 10. That you [Parliament] would have freed all trade and merchandising from all monopolising and engrossing by companies and otherwise.
> 11. That you would have abolished excise and all kinds of taxes except subsidies, the old and only just way of England.
> 16. That you would have removed the tedious burden of tithes, satisfying all improvements and providing a more equal way of maintenance for the public ministers.
> 18. That you would have bound yourselves and all future parliaments from abolishing all propriety, levelling men's estates or making all things common.[41]

Now, the purpose of these claims is to defend the private interests of men in their property and estates.[42] At the same time, however, the petition includes the following articles:

> 12. That you would have laid open all late enclosures of fens and other commons, or have enclosed them only or chiefly for the benefit of the poor.
> 13. That you would have considered the many thousands that are ruined by perpetual imprisonment for debt, and provided to their enlargement.
> 14. That you would have ordered some effectual course to keep the people from begging in so fruitful a nation as through God's blessing this is.[43]

Many of the other articles of the *Agreements* deal directly with the circumstances of the civil wars, such as demanding regular payments for the soldiers of the New Model Army,[44] and it is never clear from Leveller texts exactly how they would have provided for poor relief, dealt with debtors and so on. But these claims, along with the important and seemingly primary argument for religious toleration, should at least bring into relief the problem with the notion that the Leveller political discourse was derived principally from material or class interests.

As Houston argues convincingly, the Levellers' employment of the concept of monopoly did much to structure their arguments in favour of natural equity and liberty, rather than material and proprietary interests. The Levellers did not argue for economic equality, but 'they insisted that the laws governing property – including the rules of trade and commerce – be applied equally ... Economic opportunities were public resources; if made available to some, then they had to be made available to all'.[45] This might seem like a similar argument to that developed by the theorists of commercial society at the end of the eighteenth century. It is important to recognise, however, that it was not based on the same conceptual grounds. The Leveller belief in the benefits of free trade and private property was not founded on the Madevillian notion of private vices and public benefits. Rather, an equitable distribution of economic resources and opportunities was determined by the natural equity of man written into God's creation. Public virtue does not stem from the pursuit of private self-interest, but rather by men fulfilling their Christian duty to ensure that all are treated equally: 'To say that we are the stewards of our own souls is not to say that we are free to believe as we please, however, nor is it to say that our beliefs are irrelevant to others.'[46]

For the Levellers, then, the purpose of public power was the protection of the interests of the Christian community or commonwealth, rather than of private individuals. This is a major point of difference between the discourse of politics within which they operated and that which we find in modern liberalism. What is innovative in the Leveller's thought, however, is the notion that basis of political authority is not a direct gift from God, but rather stems from an agreement between free-born men. In their texts, then, the political domain appears in an ambiguous light. On the one hand, the sovereign public power is a necessary feature of human life, because it is its role to protect the interests of the Christian Commonwealth. On the other hand, individuals have a permanent political interest in the public power in order to ensure that natural equity and liberty, bestowed on man in God's creation, are preserved against the threat that comes from private interests. It is often thought that in rejecting the Levellers' claim that men have permanent political interests in the sovereign power, Hobbes sought to confine politics to the actions of the sovereign monarch or assembly of men. However, in the section that follows we will see that there is an important sense in which Hobbes politicises men, and that he holds a view of public power at least as ambiguous as that of the Levellers.

Hobbes

Thomas Hobbes (1588–1679) is often portrayed as an authoritarian conservative and monarchist whose major contribution to social and political thought was to claim that human beings are naturally selfish and bellicose. This is a highly misleading portrait. Indeed, in at least two senses Hobbes's work is deeply radical. It is so, first, in its context. Hobbes provided a challenge both to the basis of secular authority and to the main institutions of the Christian religion which, in his time, led to him being widely characterised as a sceptic who rejected the traditional basis of established authority, and as an atheist.[47] Second, Hobbes's texts represent contain concepts that are central to the formation of the modern radical attitude. While Hobbes's principal political concern was not to fundamentally transform the nature of the world, but rather to establish the grounds for civil peace and order, this goal did indeed require a root change in the nature of political language and life. Such change involved a rethinking of the categories in which we represent the world in general and the character of man and the citizen in particular. It is in this respect that Hobbes's engagement with the ideas of the Scientific Revolution were of such importance for his view of political, or civil science.[48] Yet at the same time that Hobbes's texts announce a profound and radical transformation in the nature of political thought, there is also at work in his writing an attempt to delimit and subordinate the political domain. Thus while on the one hand Hobbes makes men political, in a peculiarly modern sense, on the other he depoliticises them and anticipates a social order that is distinct and largely autonomous from public power.

Modestly born, Hobbes received a classical humanist education before entering the service of Lord Cavendish, Earl of Devonshire, in 1608.[49] His main role was as tutor and general adviser, and as such he accompanied the Cavendish family on a number of tours of Europe. It was during stops on these tours that he became familiar with the kind of philosophical thinking that was to play an important formative role in his writing. Early visits to Venice acquainted him with philosophers who had adopted a stance of ethical scepticism and detachment.[50] During the 1630s, his trips to Paris would bring him into contact with Mersenne, and through him the work of Descartes. Hobbes was to criticise Descartes for his theories of optics and secondary qualities, but the (qualified) sceptical attitude Descartes had adopted toward knowledge of the world in his famous *Discourse on Method*,[51] was of the kind that Hobbes had (already) come to adopt.[52] More generally, during the 1630s Hobbes turned toward the study of mathematics and the natural sciences, and in so doing came to reject his early humanist education.[53] It was at this point that Hobbes came to adopt a 'materialist' stance with respect to human action. The things that human beings did (and also thought and felt) could be understood using the same principles that natural philosophy employed in order to explain matter in motion. Accordingly, any account of the manner in which human beings behaved toward one another in civil life must involve a proper understanding of the nature of matter and behaviour. Thus Hobbes's first sketch of a major philo-sophical text was *The Elements of Philosophy*, which was to be structured in three parts: *De corpore* (of body or matter in general); *De homine* (of man); and *De cive* (of the citizen). This was never published as an entire work, with *De cive* appearing first in 1642[54] (proceded by *The Elements of the Law, Natural and Politic* in 1640),[55] and *De corpore* and *De homine* not appearing in print until 1655 and 1658 respectively. By this time, these Latin texts had been superseded (at least in the sense of fame) by Hobbes's *Leviathan: The Matter, Forme and Power of a Common-Wealth, Ecclesiastical and Civill* (1651). *Leviathan*, nonetheless, was struc-tured around Hobbes's earlier vision of the unity of the methods of natural and civil science.

Leviathan, unlike the Leveller tracts, is a work of systematic philosophy. It proceeds by setting out definitions of concepts and assessing the evidence for the truth of certain claims that employ these concepts. The 'truth' Hobbes is concerned with, however, is of a particular kind. Truth 'consisteth of the right ordering of names in our affirmations'. If a man wishes to seek the precise truth he needs 'to remember what every name he uses stands for; and to place it accordingly; or else he will find him-self entangled in words, as a bird in lime-twiggs; the more he struggles, the more belimed'.[56] Truth involves the correct naming of things and the relationship between them and in this respect appears as a public phenomenon. For Hobbes, truth is something that cannot be private in character, it cannot be established subjectively but only by the exercise of public reason. Hobbes was, and is often rightly recognised to be, a philosopher of reason, but for him 'reason' has a very specific meaning:

> For REASON, in this sense, is nothing but *Reckoning* (that is, Adding and Subtracting) of the Consequences of generall names agreed upon, for the *marking* and *signifying* of our thoughts; ... The Use and

End of Reason, is not the finding of the summe, and truth of one, or a few consequences, remote from the first definitions, and settled significations of names; but to begin at these; and proceed from one consequence to another. For there can be no certainty of the last Conclusion, without a certainty of all those Affirmations and Negations, on which it was grounded, and inferred.[57]

Though Hobbes was wont, given the conventions of the time, to capitalise the term 'Reason', he did not hold that reason was some kind of metaphysical entity that can be accessed in order to realise a higher and more general 'Truth'. The kind of reason that Hobbes is interested in is 'natural reason', that is the capacity for reasoning that people possess by virtue of being humans, distinct from animals who do not have such a mental faculty. Reason is a process that allows us to establish the cause and effects of particular things that are publicly named and conceivable. It is in this way that we can arrive at the truth, or what can be better understood as particular truths. In this respect, for Hobbes there was no sense in which as individuals we could ascertain the truth about the world as a whole.

As we will see, these philosophical considerations about truth and reason are central to Hobbes's conception of the nature of civil (or political) science and his substantive conclusions about the character of public power and its relationship to its citizens (or subjects). However, as much as it is important to treat *Leviathan* as a philosophical text, it is equally vital to recognise that it was written in a particular political context and with particular political ends in mind. Moreover, the politics of *Leviathan* cannot be divorced from questions of religion in mid-seventeenth century England; for, as we saw in considering the Levellers, in that setting matters of politics and religion were inseparable. While many expositions of the text focus on the first two parts of the work, which deal largely with the character of human nature and the derivation of the legitimate authority of the state, the third and fourth parts have often been considered ancillary to or even disconnected from Hobbes's theory of politics. In fact, parts three and four of *Leviathan* – 'Of a Christian Commonwealth' and 'Of the Kingdom of Darknesse' – should be seen as lying at the heart of the text.

As Quentin Skinner has argued, *Leviathan* can at one level be seen as a contribution to debates in England around the 'engagement' oath introduced after the execution of Charles I in 1649.[58] *Leviathan* propounds a theory of submission to the sovereign, and at the end of the Civil War the establishment of a peaceful Commonwealth required that all parties recognised the rightful authority of the new public power by swearing an oath of engagement. The details of Hobbes's argument are different from those usually given by supporters of engagement, which often amounted to the Pauline injunction to obey God's anointed rulers on earth.[59] But the effect was the same: to provide support for a sovereign power that was able to maintain peace and allow men to go about living their lives. The nature of Hobbes's argument not only lost him friends but created enemies. *Leviathan* was written by Hobbes in exile in Paris, where he had been since 1640. At that time, on the evidence of his defence of 'absolutism' in *The Elements of Law*, he was widely considered a supporter of monarchy in general (as indeed he was) and he feared persecution by the Long Parliament.[60] *Leviathan*, however, was not arguing against the leaders of the new Commonwealth but effectively in favour of obedience to them and in its detail Hobbes did not rule out the legitimacy of a non-monarchical government, that is, one constituted by an assembly of men who represented all citizens. It was thus in 1652 that Hobbes returned to England to seek the protection of the new republic from monarchist threats against his life.[61]

An important element in explaining this 'turn' (though this did not represent a change in the way in which Hobbes viewed the character of political power and legitimate authority) is the view of the Christian Commonwealth that is worked out in *Leviathan*, a view that is inextricably connected to his understanding of political power. In the last section we saw how the Levellers had supported the cause of Independency. They rejected the aspiration of the Presbyterians to create a national church that would be responsible for regulating public faith, in favour of a loose association of largely self-governing congregations with the state playing a general supervisory role, but having no direct say over doctrine and liturgical practice. In *Leviathan*, Hobbes appears to support this kind of Independency. After Elizabeth had removed the power of the papacy over the English church and the Presbyterian ambition for episcopacy had been defeated in the civil wars:

> We are reduced to the Independency of the Primitive Christians to follow Paul, or Cephas, or Apollos, every man as he liketh best: Which, if it be without contention, and without measuring the Doctrine of Christ, by our affection to the Person of his Minister, ... is perhaps the best: First, because there ought to be no Power over the Consciences of men, but of the World it selfe, working Faith in every one, not always according to the purpose of them that Plant and Water, but of God himself, that giveth the Increase; and secondly,

because it is unreasonable in them, who teach there is such a danger in every little Errour, to enquire of a man endued with Reason of his own, to follow the Reason of any other man, or of the most voices of many other men.[62]

In effect, and like the Levellers, Hobbes can be seen as arguing in favour of religious toleration. To see why, and how this argument in favour of Independency is linked to his understanding of human nature and political power, we need to consider in some more detail Hobbes's view of religion as it is set out in *Leviathan*.

In part one of *Leviathan*, Hobbes provides an account of the natural 'seed' of religion. Religion arises among men not because of the idea of God that God causes within them, but rather because of men's natural modes of thinking and behaving in the world. Men are naturally inquisitive and seek out the causes and effects of things. When they become accustomed to the regular occurrence of a certain chain of events, they are likely to explain particular instances of its happening in terms of their past experience of its causes and effects. But men do not have experience of the future, and are anxious about what kinds of things may befall them; in particular they may have a 'feare of death, poverty, or other calamity'. To deal with such anxieties, men may posit invisible forces or spirits that can be used to assuage their fears about the future. For Hobbes, however, the 'acknowledging of one God, Externall, Infinite, and Omnipotent' was more likely to stem from men's reasoning from the succession of all causes and effects to 'a First, and Eternall cause of all things; which is that which men mean by the name of God'. The invisible agents or spirits that men conceived of were taken by them to have the same incorporeal character as the human soul or reflections or things that appear in dreams: 'men not knowing that such apparitions are nothing else but creatures of the Fancy, think to be reall, and externall Substances'. It is this idea of such external spirits ('Opinions of Ghosts'), of ignorance as to how they effect the world ('Ignorance of second causes'), the worship of such spirits as if honouring men ('Devotion towards what men fear') and the attribution to them of all extraordinary events ('Taking of things Casuall for Prognostiques'), that 'consistenth the Naturall seed of *Religion*; which by reason of the different Fancies, Judgements, and Passions of severall men, hath grown up into ceremonies so different, that those that are used by one man, are for the most part ridiculous to another'.[63]

For Hobbes, this seed came to 'receive culture' from two kinds of men: one kind cultivated the seed 'according to their own invention' and the other 'by Gods commandment and direction'. However, 'both sorts have done it with a purpose to make those men that relyed on them, the more apt to Obedience, Lawes, Peace, Charity, and Civill Society'. The first kind of religion is part of 'humane Politiques', concerned with the duties of subjects to Earthly kings, whereas the second is 'Divine Politiques', concerned with the duties of subjects in the 'Kingdome of God'. 'Of the former sort, were all the founders of Common-wealths, and the Law-givers of the Gentiles: Of the later sort were *Abraham, Moses, and our Blessed Saviour*; by whom have been derived unto us the Lawes of the Kingdome of God.' In this sense, the religion of the gentiles was designed to secure social peace in part by deflecting the ill-fortune of the 'common people' and making them 'less apt to mutiny against their Governors'. Thus, 'the Religon of the Gentiles was a part of their Policy'.[64] In contrast:

> where God himself, by supernaturall Revelation, planted Religion; there he also made to himselfe a peculiar Kingdome; and gave Lawes, not only of behaviour towards himselfe; but also towards one another; and thereby in the Kingdome of God, the Policy, and lawes Civill, are part of Religion; and the distinction of Temporall, and Spirituall Domination, hath there no place. It is true, that God is King of all the Earth: Yet may he be King of a peculiar, and chosen Nation. For there is no more incongruity therein, than that he that hath the generall command of the whole Army, should have withall a peculiar regiment, or Company of his own. God is King of all the Earth by his Power: but of his chosen people he is King by Covenant.[65]

The notion that God becomes the King of his people (i.e. in biblical terms the King of the Jews) through covenant is central to Hobbes's understanding of the character of public power and the rightful grounds of sovereignty. It is indeed the case, as we shall see presently, that Hobbes derives the state out of a binding agreement between men who, in a state of nature, possess as their principal right that to self-preservation. Nevertheless, Hobbes's understanding of God and of the character of the Christian religion is an integral part of the formulation of his distinctive theory of sovereignty.[66]

J. G. A. Pocock summarises the importance of God to Hobbes in the following way:

> The Christian mystery to [Hobbes] was the belief that God had spoken in history and had said that he would return in time. The God of

prophecy and history was the only God of whom Hobbes would speak; the God of faith was the only God compatible with his political system.[67]

Hobbes's materialism was in part a rejection of what he considered to be the fantasies of ghosts, spirits and various other forms of incorporeal 'substance', which much of religion has taken to be its subject matter. The fourth part of Leviathan, 'Of the Kingdome of Darknesse', is designed to demonstrate that the fantasy of invisible, non-material powers has definite beneficiaries in history. Who benefits (*cui bono*) from the 'Kingdome of Darknesse'? At one level, it is all the priest-kings throughout history who have exercised their power over people by claiming either to be gods, spirits, and so on or to be in direct communion with them. But he also has a very specific target in mind: the papacy:

> For, from the time that the Bishop of Rome had gotten to be acknowledged for Bishop Universall, by pretence of Succession to St. Peter, their whole Hierarchy, or Kingdome of Darknesse, may be compared not unfitly to the *Kingdome of Fairies*; that is, to old wives *Fables* in England, concerning *Ghosts* and *Spirits*, and the feats they play in the night. And if a man consider the originall of this great Ecclesiasticall Dominion, he will easily perceive, that the *Papacy*, is no other, than the *Ghost* of the deceased *Romane Empire*, sitting crowned upon the grave thereof: For so did the Papacy start up on a Sudden out of the Ruines of that Heathen Power.[68]

Hobbes's criticism of established religious institutions was at the same time a criticism of their political role. We should not be too quick in drawing parallels between his approach and the atheistic rationalism of the eighteenth and nineteenth centuries which explicitly linked religious belief to political interests.[69] Hobbes maintains a belief in the role of God and religion in civil life, but as Pocock argues this is a God of history who acted in history and whose kingdom to come, as revealed in scripture, models the legitimacy of secular authority.

Hobbes's objection to the papacy may at the same time be taken as an argument against the Presbyterian desire to create a national church in England. Priests should not have authority over the character of public worship, but only the legitimate (secular) sovereign. To be sure, this means that the sovereign (but not the church) had the right to impose a single, uniform faith on his subjects, but Hobbes's support for Independency registers his concern for the maintenance of public peace.

Given the diversity of beliefs and religious practices in England in the mid-1600s, the best way to maintain order was to allow men to follow their consciences in so far as the form of public worship they adopted did not involve disobedience to or questioning of the legitimate authority of the sovereign. Catholicism, on these grounds, was not an acceptable form of public worship because it involved the belief that the pope had temporal authority over the king. Similarly, the Presbyterian claim that the church, not the king, should determine the character of public worship undermined the authority of the sovereign over the public life of his subjects.

If the sovereign were to decide on the character of public worship, how could Hobbes square this with his apparent support for religious toleration and freedom of individual conscience? The unlimited right of the sovereign to determine the rules of public conduct would seem, in principle at least, to impinge on religious freedom. This is only the case, however, if we identify religious belief and faith with its outward, public representation. For Hobbes, this view of faith is, quite simply, mistaken. A Christian's principal interest is in salvation and all that is necessary for this 'is contained in two Vertues, *Faith in Christ*, and *Obedience to Laws*'.[70] Like Luther, then, Hobbes adopts the distinction between the inner and outer man and claims that faith is purely a matter for the inner man. Even if a king were to forbid men to believe in Christ, it would have no effect 'because Beleef, and Unbeleef never follow mens Commands. Faith is a gift of God, which Man can neither give, nor take away by promise of rewards, or menaces or torture'. For the Christian, faith turns around the belief in one very simple article and that which it entails: '*Jesus is the Christ*'.[71] At the same time (and as for Luther), no man can be saved through his works alone, as all men are guilty of sin. For Hobbes, obedience to the laws of God is necessary for salvation. However, the laws of God should not be understood to be all those that are laid out in the scriptures. Rather:

> The Laws of God therefore are none but the Laws of Nature, whereof the principall is, that we should not violate our Faith, that is a commandment to obey our Civill Soveraigns, which wee constituted over us, by mutuall pact with one another. And this Law of God, that commandeth Obedience to the Law Civill, commandeth by consequence Obedience to all the Precepts of the Bible; which ... is there onely Law, where the Civill Soveraign has made it so; and in other places but Counsell; which a man at his own perill, may without injustice refuse to obey.[72]

It is the laws of nature that require Christian men to obey the civil sovereign, whether the sovereign is a Christian (who allows belief in the article 'Jesus is the Christ') or an 'Infidel'. Resistance to the latter still breaches the laws of God (which are the laws of nature) and 'rejecteth the counsel of the Apostles, that admonished all Christians to obey their Princes, and all Children to obey their Parents, and Masters, in all things'.[73]

Hobbes, then, prefers the power of the civil sovereign to that of the priest and the prophet, even if that sovereign is an infidel whose laws violate the 'Precepts of the Bible'. A man cannot justly disobey such laws, since it is the civil sovereign who is the sole arbiter of what constitutes a just or unjust law. What lies at the heart of Hobbes's argument here is his scepticism about private belief as any grounds for public order. Why do people accept the scriptures as the word of God? They cannot know that the scriptures are the word of God unless they themselves have been subject to supernatural revelation. It follows that people believe that the scriptures are the word of God on the basis of what others tell them. That is, belief in the scriptures as the word of God must ultimately spring from authority:

> He therefore, to whom God has not supernaturally revealed, that they are his [laws], nor those that published them, were sent by him, is not obliged to obey them, by any Authority, but his, whose Commands have already the force of Laws; that is to say, by any other Authority, then that of the Common-wealth, residing in the Soveraign, who only has the Legislative power. Again, if it be not the Legislative Authority of the Common-wealth, that giveth them the force of Laws, it must bee some other Authority derived from God, either private, or publique: if private, it obliges onely him, to whom in particular God hath been pleased to reveale it. For if every man should be obliged to take for Gods Law, what particular men, on pretence of private Inspiration, or Revelation, should obtrude upon him, … it were impossible that any divine law should be acknowledged. If publique, it is the Authority of the *Common-wealth*, or of the *Church*. But the Church, if it be one person, is the same thing with a Common-wealth of Christians, called a *Common-wealth*, because it consisteth of men united in one person, their Soveraign; and a *Church*, because it consisteth in Christian men, united in one Christian Soveraign. But if the Church be not one person, then it hath no authority at all; it can neither command nor doe any action at all; nor is capable of having any power, or right to anything; nor has any Will, Reason, nor Voice; for all these qualities are personall.[74]

We can now see why Hobbes's consideration of religion was so important for his understanding of legitimate public power. Hobbes's principal concern was that the plurality of competing religious beliefs that had become established in mid-seventeenth century England (and indeed in Europe more widely) threatened to engender perpetual civil war. To avoid such a possibility, it was necessary for men to submit to a sovereign power that had authority over all public conduct, including the character of public worship, without them surrendering their faith, which is entirely subjective and internal in character. Christians had nothing to fear from such a sovereign, even if he were an infidel. Salvation rests only on the heart-felt belief that Jesus is Christ and in obligation to the Laws of God, which are commensurate with the laws of nature. The very model for the constitution of just civil authority had been provided in (biblical) history by the Covenant made between the people of Israel to obey God's commandments. God in this sense was sovereign, but there was no covenant between him and the Jews; rather the Covenant was made between the people when God's laws and the promise of pro- tection obedience to them provided, was revealed by his 'Viceroys' or 'Lieutenants': Abraham, Moses and the prophets. God ruled over all men by virtue of his might, but also had *'peculiar* Subjects, who he commanded by a Voice, as one man speaketh to another'. In this regard, 'by the *Kingdome of God*, is properly meant a Common-wealth, instituted (by the consent of those which were to be subject thereto) for their Civill Government, and the regulating of their behaviour, not onely towards God their King, but also towards one another in point of justice, and towards other Nations both in peace and warre'. 'In short, the Kingdome of God is a Civill Kingdome'.[75]

While Hobbes's understanding of religion represents a bold assertion that God is to be understood largely from a historical and materialist perspective, what makes *Leviathan* such a radical and transformative text is the notion that we can in fact comprehend the character of legitimate political authority and justice without any reference to divine law. In the first two parts of *Leviathan*, the rightful character of public power is derived from the nature of human beings and the laws of nature. For Hobbes, human nature is characterised both by reason and by the pas- sions. The passions are to be understood as no more than the 'Interiour Beginnings of Voluntary Motions' in individuals, that is either the 'appetite' or 'desire' we exhibit toward an object, or the 'aversion' we have 'fromward something'.[76] The passions are psychological phenomena that result from the subjection of human beings to the physical laws governing matter in motion. While reason, as the capacity to recognise chains of causes and effects, may tell us something of how such appetites and aversions come to be formed in people, it can tell us nothing of what particular passions people should possess.[77] Accordingly, we see displayed amongst human beings a wide variety of passions and the object of some people's desires can easily repel others.

Hobbes's understanding of human nature is certainly not optimistic, but neither is it as singularly bleak and pessimistic as is often thought, since among the human passions he counts love, joy, hope, courage, benevolence, good will and charity.[78] The *bellum omnium contra omnes* that takes place in the state of nature (or what, more accurately, Hobbes refers to as 'the NATURALL CONDITION of Mankind')[79] does not arise because men are, by nature, exclusively mean-spirited and belligerent. Rather, since men are by nature largely equal in abilities they are also likely to be equals in the hope of obtaining the things they need for their conservation 'and sometimes their delectation only'. Where then, 'any two men desire the same thing, which neverthelesse they cannot both enjoy, they become enemies; and in the way to their End ... endeavour to destroy, or subdue one another'. We thus see in the state of nature equality leading to 'diffidence' and ultimately to 'warre'.[80] At the same time, however, men have passions that make them averse to death and warfare:

> The Passions that encline men to Peace, are Feare of Death; Desire of such things as are necessary to commodious living; and a Hope by their Industry to obtain them. And Reason suggesteth convenient Articles of Peace, upon which men may be drawn to agreement. These Articles, are they, which otherwise are called the Lawes of Nature.[81]

In their natural condition, men possess a right of nature to do whatever is necessary according to reason in order to preserve themselves. But for Hobbes, 'right reason' informs us that if each pursues his natural liberty to self-preservation in the state of nature there can be no security, no certainty about our relations with other men and little hope for the future. What thus takes men out of the perpetual state of war characteristic of their natural condition is their reasoned judgement that men desire one thing above all else: life. Men will therefore agree to institute whatever measures necessary for the preservation of life as a law of nature (*Lex Naturalis*), that is:

> a Precept, or generall Rule, found out by Reason, by which a man is forbidden to do, that, which is destructive of his life, or taketh away

the means of preserving the same; and to omit, that, by which he thinketh it may be best preserved ... RIGHT, consisteth in liberty to do, or to forbeare; Whereas LAW, determineth, and bindeth to one of them: so that Law, and Right, differ as much, as Obligation, and Liberty; which in one and the same matter are inconsistent.[82]

It is through natural reason, then, that men come to accept that the best means to respect the natural law of self-preservation is by contracting with one another to '*lay down this right to all things; and be contented with so much liberty against other men, as he would allow other men against himselfe*'. Men transfer their natural rights to an external power while maintaining their sole inalienable right, that of self-defence.[83] In contracting in this fashion, men create a Commonwealth in which the right over the life and death of other men is given to the sovereign power, for we cannot hope for men to maintain their covenant with one another (that is, not to harm each other's security and liberty) 'without the Sword' and without being in 'terrour of some Power' to punish them for breaches of their civil promises.[84] Having made a covenant to submit to the sovereign power, men cannot change the form of government (which may be that of one man or an assembly of men),[85] for to rebel against the sovereign would be to do an injustice by attempting to take back what was surrendered voluntarily in men's covenant:

And whereas some men have pretended for their disobedience to the Soveraign, a new Covenant, made, not with men, but with God; this is also unjust: for there is no Covenant with God, but by mediation of some body that representeth Gods Person; which none doth but Gods Lieutenant, who hath the Soveraignty under God. But this pretence of Covenant with God, is so evident a lye, even in the pretenders own consciences, that it is not onely an act of an unjust, but also of a vile, and unmanly disposition.

Moreover, the sovereign himself is no part of the covenant and is not, therefore, under any obligation as to how to wield the power that has been transferred to him:

Because the Right of bearing the Person of them all, is given to him they make Soveraigne, by Covenant only of one to another, and not of him to any of them; there can happen no breach of Covenant on the part of the Soveraigne; and consequently none of his Subjects, by any pretence of forfeiture, can be freed from his Subjection.[86]

What we see here is the invocation of the historical Covenant of the Jews to accept God's laws as a way of conceiving the contract between men in the state of nature to establish a sovereign power, that is, the state. In both instances what the covenanters receive for their obedience is protection from each other and external aggressors, but they are not granted this through an agreement with their protector. They together agree to *submit* to the power of the sovereign, and can demand nothing from him in return.

As Sheldon Wolin has claimed, Hobbes's account of political power may be regarded as 'grossly oversimplified'. The Leviathan must be a fearsome creature, capable of instilling in men a sense of terror so great that they will be bound under all (or at least the very large majority of circumstances) to obey the law. But in fact, Hobbes's sovereign is much weaker than the fabled Leviathan. In establishing public power, men effectively alienate the sovereign from them to the extent that it becomes impossible for him 'to join his subjects' will to his in the pursuit of a common endeavour'.[87] At the same time, as Harrington saw, Hobbes leaves the sovereign dependent on private power because property and wealth are things that men may legitimately use after the creation of the public power, so long as their private enjoyment does not encroach on the liberty and security of others. As the sovereign relies on 'men and arms' and not 'words and promises' to enforce his laws, he is then forced to turn to men of wealth and property to provide for the means of violence. This dependence means that the Leviathan is more suitably compared not to a great monster of the deep but to a 'mere spitfrog'.[88]

The problem with this claim is that the logic of Hobbes's theory of the constitution of sovereign power rules out private property as any kind of right that men can claim against the sovereign. Indeed, Hobbes is quite explicit in his denial of the doctrine of the right to property as an extension of self-ownership, a doctrine that was advocated by the Levellers and other radical groups in the 1640s. The call for a liberty that was freedom from laws was, for Hobbes, at the same time a demand to return to the anarchy of the state of nature.[89] Property is as much subject to the laws of the sovereign as any of the public action of men, for: 'If the Right of the Sovereign [to their goods be] excluded, he cannot performe the office they have put him into; which is, to defend them both from forraign enemies, and from the injuries of one another ... And if the Propriety of Subjects, exclude not the Right of the Soveraign Representative to their Goods; much lesse to their offices of Judicature, or Execution, in which they Represent the Soveraigne himselfe'.[90] Nevertheless, we might see Harrington's claim against Hobbes at operating

at a more general level, given that in Harrington's eyes no effective public power could be practised without enjoying the active participation of
a large number of citizens, something that could only come about
through a complex system of representation. While Hobbes's Leviathan
'represents' his subjects, there is no sense in which, after the original
covenant, subjects are able to articulate their interests to and with the
sovereign power. His 'representation' of them stops with his protection
of their lives.

The force of Harrington's criticism was that it pointed to the sense in
which the depoliticisation of subjects takes place in Hobbes's texts. It
seems hollow to call these subjects 'citizens' as they have nothing of the
liberty of citizens in the classical city republics to make the laws under
which they live. For Hobbes, men could attempt to be 'citizens' in this
sense (though ultimately this would just lead to the anarchy of the state
of nature), but he vigorously denied the claim that man was by nature
political. While Aristotle claimed that some creatures, such as bees and
ants, could be counted as political because they live sociably in the
absence of a coercive power, such sociability is not based on an agreement
since these animals are devoid of speech and reason. 'Politics' for these
creatures arises from instinct. For Hobbes, men are in contrast constantly in competition for honour and dignity; there is a difference for
them between private and common good; men recognise faults in the
conduct of their common business and aspire to correct these; men are
not at ease at peace; and the agreement of men to institute a sovereign
power is by covenant.[91] The sovereign, as Hobbes claims throughout
Leviathan, is an artificial man. Men authorise the sovereign, but having
done so they retreat into a non-political realm of sociability where they
can form attachments to others safe in the knowledge that they will be
protected by a public power external to them.

There is a sense in which Hobbes's texts involve a desire to constrain
and limit the public power so that is just performs the minimum number of functions required to maintain life and social peace. Men are
denuded of the right to determine the character of the laws they live
under and submit to a sovereign who is himself like a man in the state
of nature: he has the liberty to pursue whatever actions are necessary for
his self-preservation (though as the sovereign power is endowed with
natural reason, Hobbes expects him to equate his self-preservation with
that of his people; to do otherwise would do be to invite disobedience
and possible rebellion). But far from this view of the depoliticisation of
man entailing the reassertion of traditional authority over individual
liberty, its effect was precisely the opposite. As we have seen, Hobbes was

primarily concerned to establish what kind of institutions of government could protect the common good in a society where there was a plurality of values represented by a variety of confessions. His answer to that question was the state. Quite simply put, in early modern Europe no other institution had the power and means of violence at its disposal to enforce social peace. Yet at the same time the emerging sovereign territorial state was a new force, one that involved the uprooting of traditional forms of authority, social and political relations throughout Europe. In so far as Hobbes depoliticises man, this is precisely to accommodate a novel form of power that alone was capable of leading European society out of the destructive Wars of Religion, and in so doing creating a new set of social arrangements in which men could enjoy their liberty.

Yet if Hobbes's depoliticisation of man, in this respect, has a radical function, there is another sense in which his political thought does indeed undertake a politicisation of man. In part, this is because Hobbes's theory explicitly makes men the authors of political authority. However, Hobbes is not alone in this respect. In the context of the late sixteenth and seventeenth century, and as we have seen with the Levellers, the view that political power rests on the consent of the governed is commonplace. Yet Hobbes's civil science politicises men in another way. Men are not only the source of political knowledge by virtue of the public exercise of natural reason, but have become the objects of political knowledge. As Michel Foucault claimed, the seventeenth century witnessed the invention of 'man' as an object of scientific investigation.[92] At the same time, Hobbes's texts reflect the sense in which this newly crafted man was political man, a concept that was central to discourses of political radicalism in the Enlightenment.

3
Enlightenment, Law and Nature: Montesquieu and Rousseau

The concept of tradition has played a vital role in the composition of modern political identities. In an important sense, to be a radical is to desire a revolt against tradition, to seek the emancipation of people from mystical obligations to dead generations, releasing in them a full recognition of the boundless potential for change and innovation that is inherent in human nature. In contrast, the conservative disposition involves an affirmation of the dependent character of man. Without the practical wisdom that is bequeathed to one generation by its predecessors, a wisdom founded on the misfortunes and triumphs of immemorial experience, man becomes subjected to his most base and savage instincts. Social order is sacrificed on the altar of a 'liberty' conceived in ignorance of the dangers and vicissitudes of the human condition. Yet it would be a mistake to represent this dispute over tradition as definitive of the entire history of political thought. The formation of modern political identities required that before tradition could become an object of contestation, it had to be invented. The modern concept of 'tradition' was both founded in and, at the same moment, repudiated by the European Enlightenment. In such a way, the Enlightenment as an intellectual and social movement crafted the vocabulary of modern political life in a plenary rethinking of the form and substance of human history.

At the heart of the philosophical history that appeared in the Enlightenment were three related problems. The first question was why, if man shared a common nature constituted by his capacity for reason and his uniquely human passions, relations between men varied so widely from place to place? If such differences could not be accounted for in terms of human nature, what were their causes? Second, how had the particular kind of philosophical and historical consciousness necessary for posing this first question arisen in contemporary European society?

Reason could be understood as the defining feature of man, but what had allowed men to employ their reason to reflect on the causes of their current condition without recourse to explanations of mystical or religious character? In other words, what were the historical (and as it would turn out, social and political) circumstances that made rational, scientific knowledge of man and his human relations possible? Yet these two problems could not have been conceived of, at least in such terms, were it not for the presence of a third. If we had become aware of the conditions that both impeded and facilitated man's capacity to think rationally and to shape his relations according to rational criteria, what were the measures that could be taken to secure for the future a world fit for the practice of human liberty and reason?

With different inflexions, these three problems are posed in the texts of both Montesquieu and Jean-Jacques Rousseau. But perhaps more than any other Enlightenment thinkers they pursued them with the question of the political conditions for modern liberty at the front of their minds. In so doing they articulated the central precepts around which radical political discourse would form in the prelude to the French Revolution.

Montesquieu

The work of Charles-Louis de Secondat, Baron de Montesquieu and La Brède (1689–1751), has in the main been considered from three perspectives. It has been upheld as heralding and defending a liberal republicanism that was to provide a blueprint, moral and political, for the creation of the American system of government and modern liberalism.[1] In stark contrast, others have identified Montesquieu's texts as an appeal for the restoration of the power of the nobility against both the despotic and popular tendencies of modern government.[2] From a similar point of view, we can see his work as articulating the material interests of the aristocratic class of which he was a member, even though it may contain important conceptual breakthroughs for the social sciences.[3] The third perspective accentuates the latter point, seeing in Montesquieu the development of a method of sociological and political analysis that constitutes a central foundation for the modern social sciences.[4] For Ernst Cassirer, Montesquieu was the first thinker to outline a 'political and sociological doctrine of types' of the kind that would be central to the work of twentieth-century sociologists such as Max Weber.[5] Of course, all of these claims can to some degree be substantiated by reference to Montesquieu's texts. What would be very difficult to establish in this way, as we will show, is the portrayal of Montesquieu as a modern political radical. Montesquieu did not predict the French Revolution and it is most likely that had he lived through its events he would have been horrified by the course it took. If we had to place Montesquieu in any political category we would probably identify him as a liberal reformist, though hesitatingly since much of his political writing has a 'conservative' tone. Nonetheless, in developing a particular conception of the character of laws and of the relationship between social conditions and political institutions, Montesquieu's work is indeed radical and provides important conceptual resources for the formation of radical political knowledge in the Enlightenment and thereafter.

Montesquieu had an impeccably aristocratic background. Jacob de Secondat, his great-grandfather, was granted the barony of Montesquieu by Henry IV in 1606. Montesquieu's father had married a noblewoman who had inherited the estate of La Brède, which in turn passed to the young Charles-Louis on her death.[6] As part of the *noblesse de robe*, several de Secondats had played an active part in the *parlement* of Bordeaux. Montesquieu served the *parlement*, like his grandfather and uncle before him, as *président à mortier*.[7] By all accounts he was, however, an unenthusiastic participant in the *parlement*, and after selling his office in 1726 concentrated on producing and selling wine out of La Brède and furthering his scientific and literary interests. These were pursued with like-minded men (mainly nobles) in the Bordeaux Academy of Sciences, which he joined in 1716 and of which he was soon after to become the leading light. In the early eighteenth century, a number of such provincial scientific academies sprung up in France with royal approval. Given their nature, these were far from being hotbeds of sedition, at least in comparison to the literary salons of Paris (toward which Montesquieu gravitated after the publication of his *Persian Letters*), but as Judith Shklar remarks it was in the Academy that Montesquieu came 'to his most fundamental and enduring conviction: that science is our best moral medicine'.[8]

Montesquieu had a profound interest in the natural sciences and, as we will see, considerations of physics and biology had an important bearing on his philosophical history and science of politics. Yet his first major piece of published work was neither a scientific nor political treatise but rather an epistolary novel that was to mark Montesquieu out as a favourite of the bourgeois literary public and foe to the defenders of religious orthodoxy and the absolutist state. The *Persian Letters* was first published, anonymously, in 1721. It takes the form of correspondence between two Persian men who have journeyed to France – Usbek, the master of a large harem in Ispahan and his companion Rica – and several other protagonists, including Usbek's wives and eunuchs in the Persian seraglio. The main character, Usbek, fearing that he has created enemies in the court of his despotic sovereign for speaking honestly and avoiding corruption, has sent himself into exile. The narrative is built around Usbek's inability to control his wives from a distance, and his resort to increasingly harsh and cruel treatment via his eunuchs in a way that only serves to alienate his wives from him further. Ultimately he feels forced to risk returning to Ispahan to bring order to the seraglio. Reading the novel, we are invited to contrast Usbek's despotic and grim side with his reasoned and enlightened criticisms of the manners, political and religious life of the French. The book is thus, at the same time, both a satire and a moral fable. Yet what we are supposed to take from it is not the notion of the necessary moral ambiguity of men given their human nature, but how variation in moral qualities is related to environment. The two different sides of Usbek's character relate to their different locations and objects: Usbek is an enlightened critic in France, an irrational despot with respect to his life in Persia.

The *Persian Letters* was composed in the wake of the death of Louis XIV in 1715. Like many other publications of the time it expresses both oblique and quite explicit criticisms of the 'Sun King's' reign. Letter 37, for example, has Usbek commenting on a number of the King's personal failings.[9] The *Letters* also includes passages indicating Montesquieu's disapproval of religious centralisation and intolerance under Louis XIV. In Letter 85 Usbek argues that 'since in every religion there are precepts which are useful to society, it is well that they should be obeyed with enthusiasm, and what is more likely to encourage this enthusiasm than a multiplicity of religions'. While Louis XIV had revoked the Edict of Nantes in 1685, forcing prominent and wealthy French Protestants to flee, Usbek asserts that 'the adherents of a tolerated minority religion make themselves more useful to their country than the adherents of dominant religion, because ... they will undertake the most ungrateful social functions'.[10] The notions that religious belief performs important functions for society (in contrast to those of Pierre Bayle, who Montesquieu criticises in the *Spirit of the Laws* for arguing that atheism is no less socially useful that religion)[11] and that religious toleration is one indication of a free state, are present in all of Montesquieu's major writings. The difference between their expression in the *Persian Letters* and in *The Spirit of the Laws* is that in the latter they appear within the framework of what is intended as a rigorous science of the forms of government. In the former they operate primarily as tools of criticism of a specific regime and its policies.

That the tone of the *Letters* is satirical and ersatz does not, however, imply that they contain no important conceptual considerations of the nature of political life and, more specifically, the relation between the form of government and the character of a society. The series of letters on the 'Troglodytes', which occurs at an early point in the book, outlines at least some of the conceptual ground on which the main analytical themes of *The Spirit of the Laws* are built. Usbek tells the story of the Troglodytes to his friend Mirza in Isaphan. Mirza had written to Usbek asking for his opinion on a 'moral' question, that is 'whether men are made happy by pleasure, and the satisfaction of the senses, or by the practice of virtue'. Mirza enjoins Usbek to consider this question by expanding on a point he had heard him make in the past, 'that justice is a quality which is as proper to [men] as existence'.[12] Usbek replies to Mirza that he can best respond not with 'very abstract arguments' or 'philosophical subtleties', but rather by recounting the story of the Troglodytes. We learn that the Troglodytes were a small, unruly Arabic nation that lived under a 'king of foreign origin' who sought to curb their 'natural wickedness' through severe measures. The Troglodytes overthrew the King and agreed among themselves to create a new government led by ministers they appointed. However, 'hardly had they elected them than they found them unbearable; and they massacred them too'. Without government, they agreed not to obey anyone but that each should look 'after his interests exclusively, without considering those of others'. What followed was a series of disasters in which the pursuit of self-interest led the Troglodytes to self-destruction: a great portion of the population perished because those living on the low ground failed to share their crop with the highlanders in an arid season and when in the following year the highlanders refused to feed their lowland cousins after a flood; men took the wives and land of other men by force, leading to a cycle of vengeance; because they refused to honour their debts, a doctor from a neighbouring country who had previously cured an illness sweeping through the Troglodyte nation and who they had left unpaid, failed to respond to their pleas when the disease struck again. It was in this way that 'the Troglodytes perished because of their wickedness, and fell victim to their own injustice'.[13]

Montesquieu's recounting of the fable of the Troglodytes was designed to ridicule conceptions of the natural condition of man as one in which individuals lived by self-interest alone. If this were indeed the case, then political society would always be impossible because as soon as any authority was seen to be interfering with the interests of individuals they would cast it off and resort to their natural state of independence.

The point is made clearer by the continuation of the Troglodytes' tale. Not all of them perished and the two families left were headed by men who 'understood what justice was; they loved virtue'. They raised their children in a virtuous manner, to work in the common interest, and thus over generations '[a]s their numbers grew larger, they remained just as closely united, and virtue, so far from becoming weaker among the multitude, was on the contrary fortified by a greater number of examples'. Religion soon appeared among the Troglodytes 'to soften any roughness of manner left over from nature', and the rites of religion centred around the happiness and health of the society rather than individual wealth or good fortune. The errors of the first Troglodytes' injustices were remembered from generation to generation in fables and song. 'Nature provided for their desires as abundantly as for their needs. In this happy land cupidity was alien.' The nation considered itself as one family and lines between property blurred: 'the herds were almost always mixed up together, and the only task that was usually neglected was that of sorting them out'.[14] When foreign people became jealous of the virtue and happiness of the Troglodytes they attempted to pillage their country, but such was the Troglodytes' outrage at this injustice and the strength of their bonds that they valiantly defeated the invaders.[15]

Montesquieu here uses the device of a utopia, in a way that is common to the genre, to demonstrate the flaws of an established argument, in this instance the 'Hobbist' account of the state of nature. For any kind of society to exist, there will be a need for a commitment to the common interest that is reinforced through education and religious belief and practice. However, Montesquieu does not invoke his Troglodyte utopia, as is commonplace in utopian literature, as a token against which our existing social life should be measured and toward which we should aspire. Such virtue could only exist among the Troglodytes when their lives were simple and relationships conducted primarily on the basis of kinship ties. Yet, as Usbek's next letter to Mirza shows, this situation could not persist. The Troglodytes became tired of virtue when their numbers grew and their industriousness provided new opportunities for wealth and luxury. Yet having learnt the lessons of their ancestors, they knew better than to cast off public virtue and return to the condition of unfettered self-interest and instead sought out a king who would ensure civil peace. The old Troglodyte approached to take up the crown was dismayed. He saw that they 'would prefer to obey his laws, which would be less rigid that your own customs ... provided that you avoided falling into the worst crimes, you would have no need of virtue'. The old man then declares that his death is close at hand and that the Troglodyte ancestors whom he is shortly to meet would be grieved when he told them 'that I have left you under the rule of something other than virtue'.[16]

This conclusion to the Troglodyte fable might be thought to give weight to Keohane's assertion that '[i]n his youth, Montesquieu cast his lot with the Ancients against the Moderns, and he never reversed himself'.[17] A careful reading of the Troglodyte cycle, however, shows the premise of this claim to be questionable. Clearly we are meant to sympathise with the old Troglodyte who laments the passing of virtue, the principle on which (as Montesquieu will later show in detail) the government of the classical republic was founded. But in *The Spirit of the Laws*, and even in his earlier work, it is far from clear that Montesquieu makes a case for the superiority of the Ancients. The Troglodyte letters demonstrate that changes in the nature of government and law are brought about not merely because of the will of great men or the rational choices of individuals, but because of a change in men's circumstances and their social relations. The demise of ancient virtue is the price to pay for a society of science and commerce, and in the latter we find the means of satisfying a very large range of human needs and wants. Richter claims that while Montesquieu 'thought modern knowledge in many ways superior to that of the ancients, he did not believe in the theory of progress. Indeed, he believed in the eventual corruption of all states ...'[18] This needs some qualification. It is indeed the case that Montesquieu rejected the notion of moral progress in the sense that we can witness its growth through the ages. Moral progress in this respect does not, however, equate to progress in other areas of human life, and Montesquieu's arguments in the *Persian Letters*, placed in the mouth of Usbek, already involve a view of the development in science and technology that is worked out further in *The Spirit of the Laws*. Moreover, it would be wrong to claim that Montesquieu considers 'virtue' to be the sole register of a society's level of moral progress. As we will see, he is to an extent ambiguous about the status of transhistorical values, but it is possible to identify in his texts a prioritisation of liberty as the metric of moral standing.

In the *Persian Letters*, then, there is a focus on the relationship between a society's history, the way in which it organises the relations between individuals and disposes of property, its manners and morals and the character of its government and the law. Montesquieu pursued this concern further in his *Considerations on the Causes of the Romans' Greatness and Decline* (1734). As Shklar claims, one of the leading aims of the work (which it shares with *The Spirit of the Laws*) was to 'demonstrate the great difference between ancient and modern politics'. At the same time, the 'purpose of the enterprise was to demonstrate that history can be understood by seeking out the deep, underlying "general" causes of political changes, and not by simply recording symptomatic events, which are merely "occasional" or "particular" causes'.[19] The *Considerations* do indeed mark an important moment of transformation in modern historical understanding, contesting the notions that it is the actions of great men that constitute the most important material for historical research (as for Voltaire) and that accident and *fortuna* play the leading role in determining a society's fate (as for Machiavelli).[20] Accordingly, toward the end of the *Considerations*, Montesquieu writes:

> It is not fortune that rules the world. On this point, consult the Romans who enjoyed a series of consecutive successes when their government followed one policy, and an unbroken set of reverses when it followed another. There are general causes, whether moral or physical, which act upon every monarchy, which advance, maintain, or ruin it. All accidents are subject to these causes. If the chance loss of a battle, that is, a particular cause, ruins a state, there is a general cause that created the situation whereby this state could perish by the loss of a single battle. In a word, the principal trend carries along with it the outcome of all particular accidents.[21]

For Montesquieu, there were two main causes of Rome's decline, both a product of its imperial triumphs. First, the Roman conquest of territories 'beyond the Alps and the sea' led to a loosening of soldiers' identities as citizens. Territorial expansion empowered generals and governors, and increasingly it was toward the authority of these figures, rather than that of the Republic, that the soldiery were drawn. Allegiance was pledged to powerful generals like Sulla, Marius, Pompey and Julius Caesar, resulting in civil wars that ended only with the fall of the Republic and the emergence of Caesar Augustus as the first Emperor. Secondly, '[i]f the great size of its empire ruined the republic, the size of the city itself contributed just as much to its downfall'. In the Roman Republic, citizenship had been the exclusive privilege of those free men who dwelled within the city, yet the Roman empire rested on the toil of all Italians, 'the hands with which it had put the rest of the universe in chains'. Refused the privileges of citizenship, they revolted against Roman authority, and to ensure its survival the city was forced to bestow the rights of citizenship on people in all its territories. 'Thereafter, Rome was no longer that city distinguished by a people with a single spirit, the same love for liberty, the same hatred of tyranny.' As each city possessed its own leaders and particular interests, the respect afforded to Rome's magistrates, gods, temples, and so on was lost: 'Rome was no longer viewed with the same eyes, did not inspire the same love of country as in the past; and those modes of feeling that had once been unique to the Romans ceased to exist.'[22]

Montesquieu thus emphasises the importance of the unintended consequences of human actions for the character of particular societies and the forces exerted upon them that compel their transformation. Historians had singularly failed to recognise that, in the case of Rome, past glories could not be recaptured by great men overcoming their petty squabbles and lust for power, because such internal divisions were in the first place the very grounds on which Rome had become such a great empire. These divisions 'were necessary', 'they had always existed' and they 'should have continued to exist'.[23] Once the republic had exceeded a certain size, it became necessary to change its form of government, to create an imperial power, embodied in the person of the Emperor, which was able to use force to keep united such diverse and potentially unruly territories. Such a form of government was bound to be of a qualitatively different nature than its predecessor and was itself doomed to failure since no central authority would ever be powerful enough to pacify such a large empire in perpetuity. In short, Rome was a victim of its own success.

Montesquieu's regard for the fortunes of the Romans was prompted not so much out of historical curiosity, but by his interest in philosophical history. 'Philosophical history' here does not refer to the history of philosophy, but rather to the philosophy of 'history' understood as a distinct object of human knowledge. Montesquieu was concerned with some of the central questions of modern historiography, principally 'what is history'? From the *Considerations* it is clear that he did not believe this question to be satisfactorily answered by reference to the actions of great men or the accidental concatenation of events. For Montesquieu, the history of human societies obeys certain principles or laws that can be derived from its study. The Romans were not unique. Their fortunes were subject to the same laws that had effected earlier empires, and the fate of future empires would also be governed by them. These laws were necessary and immutable. They had the same status as causes of natural phenomena, and in this respect Montesquieu was clearly looking to the kind of physics he had become acquainted with in the Academy of Bordeaux as a model. Having recognised the law-governed nature of history as a whole, it would then be possible to establish the particular laws that determine the character of a society at any one point in its history. As Althusser remarks: 'If Montesquieu was not the first to conceive of the idea of a social physics, he was the first to attempt to give it the spirit of the new physics, to set out not from essences but from facts, and from these facts to disengage their laws.'[24]

In light of this observation, the title of Montesquieu's *magnum opus*, *The Spirit of the Laws* (1748) is already partially explained. Yet there is also something seemingly mysterious about the idea of a 'spirit' of the laws. If Montesquieu wants to eschew notions of strange essences as any part of the understanding of human history and society, then why chose such a word with all its distinctly religious connotations? To understand this, we have to see that in the title of his book Montesquieu is referring to a different order of laws than the necessary, immutable and universal principles that he takes to govern human history as a whole. The laws he has in mind as being animated by a 'spirit' are positive laws. These are laws in the form of commands that people may obey or disobey. Laws in this sense are rules of conduct that govern the relationship between states (the 'right of nations'), between the rulers and the ruled ('political right') and between the citizens of the same state ('civil right').[25] The political and civil laws of a country should relate to its geographical character, to its climate, to the way in which it organises the production of things, to the liberty it affords its people, to its religion, wealth, size of population, commerce, 'mores and manners', and to the kind of government it possesses. Montesquieu promises to 'examine all these relations; together they form what is called THE SPIRIT OF THE LAWS'.[26]

At the same time, however, at the start of the book Montesquieu indicates that positive laws are only possible given other laws that operate on man and form the conditions for society. These are the 'laws of nature, so named because they derive uniquely from the constitution of our being'. Man 'receives' these laws in the state of nature before any society has been created. The most important of them is the one 'which impresses on us the idea of a creator and leads us towards him', but for Montesquieu this does not come first in the order of natural laws. In their natural condition men will be primarily interested in securing their survival rather than enquiring into the nature of being. But, and as in the *Persian Letters*, Montesquieu rejects Hobbes's portrayal of the state of nature as one in which men have 'first the desire to subjugate one another'. Rather, because men feel inferior and scarcely equal in the state of nature they 'would not seek to attack one another, and peace would be the first natural law'. The second natural law, according to Montesquieu, is to seek nourishment, the third to seek sexual union. As well as satisfying these natural feelings, however, men also develop and share knowledge of the world, creating a bond between them, providing 'another motive for uniting'. The fourth natural law is, therefore, 'the desire to live in society'.[27]

However: '[a]s soon as men are in society, they lose their feelings of weakness; the equality that was among them ceases, and the state of war begins'.[28] Such a conception of the character of the state of nature and the generation of conflict by the creation of social bonds is also important, as we will see, in Rousseau's writing. But there, however, it plays a different role. In Montesquieu's text the notion of a state of nature presents significant difficulties given the scheme of concepts that is set out in the rest of the book. In short, the problem is how he can entertain the notion that society emerges out of a state of nature given his view of the complex causes and self-determining character of the positive laws. The early pages of *The Spirit of the Laws* might be read as indicating that what will follow is an intricate account of the derivation of social and political life from the state of nature and its natural laws, but no such account is forthcoming. The problem posed, therefore, is why Montesquieu leaves open the possibility, which he alludes to elsewhere in the text and in his earlier writings, that natural laws are in some significant sense prior to positive laws and provide an external standpoint from which the justice of the latter can be evaluated.

We will return to this problem presently, and in particular the suggestion that Montesquieu is inconsistent, because it has an important bearing on the radical character of *The Spirit of the Laws*. But we should now focus on Montesquieu's description of the various forms of government and the 'principles' that inform them. In Book 2 Montesquieu outlines a tripartite division of forms of government. There are three kinds: republics, monarchies and despotisms. He therefore departs from the ancient classification of government according to the number of people who make the laws. In both despotic and monarchic states one man governs, but with the difference that in the former government is practised according to 'fixed and established laws' whereas in the latter the ruler 'without law and without rule, draws everything along by his own will and his own caprices'.[29] On the other hand, the number of legislators is taken into account in his description of republican government, of which he claims there are two types: democracy and aristocracy.

These three kinds of government are animated by different 'principles'. Whereas the nature of government is 'its particular structure' the principle of government 'is the human passions it sets in motion'.[30] Under the different forms of government, therefore, we will expect people to feel and behave differently in relation to the public power. The principle that informs republican government, that is both democracy and aristocracy, is virtue. A popular government must be virtuous since it is the people themselves who make the laws that govern their conduct. Citizens need to act in the common interest in order to avoid the problem of corruption. Aristocratic government has greater stability than democracy because only a few have the power to make and enforce the law. But aristocracy is also open to corruption unless the nobility is able to check itself, which it can do by two means: making themselves 'in some way equal to their people' or respecting a 'lesser virtue', 'a certain moderation that renders the nobles at least equal among themselves, which brings about their preservation'.[31] In contrast to republics, the principle of monarchy is honour. Since rule is by one person alone, it is difficult to encourage subjects to be virtuous, and so political stability can be achieved only by harnessing individual self-regard to the common good. In a monarchy:

> the prejudice of each person and each condition, takes the place of political virtue of which I have spoken and represents it everywhere. It can inspire the finest actions, joined with the force of the laws, it can lead to the goal of government as does virtue itself.[32]

Finally, despotic government functions on the principle of fear. Despotism is not 'moderate' in the sense that there are no 'fixed and established laws' that constrain the power of the ruler. He rules rather by caprice and political order is guaranteed only by the dread that men have of the power of the despot. Under despotism, 'men's portion, like beasts', is instinct, obedience, chastisement'.[33]

On the face of it, the distinction between the forms of government and their animating principles is not made by Montesquieu in order to establish which is the best. Rather, each government secures political order and stability when it subscribes to the principle on which it is based as fully as possible. Nonetheless, his analysis here and later on in *The Spirit of the Laws* makes it clear that only certain forms of government can meet specific political ends, and that among the most important of these for modern societies is liberty. In Book 11, which famously sets out Montesquieu's understanding of the separation of powers, he defines political liberty as 'the power to do what one should want to do and in no way being constrained to do what one should not want to do'. In this respect:

> Political liberty is found only in moderate governments. But it is not always in moderate states. It is present only when power is not

abused, but it has been eternally observed that any man who has power is led to abuse it ... So that one cannot abuse power, power must check power by the arrangement of things. A constitution can be such that no one will be constrained to do things that law permits him to do.[34]

Monarchy is in a superior position to despotism in the sense that its internal structure can support political liberty in a way that despotism cannot. Its advantage lies in its possession of 'intermediate dependent powers', that is, bodies of men on which the monarch depends for the smooth running of the state and the protection of the laws. It is evident that Montesquieu is here thinking about the role played by 'traditional' institutions, most notably the nobility but also the church. The intermediate powers render monarchy moderate because they lessen the prospect of rule by caprice and the constant threat of popular revolution that undermines stability in despotic regimes. Thus in monarchy:

The leaders fear for themselves; they fear being abandoned; the intermediate dependent powers do not want the people to have the upper hand too much. Rarely are the orders of the state entirely corrupted. The prince depends on these orders; seditious men, who have neither the will nor the expectation of overturning the state, have neither the power nor the will to overthrow the prince.[35]

As Shklar claims, '[f]ear of despotism, rather than nostalgia for the old French feudal nobility, persuaded Montesquieu to look to the remnants of noble honour as a scaffolding on which to build a reformed monarchy'.[36] While for Hobbes the principal problem of the modern age was how to overcome religious conflict by establishing the unquestionable authority of the sovereign, for Montesquieu the most pressing difficulty with politics in the present was how to check the erosion of the constraints on the power of the sovereign. The potential existed in modern societies to support extensive liberty under the law, yet the decline of feudal institutions and relations had allowed princes like Louis XIV to gradually circumscribe men's legal freedom. However, what Montesquieu saw was that the political virtue characteristic of the republic could not be regained in modern society. This is not to say, as in the fable of the Troglodytes, that he did not lament the passing of forms of political community where individuals were motivated by 'love of the laws and of the homeland'.[37] But political virtue was only possible in societies characterised by certain social features, such as smallness in size, uniformity

in religious and civic beliefs and practices, and a simple, agrarian economy. The size and diversity of modern societies meant that they were
more suited to monarchy than republican government, and in such societies liberty could only be guaranteed by the existence and effective operation of the intermediate dependent powers.

In this respect, Montesquieu was articulating a conception of the relationship between modern liberty and modern social conditions that
emerged in the eighteenth century and was to come to constitute a central conceptual feature of political economy as it appeared in the
Scottish Enlightenment. Authors such as Adam Smith, Adam Ferguson
and John Millar held Montesquieu's work in high regard. As J. G. A. Pocock
has argued, it is however an error to characterise the kind of political
theory that is developed in the texts of Montesquieu and the later
Scottish economists as marking any straight-forward rejection of virtue
in favour of a modern concept of liberty. Rather, their work involves a
transformation in the meaning of the concept of virtue and applies it
not to the classical form of the political community, the *politicum*, but
rather to the relations between individuals in the sphere of 'civil
society', or the *commercium*.[38] It is quite misleading then to say, as Pangle
does, that '*The Spirit of the Laws* is a massive demonstration of the irreconcilable tension between virtue and freedom ... while giving credit to
the virtuous republic's claim to greatness, Montesquieu tries to show in
a dispassionate way its contradictions and its incompatibility with
human nature.'[39] The republic was clearly not, for Montesquieu, incompatible with 'human nature', but rather with the institutions, manners
and mores characteristic of modern European societies. But the central
problem of the classical republic was the same one that monarchies now
faced: that is, how to avoid arbitrary government and the corruption of
public life.

Montesquieu's argument in favour of the separation of powers made
in Book 11 of *The Spirit of the Laws* does not, therefore, as many modern
liberals have claimed, have individual liberty as its immediate or even
ultimate end. The separation of powers is one means of creating the conditions for a government and laws that are stable and provide for the
protection of the common good, the precondition for liberty in any
society. Montesquieu's liberty is not absolute licence: men should do
what they want to do only within the law. The difficulty is arranging
institutions and interests in such a way that they give rise to the requi-
site balance between the desires of the individual man and the stability
and safety of society as a whole. In chapter 6 of Book 11, Montesquieu
outlines the separation of powers in the English constitution. His

description of the way in which the three different 'powers' of government, the executive, legislative and judicial, are there exercised by different agents, has often been understood as a major statement of his support for liberal constitutionalism. In other words, Montesquieu's central contribution to liberal political thought is often said to be the juristic theory that the formal separation of powers in a constitution is the principal safeguard of liberty. What this thesis blindly ignores is most of what Montesquieu had written in *The Spirit of the Laws* up to this chapter and most of what follows after. The formal separation of powers is only established in moderate government where the social conditions for such an arrangement have already come into being.[40] As Raymond Aron points out, Montesquieu did not see the English constitution as a 'model for all countries', but rather the English system provided the 'basis of a moderate and free state, as a result of the balance of social classes and political powers'.[41]

Positive laws and constitutional arrangements have a concrete effect on the organisation of social life and provide the grounds for the exercise of liberty. But as we have seen, Montesquieu saw positive laws as the product of certain necessary conditions that gave shape to them in any particular historical setting. Books 14 to 26 of *The Spirit of the Laws* systematically set out the nature of these causal influences – climate, geography, the general spirit, mores and manners of a nation, commerce, the use of money, population and religion – in such a way that Aron comments that Montesquieu should be treated not as 'a precursor of sociology, but rather as one of its great theorists'.[42] What Montesquieu produces over the course of these books is an account of the multiple determinations of political systems and their laws that invokes the complex interaction between physical environment, biology, psychology, economics and culture. In its immediate context, this was the aspect of Montesquieu's work that had the most notable impact on his contemporaries who wished to establish a science of man and society. The political consequences of *The Spirit of the Laws* would not be grasped by radicals until the American and French revolutions.

Montesquieu's emphasis on the causal determinants of positive laws means that he has been widely perceived as a 'relativist': human values, including liberty and justice, are made possible only by a given form of society. At the same time, as we noted earlier, in invoking the notion of the laws of nature in combating Hobbes's conception of the original condition of man, he seems to recognise that there are natural rules of justice or human nature that may be employed to pass judgement on particular beliefs and actions. How can these two views be squared? For a number of commentators, such as Alisdair MacIntyre, they cannot: Montesquieu 'just *is* inconsistent'.[43] Althusser considers Montesquieu to be guilty of 'a confusion of orders': having gone to such pains to establish the scientific laws of politics he 'returns like a good boy to the most insipid of traditions: eternal values do exist'.[44] Yet if we try to understand the conceptual field in which Montesquieu was operating, there is no inconsistency. As Aron demonstrates, Montesquieu considered man's intelligence to be the grounds of his freedom. Unlike matter and animals, he is not wholly bound to causal laws.[45] There are, then, laws of rationality with respect to intelligent behaviour, but men do not always follow these because they have the capacity for independent decision-making. Montesquieu's employment of the notion of a state of nature was not designed to establish that men ever really lived in such circumstances, fully under command of the laws of nature, but instead to show that we cannot imagine this condition, as Hobbes does, to be one of perpetual war. Rather for Montesquieu war and inequality only arise in the social state. Since we cannot hope to return to this natural condition, which is only an abstract formulation, the role of politics in the social state must be 'not to eliminate war and inequality, which are inseparable from collective life, but to mitigate and moderate them'.[46] Montesquieu is arguing, then, not that there is an absolute opposition between immutable laws of reason and justice and the social state, but that the social state provides both obstacles and opportunities for securing peace, liberty and minimising inequality according to rational criteria. As Aron argues: 'Montesquieu's philosophy is neither the oversimplified determinism attributed to him by Auguste Comte, for example, nor a traditional philosophy of natural law. It is an original attempt to combine the two.'[47]

In this respect, Montesquieu's texts are much more radical than is usually thought. His support for the role of the nobility as an important intermediate dependent power was no simple reflection of his class position. Rather it involved the acknowledgement that any attempt to successfully change the social order according to ultimate objectives had to be based on an understanding of the variety of possibilities and constraints characteristic of social and political institutions and relations in any given place and time. The notion that we cannot simply invoke laws of rational or natural justice and long for a return to an idealised past is central to radical political thought and practice in the wake of the Enlightenment and the French Revolution.

Rousseau

Perhaps with the exception of Marx, no figure in the history of political thought has divided both popular and academic opinion as much as Jean-Jacques Rousseau (1712–94). On the one hand, Rousseau has been celebrated as a radical democrat whose thought was revolutionary. On this view, the sketch of the free republic in *The Social Contract* was to provide a blueprint for advocates of participatory democracy into the twentieth century.[48] If his work is not without its ambiguities, it may nonetheless be seen as articulating the concept of democracy as this would be revived and come to dominate political discourse and action in the French Revolution and its aftermath.[49] While Rousseau may be taken to have departed from some of the mainstream positions in liberal democratic thought, his work has been interpreted as a significant contribution to the tradition of modern bourgeois liberalism.[50] In contrast, Rousseau has been claimed by some Marxists to be not a partisan of bourgeois liberalism, but rather one of the first critics of bourgeois civil society whose notion of the 'general will' foreshadows the 'true' democracy that Marx believed would be established in a communist society.[51] On the other hand, Rousseau has been identified as a dangerous radical, one of the original advocates of modern totalitarianism, with his concept of the general will serving to provide ballast to theories of 'democratic dictatorship' from Robespierre to Lenin.[52] In a less polemical vein, some authors have highlighted Rousseau's critical pessimism about man's modern present and future and his scepticism about the power of enlightenment to remedy misery.[53]

Others still have argued that Rousseau's work is deeply (both psychologically and textually) ambivalent: it encompasses the hope for a political solution to the problems of modernity, while at the same time lamenting the fact that humans could never again return to their original liberty in a state of solitary communion with nature.[54] Indeed, it is this interpretation of Rousseau that is the most interesting and, at least for our purposes, fruitful to pursue. The problem, however, is that many of the studies of Rousseau's ambivalence have tended to connect it to his psychology and personal experiences, without reflecting on how it is linked to the broader political and philosophical discourse of the Enlightenment. Much of Rousseau's originality has been said to spring from his challenge to the main currents of Enlightenment thought, from his scepticism about the value of the arts and sciences in the *First Discourse*, to his rejection of the idea of representative government, in favour of an ancient model, in *The Social Contract*. Yet there are few commentators who have been prepared to locate Rousseau, as he indeed should be, squarely within the central stream of the European Enlightenment, and perhaps the most perfect representative of its ambivalent character. Rousseau is interesting in a study of the radical attitude not because he was without question of a radical disposition or because his texts provide some feasible blueprint for a radical politics in the present. By the same token, however, it would be churlish to simply dismiss him, as some authors did at the height of the Cold War, as the principal purveyor of totalitarian dictatorship or as someone whose overly romantic assessment of the natural condition of the species disqualifies his ideas from being of any relevance to politics in modernity. Rather, Rousseau's texts reflect what the Enlightenment in general bequeathed to posterity as its most equivocal legacy: the revelation of the complex but reformable character of modern public power in its relation to the subject and citizen, at the same time as a utopian dream of a moral return or overcoming in which political power would be abolished or forever tamed.

Rousseau's eventful life and the undoubted impact it had on his thought, is too rich to be usefully summarised here.[55] What we should note, at least, is the significance of his birthplace, Geneva. The 'Rome of the Protestant Reformation', Geneva had from the time of Calvin gained a reputation as a fiercely proud and independent city-republic, providing refuge to persecuted Protestants, such as the French Huguenots (from whom Rousseau was descended). In the mid-eighteenth century, Calvin was still regarded by its citizens 'as the law-giver who had made the republic of Geneva what it was'.[56] The notions of the independent republic and the law-giver are central to Rousseau's political thought, and there is no doubt that his Genevese roots had a hand in this, even if by the time of his renunciation of the rights of citizenship in 1763, he had lost patience with his city, the authorities of which had banned both his *Emile* and *The Social Contract*.[57] The grounds for the prohibition of the books were religious: Rousseau was understood to be advocating a natural religion, based on reason and dismissive of scriptural authority for divinity. Rousseau's religious views were, indeed, heterodox. He had converted to Catholicism on first leaving Geneva in 1728, later reverting to Protestantism. His belief in an original creator and the providence of the divine distanced him from the mainstream of the French Enlightenment and, above all, from his intellectual nemesis: Voltaire. But it is important to recognise that Rousseau was saying nothing particularly unusual or original with regard to the character of religion and its political functions. Indeed, his views on the relationship between reason and religion are very close to those of Hobbes and others in the natural law tradition, though as we will see his texts involve a re-evaluation and transformation of the concept of natural law.

Rousseau's first publication of political significance was his *Discourse on the Sciences and Arts* (*First Discourse*). The essay was written as an entry for the prize competition of the Academy of Dijon in 1750. For the competition, the Academy had raised the problem of: 'Whether the restoration of the Sciences and Arts has contributed to the purification of morals'. In addressing the question and winning the prize in the process, Rousseau challenged the prevailing enlightened view that it must be answered in the positive. In short, he claims that developments in the arts and sciences have corrupted men and contributed overwhelmingly to their misery in the modern world. Before the arts and sciences came to shape our manners and routine social conventions, 'our morals were rustic but natural'.[58] The politeness and propriety of modern manners and morals masks a stale and uniform 'morality' that is in fact constructed out of all kinds of vices: suspicions, petty jealousies and hatreds, betrayals and so on. In this respect, for Rousseau, life at the court of Versailles and life around the salons of Paris were equally immoral (another reason why some of the leading notables of the French Enlightenment held him in low regard). Throughout history civilisations had fallen because of the corruption engendered by progress in letters while smaller and ruder peoples had prevailed and, indeed, served as models for modern nations. At the same time that Athens had fallen into corruption in the midst of its splendour, the simple and martial spirit of the Spartans guaranteed the propagation of public virtue over the generations.[59] The development of the public arts and sciences has promoted both a dangerous curiosity and a taste for indolence. The sciences are born in idleness 'and they feed it in turn ... In politics, as in ethics, not to do good is a great evil, and every useless citizen may be looked upon as a pernicious man'. The arts and sciences promote the pursuit of unavailing, if 'true', ideas and in so doing undermine the public virtues of citizenship. Arts and letters waste time; they rely upon and perpetuate a luxury affordable only to the civilly idle. In so far as they have a use, it is to promote the fame and wealth of certain public figures. While '[t]he ancient politicians forever spoke of morals and virtues[,] ours speak only of commerce and money'.[60] At the same time, then, and like their ancient predecessors, modern societies become vulnerable when they flourish in the arts and sciences because their civic and martial virtues degenerate.

Rousseau's connection of corruption with the progress of the arts and sciences does not mean, however, that he thinks them to be causally linked as a matter of necessity. The sciences and arts, properly practised, can have beneficial effects for mankind. In order for them to do so, their study must be confined to 'those who feel the strength to go forth alone in their footsteps, and to overtake them: It belongs to this small number to raise monuments to the glory of the human mind'. Kings should accept such men into their counsel, where they can:

> contribute to the happiness of the Peoples to whom they will have taught wisdom. Only then will it be possible to see what virtue, science and authority, animated by a noble emulation and working in concert for the felicity of Mankind, can do. But as long as power remains by itself on one side; enlightenment and wisdom by themselves on the other; the learned will rarely think great things, Princes will more rarely still perform fine ones, and Peoples will continue to be base, corrupt and wretched.[61]

The *First Discourse*, then, would appear to contain a contradiction. After the bulk of the essay in which Rousseau outlines the virtue of Spartan politics (which, as Judith Shklar claims acts as one of his models of a utopia throughout his writings)[62] in opposition to the flourishing of the arts and the sciences, he then proceeds to argue that the latter may bring advantages to human societies. But they can do so only under certain circumstances, that is, where they appear as civil sciences in the sense that they function to further the welfare of citizens and more generally to promote virtue. There is thus no necessary contradiction in Rousseau's argument in the *First Discourse*. What it does demonstrate though, as Leo Strauss points out, is that his assault on the Enlightenment belief in the benefits of the widespread public diffusion of scientific knowledge was not in itself an attack on science and philosophy in the aid of society, but in one very important sense was designed to come to their defence. For Rousseau 'is shocked by the absurdity of philosophy having degenerated into a fashion or of the fight against prejudice having itself become a prejudice. The degeneration of philosophy into a prejudice would destroy forever, humanly speaking, the possibility of intellectual freedom'.[63]

Intellectual freedom, the only grounds from which the arts and sciences could properly flourish, must have as its object civic virtue and be practised virtuously. In this respect, however, they must be insulated from 'society' understood as a realm in which individual interests vie with each other for supremacy and where knowledge is an instrument of greed, vanity and pride, that is, of *amour propre*. It was not the arts and sciences that had corrupted society, but society that had corrupted the arts and sciences. It was modern manners and morals that provided individuals with the necessary motivation to corrupt and abuse this knowledge. Rousseau's novel, *Julie: or the New Heloise* and his treatise-cum-novel, *Emile*, are both addressed to the problem of the depravity of morality in the present and how the principal goal of education should be the promotion of civic virtue.[64] The question of real importance for Rousseau, then, is the proper provenance of modern manners and morals and whether these are grounded in 'human nature' or could be accounted for by the historical experience of the species.

Rousseau addresses these problems most directly in the work that made him famous (and in some quarters infamous) across Europe: the *Discourse on the Origins and Foundations of Inequality Among Men* (*Second Discourse*) of 1754. Also written as an entry to the Dijon Academy's prize competition (though it was dismissed by the judges of the Academy who had been delighted with the erudite impudence of the *First Discourse* but were clearly scandalised by the heterodoxy of the *Second*), Rousseau claimed in his autobiography that it was the product of his meditations in the forests around Saint-Germain, where he had sought to imagine man in his true nature and all that had conspired over his history to corrupt him. He reports in his autobiography that, at some stage in his reverie, his 'soul, uplifted by these sublime considerations, ascended to the Divinity; and seeing my fellow creatures following blindly the path of their prejudices, their errors, their misfortunes, and their crimes, I cried aloud to them with a feeble voice which they could not hear, "Fools, who continually complain of Nature, learn that you bring all your misfortunes upon yourselves" '.[65] Accordingly, the *Second Discourse* is set out in two halves, the first which deals with man as part of nature, while the second outlines the causes of his modern foolishness.

Rousseau makes clear in his Preface to the *Second Discourse* that what he is not attempting to do is to present a wholly comprehensive or accurate picture of the original natural condition of man or the state of nature. His inquiry into the character of human nature is concerned with what that 'is' in a quite abstract sense, that is, to imagine what it would, rather than necessarily did, entail in the absence of all 'artificial' social encumbrances. An inquiry into the state of nature does not seek to discover 'historical truths' but rather 'hypothetical and conditional reasonings' that can 'elucidate the Nature of things'.[66] It is in this regard that Rousseau's texts can be approached as a contribution to the natural law tradition; indeed, for some commentators Rousseau's reflection on the work of authors in that tradition, notably Pufendorf, Grotius and Hobbes, is key to understanding his entire political *oeuvre*.[67] But the *Second Discourse* also marks a significant departure from the natural law tradition, for it is not Rousseau's intention to establish that the laws of nature have, can have or should have any important say with respect to the social and political constitution of the present. To be sure, Rousseau laments the passing and the impossibility of recapturing man in what he takes to be his original state, but in dealing with the misery of the Moderns we should be concerned with the law of nature only insofar as it helps to reveal the causes of our current plight and how, given their ineradicable trace on the present, we may employ reason to discover remedies for their effects.

In contrast to Hobbes, Rousseau's state of nature is one of 'soft primitivism' where men are naturally 'good'. They are 'good', however, not in the sense that they live by any substantive moral code or that all their actions are altruistic, but purely in that they are uncorrupted by the morals and manners of modern society. The great error that Hobbes had made in his characterisation of the state of nature was to alienate man from civil society in the present but to leave him with characteristics that he could only have acquired in society. It is only in modern society that men are made systematically acquisitive and are driven by pride and glory. *Amour propre* is not a natural human sentiment, but is rather generated after the move out of the state of nature. In his natural goodness man has only two sentiments, 'prior to reason', that act as the principles from which 'all the rules of natural right seem to me to flow; rules which reason is subsequently forced to re-establish on other foundations, when by its successive development it has succeeded in stifling Nature'.[68] These principles derive from the impulse to self-preservation (*amour de soi-même*) that shapes man's engagement with nature external to him and the sentiment of pity we have for other sentient beings (not just humans) that we see suffering.

Given these two natural sentiments, Rousseau like Montesquieu, cannot imagine the state of nature as one of perpetual war, or even one where war is possible. While he was attempting to imagine men's pre-social history as a means of establishing in the abstract the basic features of human nature, nothing that Rousseau says explicitly rules out the possibility that this was indeed a real historical state. In that state men would have led lives that were 'simple, uniform and solitary', with the 'cry of Nature' being the only language they need to know to satisfy their needs and wants in life.[69] The only inequalities that obtain between men in Rousseau's state of nature are based on varied physical or mental capabilities, but because these natural inequalities tend to be relatively marginal, isolated men will not feel the need to combine with others in order to achieve the goal of simple subsistence: what one man lacks in physical strength he may well make up for in cunning and vice-versa. In any case, the sentiment of pity acts as a constraint on men using their natural advantages to impose suffering on others. Men live by this maxim of 'natural goodness': '*Do your good with the least possible harm to others*'.[70] The inequality of the forest-dwelling primitive is, therefore, entirely natural in character. It is not political or moral and in itself provides no impetus toward the formation of social rules and conventions. In this state of nature man is free in one sense of overriding importance: his liberty consists in not being subject to the will of another. The natural man, for Rousseau, lives his life according to his own will in communion with nature. He depends on other men for nothing:

> everyone must see that since ties of servitude are formed solely by men's mutual dependence and the reciprocal needs that unite them, it is impossible to subjugate a man without first having placed him in the position of being unable to do without another; a situation which, since it does not obtain in the state of Nature, leaves everyone in it free of the yoke, and renders vain the Law of the stronger.[71]

Part 2 of the *Second Discourse* turns to the circumstances which account for the eventual usurpation of natural right by legal and political right. As climate varies and as men multiply in numbers as a result of their ability to master nature, they find themselves having to work harder in order to subsist. Increasing contact with other men opens up opportunities for co-operative labour, but these are accompanied by great dangers to their natural freedom. Men in troops, tribes and nations, form rules of conduct governing their behaviour – in other words manners and morals – that bind them together. They develop customs associated with climate, diet, modes of labour and so on. These moral and customary codes create collective identities and differentiate groups of men from each other, and in this way provide the grounds for national pride, jealousies and ultimately warfare. But Rousseau considers the greatest threat to autonomy emerging out of the state of nature to be the advent of private property. In a famous passage, he writes:

> The first man who, having enclosed a piece of ground, to whom it occurred to say that *this is mine*, and found people sufficiently simple

to believe him, was the true founder of civil society. How many crimes, wars, murders, how many miseries and horrors Mankind would have been spared by him, who pulling up the stakes or filling in the ditch, had cried out to his kind: Beware of listening to this impostor; You are lost if you forget that the fruits are everyone's and the Earth no one's.

The following sentence is often, unfortunately, omitted when the passage is cited: 'But in all likelihood things had by then reached a point where they could not continue as they were; for this idea of property, depending as it does on many prior ideas which could only arise successively, did not take shape all at once in man's mind.'[72] Despite the rhetorical flourish, then, Rousseau's intention is not to portray private property as the point of departure for man's modern misery, nor even to claim that it is the main source of that misery. To be sure, he rejects Locke's claim that primitive rights over property can be established through the mixing of one's labour with any natural object. There can be no such pre-social rights over property in the state of nature, because they require the formation of a system of rights and a means of enforcing it, which can come into being only with the creation of rules of social conduct, their legal encoding and the power of a political state to coerce recalcitrant individuals in order to protect property. For Rousseau, it simply makes no sense to talk of 'natural property' or a 'natural right to property': property is artificial and conventional.

Rousseau's main concern, however, is not with inequalities in the distribution of private property. A just social order can, to an extent, tolerate such inequalities and still support liberty. What is inimical to freedom in any state is the existence of political inequalities, and Rousseau is interested in the status of private property from a historical perspective in the sense that it constitutes a marker of various stages of political inequality in human societies. Rules of justice for the protection of property emerged as a means by which those who denied others access to the parts of the world they had appropriated by strength and/ or cunning, could establish their moral and legal superiority. In contrast to Hobbes, it was once men entered into society that they fell into a state of war, a war principally enjoined by inequality in holdings of wealth and property. In this state of war, force alone would never be enough to provide for stability in the possession of property. Force of arms had to be combined with principles of justice in order to garner the recognition of the masses for the rightful claims of the rich to property. For Rousseau, Hobbes's covenant is a fraud: men 'ran toward their chains' because they had been duped into believing this necessary for their liberty, when in fact they enslaved themselves to the advantage of the already rich and powerful.[73]

The three forms of government that are created by men – monarchy aristocracy and democracy – each indicate, at the time of their inception, how far the society in question has moved away from the original state of nature. Monarchy represents a society most removed from the natural order, because in it the sole magistrate has come to occupy the pinnacle of a hierarchical and materially unequal society. Inequality is less in aristocracy and at its least in a democracy where men are roughly equal and where all the citizens are at the same time magistrates. The progress of material inequality is marked by the progressive distancing of the 'Chiefs' from the 'People', to the extent to which the Chiefs eventually come to be seen as extraordinary individuals who rule by dint of natural or divine nobility and grace, and are widely lauded. Social status comes to be seen as valuable in itself, something to which all men aspire. Despotism and the reduction of the masses to fawning misery do not, then, come about simply through private property, but are the products of a long process of historical development that is determined by the interplay of politics and laws, property, manners and morals. Rousseau, in contrast to Montesquieu, is a social evolutionist, but unlike the political economists of the Scottish Enlightenment and the social evolutionists of the nineteenth century, he claims that society does not progress toward liberty but moves it ever further into the distance.

Rousseau's famous declaration at the beginning of the first chapter of *The Social Contract*, that '[m]an is born free, and everywhere he is in chains', tells us that by their nature men are capable of being freed. But how is the slavery that is spawned by men's entry in to civil society to be overcome? The answer to the question is provided by *The Social Contract*, but even in its prequel, the *Second Discourse*, Rousseau had already given some consideration to the problem. The epistle dedicatory to the Republic of Geneva at the start of the *Second Discourse* portrays the Genevese constitution (through rose-tinted glasses) as one best designed to secure the liberty of the citizen and one that he would rather live under than any other. If he had not been born a citizen of the city, Rousseau writes, he would have wished to have been born in a society where 'all individuals know one another' and where the 'gentle habit of seeing and knowing one another would have made the love of one's Fatherland a love of the Citizens rather than the soil'. This country would be one 'where the Sovereign and the people could have had only one and the same interest', 'under a democratic government wisely tempered'.

He would 'have sought out a Country where the right of legislation was common to all Citizens', but 'would have fled as ill-governed a Republic where the People, believing it could do without its Magistrates or leave them no more than a precarious authority, had imprudently retained in its own hands the administration of Civil affairs and the execution of its own Laws'.[74]

In line with this account of the constitution of the free republic, the kind of government that Rousseau advocates in *The Social Contract* is a form of direct legislative democracy with an elective executive aristocracy, in the context of a small republic with rough material equality between citizens. It is only in these conditions, Rousseau believes, that we can regain something of the character of the liberty possessed by the species in its natural state. We can learn from the Ancients, with their democratic and republican forms of government, in so far as they out of all our ancestors were closest to natural liberty, but we must also learn from their errors, for they allowed their civic virtues to be overwhelmed by private interest. In short, for Rousseau the key to providing the conditions for the exercise of liberty in modern societies, that is societies in which individuals live according to their will alone and are not subject to the commands of others, is to create institutions and practices that establish and give constant succour to the *general will*.

Rousseau's concept of the general will is the most controversial and misunderstood idea in all of his writing. It is the reason why some have taken him to be a supporter of 'totalitarian democracy' and why others treat him as a radical democrat, outside the political mainstream of the Enlightenment, or as a proto-communist and precursor of Karl Marx. All of these views singularly fail to recognise that Rousseau's conception of the general will is in its context unremarkable and is drawn quite consistently and indeed rigorously, from the leading conceptions of liberty in the eighteenth century. It would be an error to claim that Rousseau was advocating a radically different conception of liberty to that of other authors in the mainstream of the Enlightenment. Like them, he believed that man was capable of being perfected through liberty, that liberty consisted in the freedom to live one's life according to rational rules of moral and social conduct, and that slavery meant subjection to the will of another.

The social contract is a just one, and liberty is achieved, when each individual agrees to live by common rules of social conduct that they themselves have rationally willed. Living in a free society cannot be a question of reaching compromise between different individual interests or simply aggregating them. A society whose rules of justice are determined by an assessment of individual interest cannot be a free society. It can only be so when it acts according to the general will, that is in the first-order interest of men as free and politically equal. Rousseau quite explicitly states that the will of all is not the same as the general will, for the reason that all may will to live in such a way that they will be subject to the will of another. Grotius and Hobbes had both argued that one may alienate command over one's self to another, but the idea is for Rousseau quite contradictory: a permanent condition of freedom cannot involve a renunciation of one's freedom as, logically, one would no longer be free in such a condition. An individual is sovereign when he makes the laws that govern his public conduct in general, and it follows that in the social contract sovereignty is, at the same time, vested in each individual and in the body politic entire. The social contract 'can be reduced to the following terms: *Each of us puts his person and his full power in common under the supreme direction of the general will; and in a body we receive each member as an indivisible part of the whole*'.[75]

As we saw in the last chapter, the Levellers advocated something like the modern doctrine of popular sovereignty in the sense that the sovereign body is authorised, through its representatives, to make the laws. But Rousseau's conception of sovereignty is qualitatively different from that of the Levellers and indeed all of the seventeenth century theorists of the social contract. For Rousseau, for a body to be sovereign it cannot authorise or alienate the law-making power that governs it to another. If we accept men as naturally free and equal, as Rousseau's picture of the state of nature insists that we must, then all men must be the sovereign authors of the laws. The refusal to recognise that men and the entire body of men are both at the same time and indivisibly sovereign, can only result in the denial of their natural liberty and their moral and political equality. Rousseau's understanding of the relationship between liberty and sovereignty, then, needs clearly to be borne in mind when considering the most abused of all quotations taken from the text of *The Social Contract*:

> Hence for the social compact not to be an empty formula, it tacitly includes the following engagement which alone can give force to the rest, that whoever refuses to obey the general will shall be constrained to do so by the entire body: which means nothing other than that he shall be forced to be free; for this is the condition which, by giving each Citizen to the Fatherland, guarantees him against all personal dependence; the condition which is the device and makes

for the operation of the political machine, and alone renders legitimate civil engagements which would otherwise be absurd, tyrannical, and liable to the most enormous abuses.[76]

For Rousseau's twentieth-century critics, the notion of being 'forced to be free' by the 'entire body' provides us with the slip that reveals the totalitarian unconscious of his system. However, this interpretation is at odds with the intention and content of the rest of *The Social Contract* and indeed all Rousseau's major political texts. He claims that the general will is never likely to impose intolerable burdens on the citizens or prevent them from pursuing their (reasonable) individual interests, because it can only ever be achieved in a certain kind of society, one that is relatively small, where the citizens are roughly equal, where all subscribe to the same customs, manners and morals and where there is consequently a need for very few laws to regulate public conduct. Certainly, Rousseau's work indicates that he would expect the same schedule of civil rights to be supported by the general will as liberals tend to claim should be guaranteed in modern societies. With the proviso that individuals do not threaten the security or liberty of their fellow citizens, all should be free to own property, to worship and speak freely, to travel where they please without rescinding the rights of citizenship and so on. Indeed, for Rousseau, in contrast to 'liberals' such as Locke, civil rights are empty and unrealisable unless they are accompanied by the political right of the individual, as an integral component of the body politic, to determine the general laws of social conduct.

Books III and IV of *The Social Contract* set out Rousseau's view of the form of institutions and practices that are necessary to establish the general will in modern societies. To reiterate, he believes that the general will can only be achieved in societies that are relatively small, equal and culturally homogenous. That does not mean to say that any attempt to design a virtuous state in a large country is destined to fail. Rousseau's later work, *Considerations on the Government of Poland and its Projected Reform* (1771) is an attempt to outline the kinds of institutions consistent with the general will in such a country. His answer to the problems of the Polish constitution is to encourage 'federative Governments, the only system which combines the advantages of large and small States', or in other words to create a confederal structure in which assemblies at the scale of regions and cities combine in appointing representatives who decide legislation at the national level.[77] In a sense this was a departure from his argument in *The Social Contract*, where he claims that the deputies of the people are merely their 'agents' and can have no final say in the determination of the laws. Representation, in its modern sense, is there derided as a product of 'feudal Government, that iniquitous and absurd Government in which the human species is degraded, and the name of man dishonoured'.[78] The provisions set out in *The Social Contract* point to a direct legislative democracy. Rousseau argues that the entire body of citizens must assemble periodically to ratify the laws, including the laws that institute the kind of government of the state. Government, that is the form of the organisation of the magistracy, is not determined by an act of contract, but rather by the laws which citizens directly ratify or rescind.[79]

It was Rousseau's advocacy of direct legislative democracy that gained him a reputation as a radical democrat and, along with his views of religion, made him a public enemy in France and his beloved Geneva. But in fact, and in line with other features of his thought and writing, Rousseau is deeply ambivalent about democracy. Democratic government needs to be 'wisely tempered'. This understanding of the dangers posed by democracy was informed by the common meaning of the concept in the eighteenth century (which can be seen operating in Montesquieu's texts), where it stood for a form of government that could not possibly meet its own high demands for virtue. As in ancient Greece, democracy allowed dominant interests, those of the rich with high social status, to determine the character of the laws. The unstructured anarchy of pure democracy thus gives way to oligarchy and, in turn, tyranny. For Rousseau, it was necessary to establish institutions and practices that could rid democratic government of these pernicious tendencies, tendencies fatal to the achievement of the general will.

In *The Social Contract* Rousseau therefore considers three main ways in which democracy may be tempered. First, there is the role of the 'Lawgiver'. This is not a permanent public office, but one occupied by an extraordinary individual like Lycurgus or Calvin, who sets out the constitution of the general will, but has himself no legislative right.[80] The second is that while the legislative power of the state should be in the hands of the citizens through periodic assemblies, they should not hold the executive power. Rather, this should be exercised by an 'elective aristocracy', by magistrates who are appointed by the citizens through their assemblies. Government is constituted by the *aristos* in the sense that the magistrates are people recognised as being the best suited for drawing up laws and upholding them in a fashion consistent with the general will rather than in the service of particular interests.[81] Third, and perhaps crucially, an ongoing means of curbing democratic excess and thus protecting the general will is provided by the institutions and practices of a 'Civil Religion'. In the civil religion it is the sovereign (i.e. the people) who constitutes the articles of faith, not the church and its priests. These articles should not be 'dogmas of religion but ... sentiments of sociability, without which it is impossible to be either a good Citizen or a loyal subject'.[82]

Rousseau's notion that freedom consists of obeying rules that are rationally determined by oneself has led to the comparison of his moral position with that of Immanuel Kant.[83] Indeed, other modern philosophers, most notably John Rawls, have taken Rousseau's social contract as involving an argument about the rational derivation of rules of moral and political conduct from a position of rational, pre-social autonomy.[84] But in fact, this reading of Rousseau as a precursor of Kantian rational moral autonomy is quite misleading. Rousseau is as ambivalent about reason as he is about democracy. The natural reason that men possess, like any of man's natural qualities, does not alone equip them for moral 'goodness' in any substantive sense. Natural reason involves recognising and following rules, but the content of those moral and political rules are for Rousseau entirely conventional and artificial once man has left the state of nature. Reason can be employed in the pursuit of particular interests and the enslaving of others as much as it can in the creation of the general will and the protection of liberty. What determines our recognition of the justice of laws that are consistent with the general will is not an autonomous reason, but our membership of the kind of political community that *The Social Contract* describes, one that is relatively small, egalitarian and in which all subscribe to the principles of the civil religion.

From a modern point of view, then, Rousseau's texts are highly ambivalent. On the one hand, they are 'radical' in the sense that they challenge constituted political authority, call for the dismantling of traditional hierarchies in church, society and the state, and place great value on the political liberty and equality of the Moderns. But this radicalism is premised on a nostalgia for the Ancients and a love of communities, like eighteenth century Geneva, with strong conservative dispositions and a fear of change to laws and customs. In this respect, Rousseau's work reflects a deeper ambivalence that runs through the political texts of the European Enlightenment, and which Reinhart Koselleck has documented with great acumen.[85] The kind of philosophical history Rousseau pursued had a profound and irreversible effect on the constitution of the modern 'science of man' in general, and on our knowledge of political institutions and practices in particular. It revealed the inherent mutability of the present and demonstrated the possibility and desirability of a fundamental reform of social and political life. At the same time, however, this philosophical history substituted for what was a political crisis in eighteenth-century Europe, as absolutism unravelled under the pressure of social upheaval and the emergence of the powerful bourgeois public, a 'moral' crisis of man conceived in universal terms. The political crisis, at bottom at contest about the character of legitimate authority and the laws appropriate for modern society and liberty, came to be seen as having a moral solution: the creation, through education and general enlightenment, of moral codes of conduct. Where Rousseau differed from the 'mainstream' of the Enlightenment, from thinkers such as Voltaire and d'Alembert, was in his strenuous denial that liberty could be secured through the actions of the enlightened prince. Reform had to be authorised by the mass of the citizens through concrete changes to political institutions and relations. Yet at the same time, what Rousseau desired above all else was an end to the moral tumult and decadence of the present by an impossible reversion to a kind of political community, the autonomous city republic, that could only operate, if at all, in those islands of civility that still bore the trace of a long-dead Europe.

4
Conservatism and Radicalism: Burke and Paine

In modern political vocabulary, conservatism stands as the antonym of radicalism. The distinction between them, as much as that between left and right, has since the French Revolution been central in the constitution of political ideologies and identities. Conservatism and radicalism are often taken to denote irreconcilably opposed world-views: the former valorises tradition and welcomes only incremental change; the latter seeks a fundamental transformation of social and political life. If, then, modern political theory is characterised by the radical attitude, there is a sense in which it is also characterised by a conservative attitude. This conservative attitude was sketched out in the late eighteenth and early nineteenth centuries principally in terms of opposition to the French Revolution and radical political change. But it would be a mistake to see this conservative attitude as little more than a reaction to revolution. While thinkers like Edmund Burke and Joseph de Maistre sought to defend 'tradition', they had to do so by engaging with and deploying the vocabulary of political modernity, a vocabulary that had been used in the Enlightenment and the French Revolution to shape the language of modern political radicalism. The political languages of conservatism and radicalism in modernity are, in this regard, far from being incommensurable. Indeed, much of modern conservatism shares with the radical attitude its ambivalent view of public power. Conservatives may tend to see political power as necessary to the construction and defence of tradition, but at the same time they have also painted politics as inherently dangerous. It needs to be constrained and it may even be possible, whether through obedience to the laws of nature or the market, to overcome it.

This chapter will focus on the formation of 'conservatism' in relation to 'radicalism' in the context of debates that took place in British political discourse at the time of the French Revolution. In particular, it will concentrate on the two main representatives of 'conservative' and 'radical' thinking at this time: Edmund Burke and Thomas Paine. In this context, both thinkers adopted an understanding of the state, politics and society and the relation between them that was moulded by the broader discourse of crisis developed in the works of the Enlightenment *philosophes* and, less obviously, the late eighteenth century theorists of commercial society. This crisis was accelerated by the French Revolution. In its wake, conservatives and radicals alike perceived a moment of irrevocable decision. While they disagreed about what was required by this decision, they were united in seeing its necessity as the product of a certain trajectory of historical development. After the French Revolution, then, both conservatism and radicalism addressed the same problem. While their answers to this problem differed in important respects, their understanding of the character of the public power and its relationship to history proceeded from the same conceptual grounds.

Burke

Edmund Burke (1729–97) is widely seen as one of the most important founding philosophers of conservatism. This reputation is built largely on Burke's famous book, *Reflections on the Revolution in France* (1790), his most coherent work of political theory. Burke's earlier writings are overwhelmingly devoted to practical political issues. In part this is because, from 1765 to 1780, and again from 1781 to 1794, Burke was a Member of Parliament and from 1783–84 held office as paymaster-general. Much of his writing thus appears in the form of letters and parliamentary speeches. Yet it is also the case that Burke steered clear of abstract political writing because of a dislike of 'theory'. His intellectual formation, against the background of British empiricism and anti-rationalism, persuaded him that experience was the criterion for judgement, whether that be moral, aesthetic or political. With respect to the latter, Burke made it his business to know in detail the events and historical background to those political problems which were to him of utmost concern: his native Ireland, the American colonies and the War of Independence, India and toward the end of his life the French Revolution. All of Burke's interventions can be understood as being politically motivated in the sense that they were designed to have specific policy effects. Nevertheless, it would be wrong to think that there is no 'theory' in Burke. His specific policy prescriptions were built around a largely coherent theoretical framework that shared much in common with other political thinkers of the time, including Tom Paine.

The resemblance between Burke's and Paine's theories of politics is to be found in a particular attitude toward the public power in relation to history. Burke was a much more subtle thinker than those who have portrayed him as the principal philosopher of conservatism and the arch-opponent of political radicalism tend to suggest.[1] To be sure, it is as least questionable whether we can see Burke as a wholly consistent 'conservative', and his opposition to the 'radicalism' of the French Revolution, while consonant with ideas he had argued for in his earlier work, may have been founded on more local and personal concerns.[2] Yet Burke's ideas must be seen in the light of the wider discursive context. The often hidden question that informs the general direction of Burke's thought is the configuration of power in the modern world and in particular the relationship between the state and society. While Burke may look to one particular vocabulary of politics that is pre-modern, that of natural right and natural law, he deploys this vocabulary to approach the same problems of modernity addressed by thinkers like Rousseau and Paine. In many important respects he arrives at the same answer: politics should be subordinate and ancillary to the providential development of history toward an ideal society, one in which the liberty of the subject is guaranteed by the elimination of the antagonisms that accompany the modern diversification of human interests.

Burke's early work was geared more toward literary, aesthetic and philosophical concerns than politics. While his first published book, *Vindication of Natural Society* (1756), was a satire on Bolingbroke's idea of natural religion, elaborating an anti-rationalist theology that was to play an important role in his attack on the French revolutionaries, the text he was best known for prior to the *Reflections* was *A Philosophical Enquiry Into the Origin of Our Ideas of the Sublime and Beautiful* (1757). The obvious influences on the book are Locke's *Essay Concerning Human Understanding* and Hume's *Treatise of Human Nature*.[3] Adopting an empiricist account of the character of aesthetic knowledge, Burke associates the experience of the sublime with the passions of self-preservation. While the sublime does not cause pain, it excites ideas of pain or danger in us and is thus 'productive of the strongest emotion which the mind is capable of feeling'. Beauty, on the other hand, excites passions that are social in character, and induces 'in us a sense of affection and tenderness'.[4] Here Burke is entirely in line with the eighteenth-century theorists of commercial society, such as Hume and Smith, in endowing passions of self-preservation, rather than those involved with sociability, with the greatest emotional intensity. Like Hume and Smith, the mature Burke subscribed to a view of social order that ultimately turns around the self-interest of individual social actors. There is from this no necessary implication of moral individualism; indeed, many interpreters of Burke rather see him as a moral collectivist, placing the interests of the nation before those of individuals.[5]

While the *Enquiry* was favourably received by a number of pre-eminent philosophers, including Kant, it was for its time a largely unremarkable account. There is no reason to believe that Burke ever repudiated the work, but it is at first sight difficult to see it as a philosophical grounding for his later take on politics and the status of modernity. In general, the *Enquiry* might be understood to affirm the priority of experience over reason in matters of taste and judgement, but this kind of empiricism itself does not entail any specific political world-view. Stephen K. White has argued, however, that Burke's language of aesthetics continued to inform his later political thought. The *Enquirie's* elevation of passion over reason represents a reaction to political modernity, as White claims Burke saw it, as the 'systematic explosion of wilfulness in politics that had a world historical significance'.[6] It may well be the case, from the point of view of the author, that the *Enquiry* was not intended as a 'political' work and indeed it was not received as such at the time.[7] Nonetheless, the intellectual and political context in which the *Enquiry* was written can be taken to have provided the problem which it addressed. It was not simply a philosophical enterprise undertaken within the dominant framework of mid-eighteenth-century British empiricism, but reflected a concern for the status of the modern world and of challenges posed to the natural and social basis of our sentiments.

In the 1760s, first under the patronage of the Irish MP William Hamilton then under that of the future prime minister, Charles Wentworth, Marquess of Rockingham, Burke became involved in Whig politics. Elected to parliament in 1765, Burke became private secretary to Rockingham, who had been called on by George III to form an administration. The 'Old' Whigs, led by Rockingham, still looked back with pride to the Revolution of 1688 and were staunchly anti-Jacobite. In so far as distinct parties could be identified in the late eighteenth century, Rockingham's Whigs stood against the Tories, many of whom continued to argue in favour of absolutism. At the same time, the Whigs were wedded to a world of politics in which it was thought the natural duty of the aristocracy-cum-gentry to rule virtuously on the behalf of the lower orders and the nation. For the Old Whigs, the constitutional settlement of 1688 was final and they had no truck, as was indeed more widely the case, with 'democracy' and social levelling.

While the link between 'ideology' and party was not well established at this time, Burke clearly subscribed to the principles of the Rockingham Whigs on entering politics. Taken with his defence of free trade, he has thus been regarded by some Marxists as a spokesman for the peculiar fusion of the aristocracy and bourgeoisie that made up the British ruling class, acting to defend the process of capitalist accumulation against reactionary feudal interests, and private property against Jacobin radicals.[8] In *Capital* Marx disparagingly remarked that Burke was 'the sycophant – who in the pay of the English oligarchy played the part of romantic opponent of the French Revolution, just as, in the pay of the North American colonies, he had played the liberal against the English oligarchy, was a vulgar bourgeois through and through.[9] In fact, the principles on which Burke argued against both the British treatment of the American colonies and the French Revolution are consistent. If Burke is dismissed as no more than a conservative mouthpiece of the bourgeoisie, what is overlooked is the extent to which the concepts he employed and his view of the present and future, overlap with those of his radical interlocutors, including Marx himself.

Burke's reputation as the leading philosopher of conservatism is based on his traditionalism, most fully developed in the *Reflections*. This traditionalism, however, should not be understood as a visceral attachment to the actual. While Burke derided the natural rights philosophy of the French revolutionaries, his later political arguments were all worked out from a largely consistent defence of the idea of a natural law that is the foundation and justification for his traditionalism.[10] Burke's conception of natural law is very different to that of thinkers like Rousseau and Paine, but his reliance on such a theory is witness to his concern with the same problems of modernity that they addressed, and in particular the relation between the state and society. The best way to begin to unravel Burke's commitment to a theory of natural law is to focus not on the *Reflections*, though as will be seen presently the same theory underpins the argument of that book, but rather his earlier and less theoretically programmatic approach toward the problems of the American colonies and of the East India Company.

In the year of Burke's election, Parliament passed the Stamp Act. The Act imposed an obligation on the American colonies to make a contribution toward the cost of defending the Empire, but can be seen as one in a line of measures designed to maximise revenues from the increasingly prosperous New World territories. The Rockingham administration of 1765–66 repealed the Act and thereafter Burke was to oppose all further attempts to introduce new taxes on the colonies. His argument was, in part, based on a conviction that free trade was to the benefit of the entire Empire. He also, however, opposed attempts by Parliament to assert its abstract legal sovereignty over the colonies. In his 'Speech on American Taxation' in 1774, aimed against the Tea Act of 1773 which provoked the Boston Tea Party, Burke declared:

> I am not here going into the distinctions of rights, nor attempting to mark their boundaries. I do not enter into these metaphysical descriptions; I hate the very sound of them. Leave the Americans as they antiently stood, and these distinctions, born of our unhappy contest, will die along with it ... But if intemperately, unwisely, fatally, you sophisticate and poison the very source of government, by urging subtle deductions and consequences odious to those you govern, from the unlimited and illimitable nature of supreme sovereignty, you will teach them by these means to call that sovereignty itself into question.[11]

At one level this constitutes a pragmatic argument against American taxation. Unlike Paine, Burke did not wish to see independence for the colonies, but he knew that effectively arbitrary taxation, in the light of the absence of American representation in the Parliament at Westminster, would only stoke the flames of rebellion. However, his denunciation of 'metaphysical descriptions' and his wish to leave the Americans as they 'antiently stood' suggest a more substantive and speculative account of what makes for peaceful social relations, both within any given social order and between them. Indeed, with respect to the latter, Burke can be seen as an important figure in the formation of modern accounts of international relations: the larger part of his political writings were, after all, concerned with affairs outside of and in relation to Britain.[12]

The episode that most clearly demonstrates Burke's concerns with Britain's relationship to its Empire and with the kind of natural law that he felt should inform this relationship, was his criticism of the East India Company and his efforts to impeach the Governor-General of Bengal, Warren Hastings. Burke's concerns with India were triggered when, in 1773, the Raja of Tanjore was deposed by the Nawab of Carnatic with the backing of troops from the East India Company. When the then Governor of Madras, Lord Pigot, attempted to restore the Raja, a coup was led against him by members of the Company who were creditors to the Nawab. Burke saw this overthrowing of a constitutional and legal government in Madras as evidence that the private interests of the East

India Company had come to take precedence over not just those of the British state and its Empire, but of the people of India themselves. The Nawab was a despot, his rule imposed over the people of Tanjore by force. It was a particular concern of Burke's, warranted or not, that the religious freedom of the Tanjore Hindus would be curtailed by the Muslim Nawab. In part this was down to his belief in an ancient Hindu constitution that was being threatened by the Muslim invaders.[13] At the same time, Burke's writings and speeches on India reveal him at his most 'liberal', in the sense that he appeals explicitly to the rights of the Indians against the injustice of tyranny. This was the language Burke employed in 1777 to announce the need for the British state to regulate the East India Company and, in 1783, to front Charles James Fox's India Bill, which sought to make the Company's court of directors answerable to an independent commission accountable to Parliament.[14]

In 1787 Burke was successful in starting impeachment proceedings against Warren Hastings. Burke accused Hastings, Governor-General of Bengal from 1772 to 1785, of gross corruption and mismanagement of government in India, not only over the Tanjore affair, but on a number of other counts.[15] In 1788 Hastings was brought to trial in front of the House of Lords.[16] Burke's opening speech charged Hastings with crimes against 'eternal laws of justice' and asserted that his fate must be determined on the basis of the rules of 'natural, immutable and substantial justice'.[17] Hastings's main line of defence was that he had ruled according to the standards of 'Asian' governments, and has thus acted in a way that respected the moral conventions and traditions of the Indians. Burke rejected this defence of Hastings's actions out of hand:

> [Hastings] has told your Lordships in his defence, that actions in Asia do not bear the same moral qualities as the same actions would bear in Europe ... This Geographical morality we do protest against ... we think it necessary in justification of ourselves to declare that the laws of morality are the same everywhere, and that there is no action which would pass for an action of extortion, of peculation, of bribery and of oppression in England, that is not an act of extortion, of peculation, of bribery and of oppression in Europe, Asia, Africa and all the world over.[18]

Against the notion that Asian government is by nature despotic, Burke declares that Muslim governments operate on the basis of a legal order and that arbitrary rule is proscribed by the Koran:

> My Lords, the greatest part of Asia is under Mahometan Governments. To name a Mahometan government is to name a Government by law.

It is a law enforced by stronger sanctions than any law that can bind a European sovereign, exclusive of the Grand Seignior.[19]

Moreover:

But it is not only here that I must do justice to the East. I assert that their morality is equal to ours as regards the morality of Governors, fathers, superiors; and I challenge the world to shew, in any modern European book, more true morality and wisdom than is to be found in the writings of Asiatic men in high trusts, and who have been Counsellors to Princes. This is to be set against the Geographical morality to which I have referred.[20]

The language used by Burke here would seem to qualify him, in the context, as a radical. There are, on this view, universal principles of justice by which all, regardless of station in life, must be judged. More strikingly, the laws of morality are said to be universal. On the face of it, this suggests Burke's affinity with the Enlightenment *philosophes* and moral rationalists. Burke's justification for the universality of such moral laws is, however, somewhat different from that of the Enlightenment *philosophes*. It is most clearly and extensively put in the *Reflections*, but a statement of it can also be found in Burke's proceedings against Hastings:

We are all born in subjection, all born equally, high and low, governors and governed, in subjection to one great, immutable, pre-existent law, prior to all our devices, and prior to all our contrivances, paramount to our very being itself, by which we are knit and connected in the eternal frame of the universe, out of which we cannot stir.

This great law does not arise from our conventions or compacts. On the contrary, it gives to our conventions and compacts all the force and sanction they can have. It does not arise from our vain institutions. Every good gift is of God; all power is of God; and He who has given the power and from whom it alone originates, will never suffer the exercise of it to be practised upon any less solid foundation that the power itself. Therefore, will it be imagined, if this be true, that He will suffer this great gift of Government, the greatest, the best that was ever given by God to mankind, to be the play thing and the sport of the feeble will of a man, who by a blasphemous, absurd and petulant usurpation, would place his own feeble, contemptible, ridiculous will in the place of the Divine wisdom and justice?[21]

Burke's claims here seem consistent with an ancient conception of natural law as the 'emanation of God's reason and will, revealed to all mankind'.[22] For Peter Stanlis, this conception of natural law runs throughout Burke's work and can be traced back to his reading of authors in the natural law tradition such as Aquinas, Bracton and Hooker.[23] It is this commitment that, for Stanlis, separates Burke from the seventeenth-century rationalism of Hobbes and Locke, as well as from revolutionary conceptions of the 'rights of man', and from later utilitarians, like Jeremy Bentham, who explicitly repudiated natural law.

Conceptions of natural law from this 'ancient' perspective, also informed more obviously 'radical' thinkers in the seventeenth century, such as Harrington and the Levellers, as well as being invoked by Calvinist thinkers in the sixteenth century to justify armed resistance to tyranny. Burke's traditionalism cannot, then, be simply read off from any commitment to an ancient conception of natural law. Moreover, the notion that Burke's mature thought can as a whole be seen as a product of a commitment to natural law is misleading. As J. G. A. Pocock has shown, Burke's defence of the English common-law tradition turns around a rejection of the very idea that we can discover founding principles of the constitution, or even principles that govern its operation at any given time. The common law for Burke is immemorial and customary: we cannot know its history as a whole and can have no complete knowledge of the 'natural' or 'ancient' principles on which it is based.[24] This view of the character of the common law is consistent with Burke's admiration for Hume and Montesquieu who emphasised the customary, historical and social character of the law.[25]

It might be thought, then, that here lies an inconsistency in Burke's thought, and it is the recognition of this inconsistency that helps us to deliver the 'radical' Burke from the 'conservative' or vice-versa. This is far from the case. Burke's view of providence is undoubtedly religious in character, but it does not follow that he adopts a consistently 'ancient' conception of natural law. Even if this were the case, the interesting question is why he would adopt such a vocabulary when around him it was being increasingly discarded? Moreover, Burke was not inconsistent in holding both that human laws are customary and immemorial in character, and that there is 'a superordinate moral authority over every political community'.[26] While the texture of Burke's argument is different to that of his 'radical' opponents, it is precisely in the reconciliation of these two ideas that he argues from the same conceptual grounds. Like the radicals, Burke believes it possible and desirable to subordinate politics and power to universal moral imperatives.

It is in his *Reflections on the Revolution in France* that Burke most fully articulates this idea. It is this book that cemented his reputation as a conservative and traditionalist. In no small part is this down to Burke's striking, and at times misinformed, condemnations of the revolutionaries. His prediction of the future bloody and anarchic course of the Revolution was spot-on, but in 1790, the year in which the book was published, the 'Revolution' was still a comparatively tame affair with the worst of the political machinations and the Terror still to come. There is no doubt that Burke's rhetorical flourishes against the revolutionaries and his occasional licence with the facts can, in large part, be explained by the character of his principal target. Concerned as he was for the future of France, Burke's more immediate pre-occupation was the future of Britain, and in particular the vision offered by those British radicals who had adopted the language of revolution and the rights of man. Initially, Burke was ambivalent about the Revolution, recognising it as a 'French struggle for Liberty' but 'not knowing whether to blame or applaud!'[27] However, he turned rapidly against the Revolution when it became clear that it was acting a spur to the British radicals. One event in particular seems to have cemented his opposition. On the 4 November 1789, Dr. Richard Price, a radical dissenting minister, gave a sermon to the Revolution Society in London at its annual celebration of the English Revolution of 1688. Price reminded his audience of the principles of that Revolution, which included 'the right to chuse our governors; to cashier them for misconduct; and to frame a government for ourselves'. He went on to praise the revolutionaries in France, adding:

> And now, methinks, I see the ardour for liberty catching and spreading; a general amendment beginning in human affairs; the dominion of kings changed for the dominion of laws, and the dominion of priests giving way to the dominion of reason and conscience ... Tremble all ye oppressors of the world! ... Restore to mankind their rights: and consent to the correction of abuses, before they and you are destroyed together.[28]

The first part of the *Reflections*, which as a whole takes the form of an extended letter to a 'young gentleman at Paris' who had solicited Burke's opinions on the Revolution, is a repudiation of Price's defence of events in France. Burke was concerned to show that the ideas of the revolutionaries and radicals subverted, rather than extended, the principles of the 1688 Revolution. The revolution in England had laid down sound procedures for checking tyranny and the abuse of power:

> The rule laid down for government in the Declaration of Right [the Parliamentary Act of 1689 stating the case against James II and laying the grounds for the legitimacy of the accession of William and Mary's], the constant inspection of parliament, the practical claim of impeachment, they thought infinitely a better security not only for their constitutional liberty, but against the vices of administration, then the reservation of a right so difficult in practice, so uncertain in the issue, and often so mischievous in the consequences, as that of 'cashiering their governors.'[29]

For Burke, as a Whig, it was clear that there were conditions under which one could not only disobey the sovereign but remove them. However:

> The question of dethroning, or if these gentlemen like the phrase better, 'cashiering kings,' will always be, as it always has been, an extraordinary question of state, and wholly out of the law; a question (like all other questions of state) of dispositions, and of means, and of probable consequences, rather than of positive rights. As it was not made for common abuses, so it is not to be agitated by common minds. The speculative line of demarcation, where obedience ought to end, and resistance must begin, is faint, obscure, and not easily definable. It is not a single act or single event that determines it. Governments must be abused and deranged indeed, before it can be thought of; and the prospect of the future must be as bad as the experience of the past.[30]

Here we see the strongly pragmatic character of Burke's thought. Political action, indeed politics more generally, should be a response only to pressing and threatening conditions and then the course of action to take must be based on a sober assessment of outcomes, not on speculative theories of human nature and right.

The real difference between Burke and the radicals is to be found in his traditionalism, and in particular his doctrine of prescription:

> By a constitutional policy, working after the pattern of nature, we receive, we hold, we transmit our government and our privileges, in the same manner in which we enjoy and transmit our property and our lives. The institutions of policy, the goods of fortune, the gifts of

Providence, are handed down, to us and from us, in the same course and order. Our political system is placed in a just correspondence and symmetry with the order of the world, and with the mode of existence decreed to a permanent body composed of transitory parts; wherein by the disposition of a stupendous wisdom, moulding together the great mysterious incorporation of the human race, the whole, at one time, is never old, or middle-aged, or young, but in a condition of unchangeable constancy, moves on through the varied tenor of perpetual decay, fall, renovation, and progression. Thus, by preserving the method of nature in the conduct of the state, in what we improve we are never wholly new; in what we retain we are never wholly obsolete.[31]

Traditional institutions like the hereditary monarchy had developed over very long periods of time and their durability was testament to their success at meeting human wants. To abolish these institutions and replace them with ones designed from abstract reason, divorced from tradition and historical experience, was a to pose a threat to the established rights and liberties that had been secured for the British over many generations.

These rights and liberties are secured by a contract or trust that is constituted by society as part of a providential order:

Society is indeed a contract ... It is a partnership in all science; a partnership in all art; a partnership in every virtue, and in all perfection. As the ends of such a partnership cannot be obtained in many generations, it becomes a partnership not only between those who are living, but between those who are living, those who are dead, and those who are to be born. Each contract of each particular state is but a clause in the great primaeval contract of eternal society, linking the lower with the higher natures, connecting the visible and the invisible worlds, according to a fixed compact sanctioned by the inviolable oath which holds all physical and all moral natures, each in their appointed place.[32]

While the laws and manners of different societies vary, what is clear from this view of prescription is that in their natural condition they will tend toward a providential order of 'physical' and 'moral' natures. It is here that we see Burke at his most 'conservative': the accreted wisdom of countless generations cannot be surpassed by the abstract reasoning of short-lived philosophers. What tradition and history have bequeathed to us should only be changed with great circumspection, and then only if it is really demanded by the status of human wants. Yet for all this 'conservatism', it is important to see that Burke's defence of tradition is not based on a direct appeal to divine or natural law. Burke explicitly adopts the notion of the 'human race' or 'mankind' as a unity and holds that it is this universal mankind that is the subject of nature and history. Providence tends toward the perfection of our rights and liberties as part of a social compact, the harmonisation of interests and the amelioration of conflict. It is striking that Burke should articulate such an argument at a time when European civilisation was facing its greatest disruption and conflict in 250 years.

It is with such conflict in mind that Burke saw the state principally as a coercive body. While Rousseau had lamented the curtailing of the passions by law and the state, Burke argued that their natural function is to hold the passions in check:

> Government is a contrivance of human wisdom to provide for human *wants*. Men have a right that these wants should be provided for by this wisdom. Among these wants is to be reckoned the want, out of civil society, of a sufficient restraint upon their passions. Society requires not only that the passions of individuals should be subjected, but that even in the mass and the body as well as in the individuals, the inclinations of men should frequently be thwarted, their will controlled, and their passions brought into subjection. This can only be done *by a power out of themselves*; and not, in the exercise of its function, subject to that will and to those passions which it is its office to bridle and subdue.[33]

This passage has sometimes been taken as prima facie evidence of Burke's conservatism, and a sign of his tendency toward authoritarianism.[34] Its language, though, should be scrutinised carefully. Burke writes of a 'sufficient restraint' on men's passions. This sufficient restraint is the state, 'a power out of themselves'. The notion that the 'inclinations' of the 'mass and the body' should be controlled by the state was undoubtedly written with the 'mob' in mind. Burke's experience of the mob was not confined to a second-hand account of the storming of the Bastille and the detention of Louis XVI and Marie Antoinette. In 1778 Burke had supported Sir George Savile's Relief Act, which provided for partial Catholic emancipation. Two years later, some 60,000 members of Lord George Gordon's Protestant Association went on the rampage through London, targeting Catholics and those, like Burke, who had supported the Relief Act. Burke was appalled not just by the cost to life (around 300 people were killed) and property (in excess of £100,000) caused by the Gordon Riots, but also by the intolerance and irrationality of the mob's behaviour.[35]

It was such 'passions', then, that Burke most likely had in mind to 'bridle and subdue'. With respect to the French Revolution, Burke was clearly arguing that government should not act to support such mobocracy, but rather to suppress it. Understood in this way, the above passage is very much in line with what Burke's 'radical' contemporaries thought about the coercive function of the state. Virtually all political thinkers accepted the necessity of government for restraining the passions in order to protect civil peace and liberty. There were, of course, exceptions, the most notable of them being William Godwin.[36] By and large, however, most eighteenth century political thinkers, 'radicals' among them, did not consider the possibility of a peaceful society in the absence of a coercive power outside of individuals. Burke's argument cannot, therefore, be treated as exceptional or even in its context particularly 'conservative'.

For Burke, the state is part of a providential natural and historical order. Government is seen as a product or 'contrivance' of already social beings to meet their wants. This tends to suggest a view of political power as a restricted if necessary feature of a social order whose major function is to keep the passions of society in check. Burke also, however, clearly considered laws and manners to be closely related and the public power must thus play a role in shaping the conduct of social actors. As Burke saw it, the danger of the French Revolution was that the public power took on a role greater than that which providence has determined for it and on the basis of a misguided philosophical rationalism sought to shape the world according to its will.[37] At the same time, it is clear from his thinking on America and India that Burke was quite willing to contemplate a wider role for political action when the circumstances dictated. More precisely, political action – to remove a corrupt leader, to shape manners according to moral precepts – is necessary as a reaction to *crisis*. Although he did not employ the term routinely, Burke very clearly subscribed to the concept of crisis. The French Revolution for him did, indeed, mark a moment of crisis that required an irrevocable political decision: not to extend, but to defeat it.

In his later writings on the Revolution, Burke would become ever more insistent on the necessity of the military defeat of the revolutionaries and in particular of Jacobinism. In his 'First Letter on A Regicide Peace', written in 1776 to urge against any peace settlement between Britain and France, Burke claimed that the Jacobins exhibited a 'determined hostility to the human race' and a threat to the 'community of Europe', 'virtually one great state having the same basis of general law', that had to be defeated by force of arms.[38] There could be no compromise with the Jacobin threat to the prescribed laws and customs of Europe. The Jacobins were the enemy not just of the national interests of the British, but of a balance between laws and manners that had become prescribed in the history of European civilisation. Like the radical revolutionaries, then, Burke had adopted the language of a crisis that operated on the terrain of universal interests. For all his seeming hostility to a universal morality, Burke saw the defeat of the Revolution as, at the same time, a defence of 'mankind' or the 'human race' against the atheism and rationalism of Jacobinism.

Leo Strauss has argued that 'Burke's intransigent opposition to the French Revolution must not blind us to the fact that in opposing the French Revolution, he has recourse to the same fundamental principle which is at the bottom of the revolutionary theorems and which is alien to all earlier thought.'[39] That principle is 'secularisation', or more precisely the secularisation of religious concepts that takes place in modern philosophy and science. For Strauss, Burke's conception of providence had been secularised in so far as he was prepared to consider, in the crisis constituted by the French Revolution, that its victory might itself have been countenanced by providence. This was not providence in the sense of a mandate from God, but rather in the sense that history, through its 'great variety of accidents', ensures that there are powerful currents in human affairs that cannot be reversed. It is not human will that shapes the world; the world is only there to be understood through the medium of a philosophy of history and nature. Strauss argues that Burke's defence of the British constitution rests precisely on such an account. Despite Burke's invocation of the language of natural right, the constitution cannot ultimately be defended by recourse to any principles outside those which it affirms: 'Transcendent standards can be dispensed with if the standard is inherent in the process; "the actual and the present is the rational".' Hence, for Strauss, in Burke's defence of the constitution we see an anticipation of Hegel's philosophy of history.[40]

Burke was not a systematic philosopher, and it would wrong to view him through the lens of Hegel in order to make him appear to have been so.[41] Yet, as Strauss argues, the obvious 'practical' bent of Burke's thought should not disguise the reliance of his thinking on the concepts constitutive of political and philosophical discourse in his context. Despite his frequent references to natural law and a moralising rhetoric that runs through much of his writing, Burke's thought shares with that of many of his radical opponents a certain understanding of the notions of history and political power. In Burke's work, history appears as a process that has the human race or mankind as its subject, but which is not itself driven by the rational volition of man. History is the accrual of the practices of generations. While Burke eschews the notion that this history operates according to any rationally discernible principles, the historical condition we find ourselves in at the present moment is nonetheless the outcome of natural providence, the character of which we are capable of conceiving. For Burke, like many of his radical adversaries, the French Revolution marked the arrival of history at a point of crisis, a crucial moment for the determination of the future of civilisation. Yet despite his denunciations of the 'evil' that was Jacobinism, Burke's conception of history filled him with the fear that what the French Revolution had unleashed was a powerful and providentially determined transformation in the manners of civilisation that could not be reversed.

Here, then, Burke was arguing from the same conceptual grounds as his radical interlocutors. They too subscribed to philosophies of history that had in common the postulate of an irrevocable crisis in the modern world. Burke's 'traditionalism' was not, and could not be a simple resuscitation of ancient principles. The reason that Burke's work is so often identified as an 'advent', that is, the advent of conservatism, is because he articulates a view of the world that is distinctly modern. It is so not solely because of his subscription to a modern conception of history. Burke's view of political power is also a modern one, and one again that he shares in common with his political adversaries. On the one hand, Burke seems to provide us with a notion of the modern state as a realm of coercion designed to protect the wants of men in the sphere of society. The 'political' is that sphere so defined. If anything, this is a distinctly liberal understanding of public power, one that is common in the late eighteenth century. At the same time, however, Burke's arguments concerning America, India and France make it clear that he believes in the necessity for political power to exceed its normal bounds in moments of crisis of authority. In the American and Indian cases, this meant a challenge to and possible overthrow of existing authority. While he did not recognise the legality of the French revolutionary state, Burke's attack on the French Revolution can be seen in the same terms. His calls for the defeat of the revolution by military means make it clear that in his eyes the resolution of the crisis had gone beyond the usual legal and political routes. The struggle for the future of European civilisation was a political struggle in a broader sense. It was one in which the future of the human race was at issue. The revolutionaries did not disagree.

Paine

Thomas Paine (1739–1809) was one of the few figures to play a leading role in both the American and French revolutions. While he has been variously portrayed as a revolutionary atheist (by his enemies),[42] radical liberal[43] or liberal turned radical,[44] none of these labels adequately capture the character of Paine's thought. By virtue of his political commitments Paine was certainly, in his context, a radical and a revolutionary. But to claim Paine as the major instigator of a radical, revolutionary or demo-cratic tradition is no more edifying than attributing to Burke the paternity of modern conservatism. As for Burke, Paine's texts must be seen as a response to a widely conceived crisis of the modern world. While Paine's sense of urgency shines through more than Burke's, this is because of his idiom and the audience for which he wrote. All of his major works had clear political goals and were mainly written to appeal to those working men and women who had neither time nor training to ponder exten-sively the principal problems of philosophy. That is not to say that Paine's work is not imbued with ideas that are drawn, consciously or otherwise, from the philosophy of the Enlightenment. Perhaps more than any of his 'radical' contemporaries, Paine draws together the central strands of Enlightenment conceptions of history and of the relationship between the social and the political domains to articulate a coherent and largely non-utopian vision of the future and its means of achievement: revolution. Yet just because Paine paints a more vibrant and appealing picture of revolution than any of his contemporaries, in his work the public power recedes almost to the point of disappearance, while at the same time his appeal to revolutionary republicanism surreptitiously politicises the social to an unprecedented degree.

Born the son of a Quaker tenant-farmer, Paine's early life was a mix of adventure – in his teens he spent time aboard two privateers – and of the mundane, following his father into the profession of corset-maker before becoming an excise officer in 1762. Dismissed from the latter post for a minor oversight, he spent time teaching in London before being reinstated to the excise in 1768. He migrated to America in 1774, but it seems that in the meantime he became politicised. During his stay in London he attended the lectures of Benjamin Martin and James Ferguson. Martin and Ferguson were committed to bringing scientific ideas, principally those of Newton, to a non-specialist audience, largely made up of artisans and shopkeepers from dissenting backgrounds.[45] Members of these audiences tended toward political radicalism, some of them being associated with the 'Club of Honest Whigs' among whose members was then London resident Benjamin Franklin. It was through a meeting with Franklin in 1767, organised by Martin, that Paine received a letter of introduction helping him to start his new life in America.[46]

Like many largely self-educated dissenters of the time, it seems that Paine was fascinated by Newtonian science and its practical applications. He would retain this practical commitment to science for the rest of his life. He sought to construct a single-span bridge during his first American sojourn, and it even seemed for while that this rather than politics might become his main interest in life.[47] At least as importantly, the Newtonian view of an ordered universe operating according to rationally comprehensible laws of nature meshed with the dissenting religious and radical political ideas of mid-eighteenth-century Britain. Paine's Quaker background had already given him access to the idea of the natural equality of men in the eyes of the divinity, and his understanding of Newtonian science probably strengthened his egalitarian convictions. Violations of this natural equality of man, however, appeared everywhere in Paine's early years in England. While this period in Paine's life is not in general that well documented, it is certainly the case that when he left England he was at the very least unhappy with what it had to offer men of his social standing. By that time Paine had already had his first taste of direct political engagement. In 1772 he penned a pamphlet, *The Case of the Officers of Excise*, which made the argument for an increase in the excise officers' salaries. To the same end a petition was signed by nearly all the officers in the country. That the Excise Board and Parliament flatly refused to acknowledge the officers' grievances can hardly have hindered Paine's decision to leave for new shores.[48]

It is almost certain, then, that when he arrived in America Paine had a fairly coherent view of the problems affecting British society and some idea of how to deal with them. To an extent, these ideas overlapped with those of British radicals such as Joseph Priestley, Richard Price and James Burgh. These thinkers themselves had an important impact on the formation of radical opposition to the British monarchy in America.[49] While Paine did not, broadly speaking, differ from them on grounds of principle, he was a much more cosmopolitan thinker. In part this was down to his circumstances. His work could not help but focus on the international given that he was directly caught up in the maelstrom of the greatest upheaval in the West since the Reformation. At the same time, Paine's arguments, while they often had America, France and Britain as their specific objects, were designed to have a truly global reach. In his *The Rights of Man*, the revolution that had started in America appears to have unstoppable momentum:

> And as the tide of human affairs has its ebb and flow in directions contrary to each other, so also is it in this. Government founded on a *moral theory, on a system of universal peace, on the indefeasible, hereditary rights of man*, is now revolving from west to east by a stronger impulse that the government of the sword revolved form the east to west. It interests not particular individuals but nations in its progress, and promises a new era to the human race.[50]

As we will see, Paine was perhaps the first modern thinker to conceive so openly of revolution on a global scale. Yet before Paine came to a full realisation of the revolutionary process and the radical break it constitutes with the history of the old world, he was moulded by his experience of the new world and its forging of a distinctive idea of its own identity.

In 1776, just two years after arriving in America, Paine found himself at the forefront of the articulation of that identity. His connections with Franklin had helped him to find work as the editor of the *Pennsylvania Magazine* and from this position he was able to pen his famous pamphlet, *Common Sense*. After the clash between the British and American militiamen at Lexington and Concord in 1775, reconciliation between the two sides seemed increasingly unlikely and many Americans now called openly for independence. *Common Sense* provided full-blooded support for that call, though it was couched not in terms of its prudential benefits for Americans, but rather in terms of their rights and the natural superiority of republican government over hereditary monarchy. In his Introduction Paine provides an early indication of his understanding of the global significance of events unfolding in America:

> The cause of America is, in a great measure, the cause of all mankind. Many circumstances have, and will arise, which are not local, but universal, and through which the principles of all lovers of mankind are affected, and in the event of which their affections are interested. The laying of a country desolate with fire and sword, declaring war against the natural rights of all mankind, and extirpating the defenders thereof from the face of the earth, is the concern of every man to whom nature hath given the power of feeling; of which class, regardless of party censure, is.[51]

Here Paine commits to print ideas that were quite common in the Enlightenment discourse with which he had become familiar: natural rights are a universal concern of mankind since, through nature, we are each bestowed with the capacity for fellow-feeling. Where Paine departs from the mainstream, however, is in his declaration of a clear distinction between the state (or what he more usually refers to as 'government') and society. This distinction plays an explicit role throughout Paine's texts in his understanding of the character of power in the modern world.

In framing the distinction, Paine was in no doubt of the very different functions of state and society and the desirability of the subordination of the former to the latter:

> Some writers have so confounded society with government as to leave little or no distinction between them; whereas they are not only different, but have different origins. Society is produced by our wants and government by our wickedness; the former promotes our happiness *positively* by uniting our affections, the latter *negatively* by restraining our vices. The one encourages intercourse, the other creates distinctions. The first is a patron, the last a punisher.
>
> Society in every state is a blessing, but government, even in its best state, is but a necessary evil; in its worse state an intolerable one; for when we suffer or are exposed to the same miseries *by a government*, which we might expect in a country *without government*, our calamity is heightened by reflecting that we furnish the means by which we suffer. Government, like dress, is the badge of lost innocence; the palaces of kings are built upon the ruins of the bowers of paradise.[52]

Paine appears, then, as a reluctant supporter of the notion that government is necessary where, out of the state of nature, human needs are produced that cannot be satisfied by the natural sociability of man. He attaches the state/society distinction to an account of representation that seeks to undermine any justification of authority on the grounds of prescription. While Locke and those authors of the American Constitution strongly influenced by him, like James Madison, supported the notion of some form of 'natural' aristocracy and hereditary title to rule, Paine dismisses the idea out-of-hand. For Paine, the only legitimate government derived from the state of nature is one established on the basis of the explicit consent of the members of society.[53]

Paine's construction of the distinction between the state and society and of the origins of legitimate government out of the state of nature, were designed to meet one aim: the justification of the republic as the only acceptable form of government in the modern world. Paine's republic, however, is not Rousseau's.[54] For Paine, modern societies were simply too large to allow citizens to directly participate in the public power. Of course, as we have seen, Rousseau also recognised this and in his scheme for the government of Poland supported the idea of a representative legislature. Yet while for Rousseau the practical necessity for such a form of government was the price to pay for his reluctant acceptance of modernity, Paine more readily embraced the modern world. Like the theorists of commercial society, Paine believed that the multiplication of wants and the social means of meeting them made for a more secure and profound liberty than that enjoyed in the ancient republics. Here, then, he was on similar ground to Burke. The martial and ascetic virtues of classical antiquity made for an impoverished and restricted liberty. In Paine's eyes, this 'liberty' was meaningless under any conditions other than those of the democratic republic. Virtue, in so far as this appeared as an object of Paine's discourse, was a quality that characterised the relations between individuals in society or, more precisely, 'civil society'. By adopting this term, and contrasting it to 'government' or the state, Paine was challenging the classical understanding of 'civil society' as a unified political community.

For Paine, the representative republic constitutes the only legitimate form of government in the modern world since it is the only one that is based on 'the common interests of society and the common rights of man'.[55] In contrast, monarchy is a form of government based on power with most monarchies founded on usurpation and conquest. Subjects do not consent to the laws but are coerced by them. Sovereign power inheres in the person of the king, not in an impersonal system of government in which all are equal before the law. In this respect, Paine rejected the notion that there was any qualitative difference between the character of government in Britain and France. While the French lived under the tyranny of 'absolutism', it was the claim of defenders of the British constitution, including Burke, that the settlement of 1688 had curbed monarchical power and ensured government by representation through the House of Commons. But while the English were 'wise enough to shut and lock a door against an absolute monarchy, ... at the same time [they] have been foolish enough to put the crown in the possession of the key'. '[T]he fate of Charles the First hath only made kings more subtle – not more just'.[56]

For Paine, monarchy was contrary to the natural order and destroyed the equality of mankind that was originally written into creation. In

Common Sense, Paine was quite prepared to turn to scripture to establish this claim: the Israelites' clamour to copy other nations in having a king went against the teaching of Samuel and of God himself.[57] His later book, *The Age of Reason*, repudiates scriptural authority and makes reason the criterion for judging human institutions. Nonetheless, Paine's position in both works is consistent: kingship violates the natural rights of men and serves the interests only of those few who, by wielding power, have violated the natural order. The English became subject to such violation when, in one of several such references, a 'French bastard' (William the Conqueror) and his 'armed banditti' established his kingship through conquest 'against the consent of the natives'.[58] We have come across a similar claim before in the writings of the Levellers. Unlike them, Paine did not wish to argue that the pre-Norman yoke was a state of perfect liberty: the pre-Norman English still lived under the rule of kings. Rather, legitimate government can only be established on the basis of the consent of its citizens, that is, in a republic. As Paine makes clear later in *The Rights of Man*, only two governments in the world could claim such legitimacy: the American and French republics in the wake of their revolutions.

Common Sense enjoyed huge popularity in America, with 150,000 copies sold by the end of 1776. It may not be an exaggeration to say that it 'turned the tide of American opinion in favour of independence'.[59] The idea that 'a government of our own is our natural right'[60] was one that won increasing approval. It did so in the light of a widespread view of crisis that *Common Sense* did much to foster. Many took to arms in what was seen as the defence of liberty against British tyranny, but there is little doubt that throughout the colonies this was done not simply out of self interest, but from political and, very importantly as Bernard Bailyn has argued, religious commitment.[61] Despite the significance of the religious aspect of the American 'revolution', it differed fundamentally from the English 'revolutions' of 1649 and 1688 in that the language used to justify it was largely secular. It was natural rather than divine law that was invoked, even if the natural order was ultimately seen as the product of the divinity. In the discourse of politics in America at this time, the notion of crisis undergoes a secularisation. No better indication is given of this then Paine's famous introduction to another pamphlet published in 1776, aptly entitled *The Crisis*:

> These are times that try men's souls. The summer soldier and the sunshine patriot will, in this crisis, shrink from the service of his country; but he that stands it *now*, deserves the love and thanks of

man and woman. Tyranny, like hell, is not easily conquered; yet we
have this consolation with us, that the harder the conflict, the more
glorious the triumph.[62]

The use of religious concepts in this passage – the soul and hell, the
implicit promise of salvation to those who stand up to tyranny
(the glorious triumph) – is used to fire up secular passions of patriotism.
The glory of the triumph, then, carries with it not just hidden religious
significance, but also involves a certain idea about the rewards of virtue
that come to the citizen in the form of service to his country. This concatenation of religion and civic virtue appeared in the context of the revolutionary moment, what Paine sought to capture in his use of the term
'crisis'. While in 1776 Paine did not use the word 'revolution' routinely,[63]
it was entailed by his concept of crisis joined with the notions of the
exclusive legitimacy of representative republicanism and the historical
significance for mankind of the American struggle for independence.

It was events in France in 1789, rather then in America in 1776, that
were to establish a fundamental transformation of the concept of revolution. While the term revolution, with its root in the latin verb *revol-
vere*, had been used in political discourse in the West since antiquity to
signify changes in type of government, traditionally between monarchy,
aristocracy and democracy, it had the sense of a fixed and repetitive pattern, a sense that was taken up by astronomers to describe the regular
movement, or 'revolution', of the planets.[64] In the wake of the French
Revolution, it would increasingly come to stand for a fundamental
change in the nature of social life, a rapid transformation that saw the
annihilation of the old regime and the introduction of a new order of
human affairs. The eschatological content of this concept is clear and
cannot be separated from the discourse of crisis that had developed in
the West from the seventeenth century. In its clearest relief, the crisis
stood for the clash between political power represented in the state, and
the universal interests of mankind represented by society. Yet what was
perceived to lie behind this conflict was not simply a clash of interests of
different social groups. This explanation for crises of authority was as
least as old as Greek antiquity. Rather, the clash of social interests in the
present – between the monarchy and aristocracy on the one hand and
the class of merchants, traders, financiers, industrialists, artisans and
tenant-farmers on the other – was the manifestation of deeper currents
in the trajectory of human history that could only be seen through a
philosophy of history. It is a view, as we have seen, that informs Burke's
thought in his understanding of providence and his fear that it pointed

toward the French Revolution as the natural course of history. Even so, Burke's support for an extra-legal counter-revolution, in the form of all-out war on the revolutionaries, points to his conviction of an inescapable turning point in the history of civilisation. As we will see, despite Paine's opposition to Burke's *Reflections*, he shares a similar conception of the historically constituted nature of the crisis and its determination of the revolutionary situation.

After *Common Sense*, Paine had continued to make a significant contribution to the American war effort, serving under Generals Nathanael Greene and George Washington, acting as an envoy of a Congressional commission to reach peace with the Susquehanna, and setting up the Bank of North America to fund the revolutionary army. After the Silas Deane affair, in which Paine rightly accused Deane, a businessman whom Congress has appointed to procure military supplies from the French, of profiteering, Paine's stock in America suffered. Many resented Paine, as an outsider, attacking someone who was widely seen as an American patriot.[65] Subsequently, Paine withdrew for a while from American public life and, in 1787, travelled to France. He was to spend the greater part of the next few years in transit between England and France and so it was, at first as an occasional resident of Paris and later as an honorary member of the National Assembly, that he was a first-hand witness to the events of the French Revolution.

From the start Paine was a strong supporter of the Revolution. He saw it as an opportunity to create republican government at the heart of the old European order. It would act as a catalyst to a wider revolution in which the principles of the natural rights of man and republican government would be adopted around the world. When he heard of Burke's intentions to repudiate the revolution, Paine was at first surprised but then resolved to write a response as soon as the former had published his thoughts. Such was the violence of both Burke's polemic and Paine's response to it that the friendship they had developed over their shared views of America was irretrievably broken. The first part of Paine's *The Rights of Man*, published in 1791, is a sustained attack on Burke. It opens with a refutation of his doctrine of prescription:

> The circumstances of the world are continually changing, and the opinions of men change also; and as government is for the living and not for the dead, it is the living only that has any right in it.[66]

As it is only the living and not the dead that have any rights over government, Paine dismisses Burke's defence of the constitutional settlement of 1688. For Burke, the settlement had established the completion of the Revolution by parliament's confirmation that the people would '*submit* themselves, their *heirs* and *posterity*, FOREVER [to William and Mary and their successors as rightful sovereigns]'.[67] On Paine's understanding of the legitimate basis of government, sovereignty can only be conceived as an express delegation of power from society to government, with the governed retaining the right to revoke sovereign power as they see fit. Sovereignty cannot be understood as having been established for all time by one generation, successive generations thereby being bound by the original agreement. Such an agreement would violate the natural right of man to property in himself: 'Man has no property in man; neither has any generation a property in the generations that are to follow.'[68]

As we have seen, it was not Burke's intention to deny that men had rights. However, the origin of those rights and the grounds of their legitimacy were to be located in the sum of the laws and customs that, for Burke, were constitutive of a legitimate constitution. For him, liberty could only successfully operate within the framework of historical institutions. In contrast Paine denied that tradition has any such legitimating function. It is here that we find Paine at his most rationalist: it is reason independent of experience that is the only means of establishing the legitimacy of laws and social institutions. Whenever those laws and institutions can be seen to rest on the explicit consent of citizens they are legitimate. However, Paine needed to demonstrate that, in the first place, laws and social institutions are a necessary feature of modern societies. He did this by distinguishing between natural and civil rights:

> Natural rights are those which always appertain to man in right of his existence. Of this kind are all the intellectual rights, or the rights of mind, and also all those rights of acting as an individual for his own comfort and happiness, which are not injurious to the rights of others. Civil rights are those which appertain to man in right of his being a member of society. Every civil right has for its foundation some natural right pre-existing in the individual, but to which his individual power is not, in all cases, sufficiently competent. Of this kind are all those which relate to security and protection.
>
> The natural rights which he retains are all those in which the power to execute is as perfect in the individual as the right itself ... The natural rights which are not retained are all those in which, though the right is perfect in the individual, the power to execute them is defective. They answer not his purpose. A man, by natural right, has a right to judge in his own cause; and so far as the

right of mind is concerned, he never surrenders it: but what availeth it him to judge, if he has not power to redress? He therefore deposits this right in the common stock of society, and takes the arm of society, of which he is a part, in preference and in addition to his own. Society *grants* him nothing. Every man is a proprietor in society, and draws on the capital as a matter of right.[69]

The purpose of social life is to protect and extend the enjoyment of the natural rights that obtain in each man. Government, in so far as it is emerges with the consent of individuals, is designed to protect and secure natural rights, one of the means by which a man can make effective his natural right to judge in his own cause. It is important to note, however, that Paine emphasised the inalienability of the right of man to judge himself in matters of 'right of mind'. In other words, the inner-world of private conscience appears as the inviolable, non-social sanctum of the individual. As we have seen in previous chapters, this isolation and protection of the world of private conscience from the public power is, from Luther onwards, the condition for the realisation of the social as a domain distinct from and ultimately superordinate to the political.

While Paine departed from the theorists of commercial society, most obviously Hume and Smith, in advocating the notion of a pre-social grounds for right and justice, he nonetheless accepted their understanding of the mutual benefits of society. He pursues this idea most fully in the second part of *The Rights of Man*, published in 1792: 'The mutual dependence and reciprocal interest which man has in man, and all the parts of a civilised community upon each other, create that great chain of connection which hold it altogether.'[70] The role that government plays in the satisfaction of human wants is limited and, moreover, in most areas of social intercourse its interference is likely to do more harm than good:

All the great laws of society are laws of nature. Those of trade and commerce, whether with respect to the intercourse of individuals or nations, are laws of mutual and reciprocal interest. They are followed and obeyed, because it is the interest of the parties so to do, and not on account of any formal laws that their government may impose or interpose.[71]

Paine's defence of commerce has been considered to place him within a broad tradition of Anglo-American thought that springs from Locke's *Second Treatise of Government* with its defence of self-ownership, private property and minimal government. From a Marxist perspective, the emphasis on commerce in *The Rights of Man* appear to establish Paine, alongside Burke, as a bourgeois liberal. Yet Paine's defence of commerce is in a number of important respects different to that of the theorists of commercial society. There is little indication that he saw commercial society as the highest stage of civilisation, as did Adam Smith. In particular, Paine saw agricultural production as, if anything, a more certain and sound basis of a society's wealth than commerce.[72] Moreover, in the second part of *The Rights of Man* and a pamphlet of 1797, 'Agrarian Justice', Paine called for an expansive, proto-welfare state.[73] This would involve, among other things provision for the poorest families and the aged, universal education, allowances for births, marriages and funerals, and a guarantee of work 'for the casual poor in the cities of Westminster and London'.[74] All of this would be funded from taxation collected and distributed by the state.

In their context, these were radical and non-utopian proposals for social reform. They could not be achieved, however, without a revolution against monarchical and in favour of republican government. Paine's argument for republicanism, as we have seen, is not prudential in character. He did not argue, as for example James Mill would, for representative government on the grounds of utility.[75] The significance of republicanism was that it was world-historic. The principal theme that Paine took from the theorists of commercial society was the congruence of commerce with modern manners, the latter being pacific and socially-oriented in character. Modern societies contained the potential for a virtuous ordering of social life, with social intercourse centred around voluntary associations that would further human enlightenment. The benefits of the commercial republic were not just confined to individual states: trade and social intercourse between nations presented the greatest obstacles to war. The principal beneficiaries of war in the old world were monarchical and aristocratic tyrannies, with the threat of constant war justifying arbitrary taxation and suppression of their subjects. The revolutionary inception of the republic would, then, provide the conditions for a more just ordering of social life according to the doctrine of natural rights and at the same time open a new era in human affairs in which peace and the disinterested pursuit of knowledge in the name of the advancement of mankind would prosper.

Paine's radicalism thus presents us with detailed proposals concerning political and social reform that are non-utopian. The republic is to be established on the basis of a constitution, like that of the United States, which obtains the express approval of all citizens.[76] It is the duty of the state to effectively uphold the rights of citizens, including the right to a minimum standard of wealth and social security. At the same time, however, there runs through Paine's texts a sense of urgency and millenarianism that does indeed reflect a utopianism born of a belief in a philosophy of history. The character of that philosophy of history is laid bare in Paine's last major piece of writing, *The Age of Reason* (1796). This Deistic tract, which saw him widely shunned by Protestant America in the remaining years of his life, rejected established religion and scriptural authority as the bases for morality. The intentions of the creator are to be found in creation alone, not in the words of man. Man's moral duty:

> consists in imitating the moral goodness and beneficence of God manifested in the creation toward all his creatures. That seeing, as we daily do, the goodness of God to all men, it is an example calling upon all men to practice the same towards each other; and consequently, that everything of persecution and revenge between man and man, and everything of cruelty to animals is a violation of moral duty.[77]

Paine's Deism probably sprang from his Quaker roots (while Quakers' were not Deists they were, according to Paine, 'nearest of all others to true Deism, in the moral and benign part thereof'[78]) coupled with his knowledge of Enlightenment supporters of the doctrine, such as Voltaire. Even in this, the most philosophical of his texts, there is thus a political motivation. Deism stood for a rejection of the tyranny of the priest and his word over the ordinary man, and it was the priesthood that, for long, had provided the most rigorous support to monarchical despotism. The real significance of Paine's incipient Deism throughout his earlier political works is that it performs as the ultimate marker against which actions are to be judged. Man should strive to achieve the harmonious order manifest in creation as a moral mission ultimately overriding all prudential considerations. While Paine did not licence violence lightly, for example as a deputy to the French National Convention he bravely opposed the execution of Louis XVI in the face of hostile Jacobin opposition,[79] he saw revolutionary war as a legitimate and necessary means of breaking the crisis.[80] Even where war was not its explicit means of realisation, he saw the global progress of republicanism in martial terms:

> An army of principles will penetrate where an army of soldiers cannot; it will succeed where diplomatic management would fail; it is neither

the Rhine, the Channel, nor the ocean that can arrest its progress; it will march on the horizon of the world, and it will conquer.[81]

If Paine viewed the political as a necessary evil, a realm of conflict and coercion that any well-ordered and just society will keep to a minimum, his view of the historical destiny of republican government committed him to a global revolution that involved an unprecedented politicisation of social relations. His understanding of political power and its relation to the social is thus deeply ambiguous. His republicanism requires a conception of the *vita activa* in a context that is free from political conflict, and on these grounds his thought was clearly utopian. This sits uneasily with his frequent recognition that the diversity of wants created in modern societies could only be satisfied peacefully with the mediating influence of law-governed social institutions and the state.

Paine's anti-politics was not simply a product of his distrust of the venal politicians he came across in his career. It was tied to his providential view of the character of the universe and the possibility it held out of a future society freed from political conflict. In comparison, Burke may seem more of a 'realist', prepared to accept without question the absolute necessity of public power in the ordering of social life. Yet as we have tried to show in this chapter, this widespread interpretation of Burke and his relationship to Paine is open to question. The dispute between the two over the French Revolution was in one respect theoretical: it involved different ways of conceiving the character of rights in modern societies. At some level both men appealed to 'natural law'. While for Burke the character of that law could only be gleaned through the providential constitution of the present by tradition and not by reference to a moment of origin, for Paine it could be understood only from a perspective outside the present and which went beyond that we know as the past. To establish the character of natural rights we need to posit man in a state that is natural and pre-social, that is, the state intended by creation. Reason and nature, not tradition, are the criteria of justice for any given social order.

It is, however, misleading to say as Fennessy does that 'there is no actual controversy between Burke and Paine – that is no exchange of argument, reply or counter-argument – but simply two appeals to English political opinion, from two entirely different and irreconcilable points of view'.[82] Burke and Paine were deeply engaged, not just in the sense that they wrote about the same events, but in that they employed concepts that were moulded by late eighteenth century discourse of the crisis of mankind. Burke's 'conservatism' was not simply a reaction to this crisis. Its view of history as determinate process, and of mankind and the state as objects of that process, is entirely consistent with that held by his radical contemporaries, including Paine. In turn, the modern doctrine of conservatism, with its acceptance of the global crisis and the necessity of its immanent resolution, served to further entrench the radical attitude toward modernity.

5
Democracy and Revolution: Tocqueville and Marx

The French Revolution resounded through the nineteenth century, shaping political identities and acting as the focal point for political and ideological conflict. For radicals, the Revolution had an ambiguous legacy. On the one hand, it had at its foundation the desire to escape the shackles of absolutist monarchy and to establish political, civil and social equality. At the same time, however, the Revolution had given way to internal conflict and repression, war and ultimately, in the person of Napoleon Bonaparte, a form of despotism that appeared considerably more powerful and far-reaching than that of even Louis XIV. 'Conservative' thinkers, like Burke, had seen the despotic denouement of the Revolution as a direct outcome of its original character: once the revolutionaries had taken the first step by destroying the institutional and customary basis of monarchy, all kinds of nefarious measures for imposing a 'rationalist' blueprint on society became acceptable. For others, like Paine, there was nothing inevitable about the corruption of the Revolution. It took the course that it did because of the mistaken and often venal actions taken by its leaders. For both Burke and Paine, however, the Revolution was so significant because in an important sense it was determined not by the conscious activities of men, but by historical forces that worked behind their backs. The problem was, first of all, to determine what these forces might be and then to register what kind of conscious choices men should make in response to them.

It is this problem that constitutes a central and recurrent theme in the texts of both Alexis de Tocqueville and Karl Marx. For both men the future of the world was to be gleaned through a reflection on alien cultures: for the French Tocqueville, democracy in America; for the German Marx, industrial capitalism in England. The writings of both were astonishingly prophetic, and they were able to grasp better than any other authors of the nineteenth century the social and political constitution of the present and its possible trajectories. Tocqueville and Marx are often seen as inveterate optimists, where in fact their assessment of the present is often ambiguous and pessimistic. Both, as we will see, are 'democrats', but not in any conventional sense. Tocqueville and Marx are, in different ways, 'social' democrats. Their view of public power is that it results from social relations and, in the modern world, should be used only as an instrument of the social interests of men. It is in this subordination of the political to the social, then, that we see in Tocqueville and Marx the kind of aversion to power and politics that is one of the definitive features of the modern radical attitude. But we must be careful not to place too great an emphasis on this aspect of their works, because it does not vitiate the significance and continued relevance of their reflections on the character of political modernity. We should read Tocqueville and Marx today, and preferably in concert, because their texts both reveal much about modern social and political conditions and, at the same time, have made an essential contribution to the formation of contemporary political identities and contests.

Tocqueville

Like Montesquieu, Alexis de Tocqueville (1805–59) was born into the French aristocracy. Montesquieu's work was to be a considerable influence on Tocqueville throughout his life, but unlike him he sought not to re-entrench the role of nobility in French society, but rather, in the wake of the Revolution, to recognise its irretrievable dissolution and the need to find a new form of social and political settlement. The Revolution had profoundly affected Tocqueville's family. In 1794 his famous grandfather, Malesherbes, who had defended Louis XVI to the Convention and other members of his family were tried and guillotined in. Although Tocqueville's parents were imprisoned, they escaped the same fate and after the fall of Robespierre were able to build a comfortable aristocratic life, partly as the result of property inherited from their executed relatives.[1] Malesherbes' decision to defend Louis XVI, even though he had been an enlightened critic of royal despotism, evidently greatly impressed Tocqueville. He wrote: 'I am the grandson of M. de Malesherbes: Malesherbes defended the people before the King and the King before the people. His is a double example that I have not forgotten, and shall never forget.'[2] As Larry Siedentop suggests, the example of the grandfather must have had some impact on Tocqueville's conception of aristocracy as 'having more to do with quality of motives than with prejudice of caste'.[3]

The fate of Tocqueville's most illustrious ancestor thus seemed to point him toward a life of politics and public service. He studied law in Paris in the 1820s, and in 1827 was appointed as a junior magistrate in Versailles. After the revolution of 1830, where Charles X was deposed after having attempted to reintroduce the privileges the aristocracy had enjoyed under the old regime, Tocqueville perceived that his progress in the legal profession would now be blocked, mainly due to his aristocratic background. Along with his friend, Gustave de Beaumont, Tocqueville thus set out on a journey to America, one that he had been planning for some years, while retaining his magisterial position by claiming that the trip was designed to investigate reforms to penitentiaries in Philadelphia and New York. The nine-month visit to America was to provide the material used in the writing of Tocqueville's most famous book, *Democracy in America* (volume 1 appearing in 1835, volume 2 in 1840). Yet while *Democracy in America* is indeed the most important of Tocqueville's texts, it is often taken to be so for the wrong reason. *Democracy in America* tends to be widely lauded in America as the classic work on American government and society, more significant even than Madison, Jay and Hamilton's *The Federalist*. It is indeed a highly perceptive account of the relationship between American society and government, but in a very important sense it is *not* a book about America. Tocqueville's interest in America had grown through the 1820s, but principally because of the attention he was paying to the debates of the time about French and European history. A central feature of these debates was the notion of a dual process of atomisation and centralisation that had come to define modernity. The idea was particularly prominent in France where it had been employed to try to explain why the country had gone through Revolution, and why that Revolution had degenerated into tyranny.

The debate with respect to atomisation-centralisation took place largely within liberal circles in 1820s Restoration France. At this time liberal authors and politicians, such as François Guizot and Pierre Royer-Collard, had launched a sustained attack on those ultra-royalists in government who were attempting to turn the clock back to the old regime by restoring the privileges of the church and aristocracy. What the ultras failed to recognise, the liberals claimed, was that the social conditions that supported aristocratic government no longer existed in France and could not be reinstated by acts of political will. Aristocratic society had been in decline over the course of at least four centuries. Accordingly, Guizot and Royer-Collard came to think of the Revolution as 'formalising changes in French society and adjusting the structure of

French government to those changes, rather than being in itself the primary source of social change'. For Siedentop, these '[l]iberals learned to make a careful distinction between social structure and political institutions. They also assumed that the former had causal authority'.[4] The Revolution thus appears as the result of long-term changes in the structure of French society, transformations that tended toward 'atomisation' or the increasing individuation of social life as traditional feudal social structures fell into decline. The decay of the nobility had weakened the system of local administration to the extent that, first under the absolutist monarchy and then under Napoleon, a highly centralised form of political administration had been allowed to emerge. Montesquieu addressed very much the same problem in his *The Spirit of the Laws* when he called for a revival of the intermediary dependent powers in curbing the threat of monarchical despotism. Yet the liberals of the 1820s could not, given their understanding of the irreversible and socially constituted decline of the old order, countenance a return to the nobility and church as a means of mediating between individuals and the sovereign power. Rather, they sought out constitutional and representative means of constraining the power of government and protecting the realm of private freedom.

Guizot and other Restoration liberals had looked to England, as had Montesquieu, as a model for non-despotic, representative government that protected the liberty of the modern individual. England's constitutional settlement of 1688 had managed to reign-in monarchical power without unleashing the anarchy that followed the in the wake of both the first English Revolution of 1649 and the French Revolution of 1789. As François Furet points out, the Restoration liberals had looked to England in 1688 as a sign of hope: the English had managed to secure freedom under representative liberal government only after 40 years had come to separate them from their initial revolution against absolutism.[5] But while Tocqueville had taken from Guizot the idea that the study of comparative history was central for the divination of France's future trajectory, through the 1820s he became sceptical of the idea that England stood as the most important comparator. Like the Restoration liberals, Tocqueville was concerned with the question of how liberty could be maintained in societies in which conditions were becoming ever more equal. But unlike them, he did not believe the notion of 'democracy' was exhausted by the character of free institutions, such as those in England. As Furet shows, Tocqueville was increasingly convinced that England was not a democratic society, but rather remained largely aristocratic with a 'mixed' political constitution.[6] If we wanted to understand the (possible) future of French and European society (including the future of England), then 'democracy' had to be seen as a term that was applicable to social conditions in general. There was only one society in the world at this time that could be said to be egalitarian, and thus 'democratic', in this sense: America.

Tocqueville's voyage to America was, then, planned ahead by a number of years not simply because of his general curiosity about the country, but rather because he had come to believe that a proper study of American democracy was crucial for an understanding of the future of France and of European civilisation more broadly. In the Introduction to *Democracy in America* (1835), this point is clearly made: his interest in America is borne out of a realisation that it offers a glimpse into civilisation's future as this has been determined by the 'gradual unfurling of equality in social conditions ... a providential fact which reflects its principal characteristics; it is universal, it is lasting and it constantly eludes human interferences'. The inexorable movement toward social equality and the decline of a society characterised by inequality, that is, aristocracy, meant that, '[a] new political science is needed for a totally new world'. But this new political science had to proceed on the basis of an examination of a social state that most closely approximated the future of the world. For Tocqueville, it was America that fulfilled this role. Thus he was prepared to 'confess that in America I have seen more than America itself'.[7]

America was important for Tocqueville since it already existed as a democratic social state. It was not to be understood as a democracy simply because it possessed representative-democratic political institutions. To be sure, Tocqueville claims in the course of *Democracy in America* that the nature of these institutions and the character of their political constitution were important factors in explaining why Americans had not succumbed to despotism after their Revolution. However, American democracy was to be discovered in the peculiarities of its society as these were evident from its foundation. The original settlers of America were of two types. In the south they were initially speculators and adventurers seeking a fortune in precious metals, shortly afterwards followed by lower-class craftsmen and farmers. Slavery was established relatively quickly in the southern colonies, an important factor for Tocqueville since 'it brings dishonour to work; it introduces idleness into society together with ignorance and pride, poverty, and indulgence. It weakens the power of the mind and dampens human effort'. Accordingly, '[n]o noble views, no spiritual thought presided over the foundation of these new settlements'.[8] In contrast, the northern colonies were settled by

Puritans who had left England not 'in order to better their lives or to increase their wealth', but 'to obey a purely intellectual need; by suffering the inevitable deprivations of exile, their object was the triumph of an *idea*'. For Tocqueville, this 'idea' was not just religious in character but 'linked itself in several respects to the most prominent democratic and republican theories'. The radical Puritans, facing political persecution and social ridicule for their ascetic practices, 'sought out a land so rough and so neglected that they might be allowed to live there as they wished and to worship God without restriction'.[9]

While these differences between the settlement of the north and south would have an important bearing on the future cohesion of the American Union,[10] Tocqueville believed that they contributed toward the substantive political and social independence of the settlers from the English colonial power. Such independence was further entrenched by the practice, peculiar to the English of all colonising empires in the seventeenth century, of granting Royal Charters to settlers, specifically those in New England. These Charters effectively bestowed on the colonists the right to govern their territories as they saw fit, so long as this was consistent with the Crown's ultimate sovereignty. In New England forms of self-government, first through the religious congregation of Puritans and later through village and town councils, were created before the granting of Charters. The Charters bestowed legitimacy on forms of government already set up in the colonies of Rhode Island and Connecticut, and towns like Plymouth and New Haven. For Tocqueville, the laws passed by the early settlers of these New England territories provide 'the key to the great social mystery which the United States presents to the world'.[11]

The Puritans introduced laws that claimed scriptural authority and imposed an austere discipline on personal habits. The penalty for blasphemy, witchcraft and adultery was death and other ungodly forms of behaviour, from drunkenness to sporting long hair, were met with a range of legal sanctions and social censure. But these fanatical penal laws emanated from a system of law-making that enshrined conceptions of political liberty not to be widely embraced in Europe for a further two centuries. The original government of New England established general principles such as: 'the involvement of the people in public affairs, the free vote on taxes, the personal responsibility of those in power, individual freedom, and trial by jury'. In the towns of New England, laws were created not by Crown-appointed officials, elders or even representatives, but rather 'the affairs which effected everyone were discussed, as in Athens, in the public squares or in the general assembly of the citizens'.

Social and material conditions were largely equal and the town oversaw a variety of measures to provide support for the poor, maintain roads and public property and provide publicly funded education for children.[12] Thus, for Tocqueville, in New England we could witness the expression of a religious fanaticism that had been driven out of Europe, existing alongside a form of government enshrining political liberty and concern for public life that under absolute monarchy in the early seventeenth century was unknown: 'The founders of New England were both sectarian fanatics and noble innovators.' It was on this foundation that the character of American civilization emerged:

> This civilization is the result (and this is something we must always bear in mind) of two quite distinct ingredients which anywhere else have often ended in war but which Americans have somehow suc-ceeded to meld together in wondrous harmony: namely the *spirit of religion* and the *spirit of liberty*.[13]

From the outset Americans were provided with solutions to the problem of atomisation-centralisation that were not available in Europe. The destruction of feudal forms of local government and the increasing preponderance of commercial relations had created a process of atomisa-tion, one that could not be tempered by religion. In Europe the Reformation and the wars of religion had contributed to the gradual sec-ularisation of society and the belief that acts of public worship and acts of law-making should be kept distinct. The Puritans, in contrast, drew on the Calvinist idea of church government to argue that there could be no clear division between matters of faith and public law. The Puritans were radicals, however, in the sense that they believed that it was the congre-gation of faithful families that constituted the sovereign body in a Christian community. Of course, church and state were to become sepa-rate in America, but what remained was the conviction that the family operated as the 'natural horizon' for religion.[14] The religious values that united Americans were dispersed over the generations and provided a method of 'social control', a way of dealing with 'the political crisis cre-ated by equality'.[15] Religion remained robust in America, while in Europe it had fallen into decline. The French Revolution was, at least on first sight, a revolution against religion. The problem of atomisation could not be dealt with in Europe by religion or at least traditional, established religion. However, as we will see in considering Tocqueville's work on the Revolution, that event could itself be seen as acting in a very similar manner to a religious revolution, propagating a universal ideology that called on men to forge a new, universal community of values.

While the wide distribution of religious values in America acted as a means of promoting social solidarity, from the outset the presence of a tradition of political liberty obviated the tendency toward an absolutist form of government. Tocqueville makes a distinction between two different forms of centralisation: governmental and administrative. The former refers to '[c]ertain concerns that are shared by all national groups, such as the formation of general laws and relations with foreign nations', whereas the latter involves '[o]ther concerns ... of special interest to certain national groups, such as, for example, business undertaken by the townships'.[16] America had, in the commissioning of a federal system in 1787, created a centralised system of national government, but at the same time it had retained the administrative decentralisation of the colonial period and entrenched it by providing constitutional recognition of the legislative rights of states, counties and townships. This federal system was designed by the founding fathers of the American constitution as a means of protecting individual liberty, of allowing individuals to pursue their own private and material interests in the absence of arbitrary authority. Much of part 1 of book 1, volume 1 of *Democracy in America* is primarily concerned with demonstrating how the combination of governmental centralisation and administrative decentralisation functions in the federal system 'to combine the several advantages which stem from the large or small size of nations'. In America the liberty exercised by men in small states is preserved at the same time as they enjoy the security and prosperity achieved only in large states.[17]

The federal system of government serves to underpin American democracy as it stands for the rough equality of social conditions in American society. It functions, as James Madison had argued it would in the famous tenth paper in *The Federalist*,[18] to militate against the emergence of all-powerful national factions. But there might appear to be a paradox here, for as much as there is political equality in America there are, as Tocqueville recognised, great extremes of wealth and rich men often try to obtain and succeed in exercising a disproportionate influence over legislative power. However, for Tocqueville this was no bar to the portrayal of American society as egalitarian. The fact that relatively few men held great wealth and occupied political office was not tantamount to aristocracy in America. The reason was that wealth in America was not, on the whole, tied into an aristocratic system of property rights and inheritance based on the aristocratic principles of entail and primogeniture (though some vestiges of the influence of English aristocratic proprietary practices remained, particularly in the south). At the same time, the vast expanse of territory in America meant that there were plenty of opportunities for land acquisition, particularly for those prepared to live the life of frontiersmen as the boundary of the western United States was pushed ever further toward the Pacific. In general while there was a restlessness for the pursuit of property in America and a widespread acceptance of inequality in possessions, 'wealth circulates with astonishing speed and experience shows that rarely do two succeeding generations benefit from its favours'.[19] It is this rapid circulation of wealth that ensures the maintenance of equality in America; not, that is, an equality of material conditions but rather of opportunity to acquire riches. In volume 2 of *Democracy in America* Tocqueville did recognise that the development of an industrial economy and the entrenchment of permanent inequality of social conditions posed a threat to this circulation of wealth and therefore to the persistence of democracy in American society.[20] But in the early nineteenth century this danger had not been realised and could still, he argued, be countered through law and custom.

The picture that Tocqueville presents of American society, then, is one where equality of opportunity to acquire wealth sits alongside a widely accepted philosophy of self-interest and commercial competition. But as we have seen, Tocqueville does not think this individualism operates as a necessary threat to the coherence and civic virtue of American society and government. Shared religious values serve to promote and enhance beliefs in democratic participation; local self-government is the norm; the constitution and character of the political institutions of the United States serve to provide a system of checks and balances, particularly through a politically independent judiciary, which ensures that no powerful interest groups can come to dominate American public life; and widespread participation in political and civil associations ensures that citizens have a collective voice in political decision making.[21] But it was not Tocqueville's intention, as he makes clear at the opening of the book, to compose a 'hymn of praise'.[22] American democracy, while it had to date managed to secure a balance between the liberty of its citizens and virtue in the conduct of public affairs, contained many dangers. The mechanisms that maintained democratic equality in American society could easily have led to the creation of tyranny. The despotism that America contained in seed was not the kind of monarchical despotism peculiar to Europe in the early modern period, but rather a democratic despotism or, as Tocqueville refers to it, 'the tyranny of the majority'. There is no guarantee in America that the majority may not ride roughshod over the rights of the individual. The principle of the majority in American life provides a kind of arbitrary power, characteristic of traditional European despotism, to public officials who can effectively claim to have the weight of the people's support behind them. At the same time, majority opinion has an overarching influence on thought and public discourse, to the extent that Tocqueville claims, 'I know of no country where there is generally less independence of thought and real freedom of debate than in America.'[23] Finally, the tyranny of the majority opinion in America expresses itself in an unreflective patriotism, eager deference to leaders, and a lack of independently minded and charismatic public figures.

Volume 2 of *Democracy in America* is in an important respect a continuation of this investigation into the power of the majority over the beliefs and customs of American life. But while Tocqueville sees the character of American customs as potentially dangerous to the continuation of liberty, at the same time he claims that they act as its main support. By 'customs' here, Tocqueville means 'the term used by the classical writers when they used the word *mores*; for I apply it not only to customs in the strict sense of what might be called the habits of the heart but also the different concepts men adopt, the various opinions which prevail among them and to the whole collection of ideas which shape mental habits'.[24] The equality of social conditions that characterises American society is itself a condition for the operation of the democratic customs that Americans possess, but at the same time those customs tend to reinforce equality of social conditions. In this respect, customs take priority over laws and laws over 'physical conditions' in the maintenance of the democratic republic in the United States.[25]

This argument concerning the subordination of physical environment to laws of and laws to customs is important for the conclusions Tocqueville wishes to draw from his study of America for the future direction of democracy in Europe: 'If nations with a democratic social state could only remain free as long as they live in a wilderness, we would have to despair of the future destiny of the human race; for men are rushing toward democracy and the available wildernesses are filling up.' Liberty in America, however, has been established and so far safeguarded by laws that enshrine administrative centralisation and customs that promote democratic equality of conditions. Tocqueville 'is very far from thinking that we should follow the example represented by American democracy or imitate the means she has used to achieve this aim for I am well aware of the influence of the nature of the country and of previous history upon political constitutions and I would regard it a great misfortune for mankind, if freedom should assume the same features in all places'.[26] But nonetheless, America offers hope for the future of European civilization in the sense that the relentless march toward the equalisation of social conditions does not bring with it an inexorable threat to the liberty of modern men. For Tocqueville, optimism for the future depends on crafting laws and customs in the present that will foster self-interest 'properly understood'. This is self-interest tempered by the tying of men into public life through both institutional and customary means: '[t]he doctrine of self-interest properly understood does not inspire great sacrifices but does prompt daily small ones; by itself it could not make a man virtuous but it does shape a host of law-abiding, sober, moderate, careful, and self-controlled citizens. If it does not lead the will directly to virtue, it moves it closer through the imperceptible influence of habit'.[27]

It is possible to see Tocqueville's argument in *Democracy in America* as recapitulating the central theme of the philosophical history of the Enlightenment: that men, their laws and political institutions are caught up in a tide of history from which they cannot escape. The sphere of public power is doubly subordinated: first to the realm of the social, expressed mainly by Tocqueville in terms of the 'customs' characteristic of different kinds of society; and second to the movement of history as a 'providential march toward equality'. What renders Tocqueville's understanding of historical development even more problematic is this emphasis on 'providence'. For Marxist critics, it is entirely appropriate to attempt to distinguish laws of historical development and to seek out their manifestation in particular kinds of social and political arrangements. Tocqueville, from this point of view, adopts a Panglossian view of the present that articulates the interests of the class that benefited most from the 'equality' of social conditions: the bourgeoisie. It was the bourgeoisie, not a universal mankind as Tocqueville tends to suggest, that had reaped most from the decline of the old regime, as the legal privileges over private property enjoyed by the nobility were gradually rescinded and the space opened up for the development of a market economy. While Tocqueville was clearly aware of the importance of changes in the legal character of property, from a Marxist point of view what he singularly failed to recognise was how the distribution of property in modern bourgeois society was inextricably linked to the exercise of political power by the capitalist class.

However, it was not the case that Tocqueville was attempting to seek out 'laws' of historical development. Indeed, as Raymond Aron has written, Tocqueville 'differed from so-called classic sociologists like Comte and Marx in his rejection of vast syntheses intended to forecast history. He did not believe that past history is governed by inexorable laws or that future events are predetermined'.[28] The 'march toward equality' is 'providential' because it provides the potential, in a way that Marx also acknowledged, for human beings to live freer and richer lives, not because it is determined by the hand of Providence. The equalisation of social conditions, for Tocqueville, is the outcome of a host of historical tendencies and events that could never hope to be adequately captured in their entirety by general laws or principles of philosophical history. At the same time, Tocqueville's texts and political activities point toward an understanding of politics that is far more complex than is suggested by the idea that he was a principal representative of the material interests of the bourgeoisie. As Wolin claims: 'The abiding concern of Tocqueville's thinking, the referent point by which he tried to define his life as well as the task before his generation, was the revival of the political: in his phrase *la chose publique*. The elevation of the political and the making of a public self were conscious gestures of opposition to privatising tendencies for which he, as much as any writer of his time, provided the authoritative critique.'[29] Tocqueville differed quite considerably from bourgeois liberals, such as John Stuart Mill, who tended to take the possessive individual of classical political economy as a given rather than a product of particular kinds of social and economic relations.[30] In a was that renders Tocqueville's work radical in its context, he saw how the modern individual was a product of historically contrived circumstances and how the future of the individual rested upon the character of the public life into which he was necessarily drawn.

This concern with the character of public life is already apparent in *Democracy in America*, but if anything it is even more evident in Tocqueville's other major work, *The Old Regime and the French Revolution* (1856). In the Preface to the book he writes:

> Liberty alone can effectively combat the natural vices of these kinds of societies and prevent them from sliding down the slippery slope where they find themselves. Only freedom can bring citizens out of the isolation in which the very independence of these circumstances had led them to live, can daily force them to mingle, to join together through the need to communicate with one another, persuade each other, and satisfy each other in the conduct of their common affairs. Only freedom can tear people from the worship of Mammon and the petty daily concerns of their personal affairs and teach them to always see and feel the nation above and beside them; only freedom can substitute higher and stronger passions for the love of material well-being, give rise to greater ambitions than the acquisition of a fortune, and create the atmosphere which allows one to see and judge human vices and virtues.[31]

For Tocqueville, this was the form of freedom the Revolutionaries of 1789 had hoped to achieve, one in which the liberty of the individual was tied into a democratic and thriving public life. Yet the Revolution gave way first to the Terror and then to the despotism of Napoleon Bonaparte. It might have been easy and self-gratifying for Tocqueville, given the fate of many of his relatives in the Terror, to have explained the decay of the Revolution in terms of the personal and ethical short-comings of leaders such as Robespierre. However, in answering the question of why the Revolution failed to achieve its aim of liberty and succeeded rather in constituting despotism, Tocqueville looked not to the character of historical actors but to long-term tendencies in social and political life in France.

In their Revolution the Americans had attempted to forge a national unity by the creation of a constitution and a political culture to which all Americans could subscribe. One of the central tenets of this political constitution was administrative decentralisation, the notion that liberty rested on the capacity of individuals, civil associations, towns, counties and states to legislate their own affairs. Now the French Revolutionaries has similarly seen the importance of creating a centralised political identity for all Frenchmen, something that had not existed under the old regime because of the continued division of society along the status lines that were the trace of a dying feudal social system. Accordingly, the Revolution abolished 'the political institutions which for several centuries had reigned unopposed among the majority of European peoples, and which we usually call feudal institutions. It did so in order to replace them with a more uniform and simple social and political order, one based on social equality'.[32] However, in contrast to what a number of historians of the French Revolution had thought, it did not create a centralised administrative state: rather this was its inheritance. Tocqueville's original historical argument at the centre of *The Old Regime* is that under the absolutist monarchs a highly centralised and bureaucratic administration had been created in France, reaching its apogee in the eighteenth century.

After the Revolution the revolutionaries utilised this centralised state as an instrument with which to destroy the remnants of the old regime, but in doing so undermined the kind of political liberty they wanted to achieve. Tocqueville's point here is not that the future direction of the revolution was solely determined by the political choices made by its leaders, but rather that the existence of administrative centralisation had narrowed down the range of such choices available after the Revolution. For Tocqueville, the Revolution itself was 'inevitable' in the sense that the irrepressible march toward democracy, as the levelling of social conditions, made the continued existence of feudal institutions and social practices ever more unlikely. But the development of administrative centralisation in France had created political institutions and a public culture that were as likely to produce democratic despotism as a decentralised system capable of supporting political liberty. As François Furet and Françoise Mélonio suggest, the argument that Tocqueville makes here represents something of a shift in his perception of the relationship between social change and political institutions. Tocqueville sees administrative centralisation as something that precedes the development of a democratic social state and which appears again in the nineteenth century after France has gone through a democratising process. Tocqueville's inversion of this relationship between the social state and the political regime may be seen, as Furet and Mélonio claim, as a product of his experiences as a liberal politician in France during the 1840s and during Louis Bonaparte's coup d'état of 1851, to which he was strongly opposed. Tocqueville saw that '[t]he Republic of February 1848 was not the victory of one class over another but an imitation of the French Revolution. The coup d'état of December was made possible by the combination of a prestigious name [that of Louis Bonaparte, Napoleon's nephew] and a bureaucratic state that was independent of society. Through the history of this bureaucratic state, Tocqueville began his inventory of the old regime'.[33]

The course of the French Revolution had, then, been determined by the effects of a history of administrative centralisation, as the bureaucratic apparatus of the absolutist state became more developed over the course of two centuries, alongside the equalisation of social conditions that occurred with the decline of the feudal social structure. Absolutism in France had closed the space for the exercise of political liberty in a secure social sphere; the same opportunity for active involvement in public life through civil and political associations did not present itself to the French as to the Americans. Cut off from the political domain, the intellectual leaders of the French Revolution, Enlightened *hommes des lettres*, were more attracted to abstract ideals and universal values than to practical measures of social and political reform. This explains why, for Tocqueville, the French Revolution had the character of a religious revolution. It adopted the belief in a universal community, extending beyond the borders of France, in which men were endowed by their creator with inalienable rights; it 'became a new kind of religion, an incomplete religion, it is true, without God, without ritual, and without a life after death, but one which nevertheless, like Islam, flooded the earth with its soldiers, apostles, and martyrs'.[34] In pursuit of these quasi-religious ideals the people in the French Revolution rejected the idea of gradual reform in favour of the abolition of everything associated with the old regime. But in doing this they 'had accepted as the ideal society a people without any aristocracy other than government officials, a single and all-powerful administration, director of the state, guardian of individuals. In wishing to be free, they did not intend to depart in the slightest from this basic idea; they only tried to reconcile it with the idea of freedom'.[35] For Tocqueville, the French Revolution was bound to degenerate into despotism at the moment it came to be seen as a means of radically transforming French society using the tool of the centralised administrative state. Political liberty rather required the gradual decentralisation of administration and the encouragement of democratic social customs. In contrast, the Revolution entrenched the bureaucratic state and left it beyond political control, while at the same time promoting a view of citizenship as unquestioning loyalty to, first, the revolutionary state, then the interests of the nation and finally, under Napoleon, the Empire.

Tocqueville, then, was a critic of the French Revolution, but not in the same fashion as Burke. Unlike Burke, Tocqueville recognised and embraced the revolution insofar as that meant the gradual and irrevocable replacement of aristocratic by democratic society. In this respect, Tocqueville's view of the Revolution was much closer to that of another Frenchman and contemporary, Pierre-Joseph Proudhon. Proudhon, the original 'anarchist', also believed that the old regime had to die for a new liberty to be born. Liberty could only be achieved and sustained in a society where individuals had the freedom to enter into (and freely exit from) mutual associations of independent producers. Tocqueville's conception of democracy and its relationship to sovereignty is not so different from Proudhon's: he too believed that liberty was only possible in a politically decentralised society, where social life was organised on the basis of self-interest 'properly understood'. Both also saw the kind of democratic despotism associated with the Jacobins and Napoleon as inimical to liberty. But while Proudhon's free man joined together with other men largely out of necessity in order to meet his material needs and wants, for Tocqueville association was itself the key to *political* liberty. The radicalism of Tocqueville's texts lies not so much in their support for 'Revolution', but in their recognition of the importance that political and civil life have for the exercise of freedom in the modern world. The connection between community and freedom is also clear in the work of Karl Marx, but as we will now see for Marx the achievement of freedom requires the overcoming of political power.

Marx

Karl Marx (1818–83) is widely acknowledged as a deeply radical thinker whose work effected a transformation in the way people thought about the world as well as providing the main impetus for the development of a new, revolutionary force in politics: international socialism. Marx inherited from the radical Enlightenment both its profound dissatisfaction with the world as it was constituted and the desire to establish a form of human social life in which each and all governed their conditions of existence. It was in this respect that Marx was a 'social democrat', consistently advocating throughout his life the need for people to lead autonomous lives in order to be properly realised as human beings. Marx's vision of a communist society is one in which heteronomy has been abolished and where individuals freely cooperate with each other in order to express their creative powers. In this communist society, man will have achieved genuine autonomy through his mastery of nature and liberation from the command of others.

Many of Marx's critics have focused on this 'utopian' vision of communism. They deny such a state is ever possible because, for example, human beings are naturally dependent creatures who require command to make sense of their lives or in contrast because man's attempted mastery of nature through science and instrumental reason can only lead to mastery of others and thus the frustration of autonomy.[36] But it is misleading to portray Marx as 'utopian' in this sense. Marx understood that people in communist society might have to do things they found disagreeable, to respect the commands of others in order to meet collective goals and to recognise that nature imposed limits on what men could successfully do. There is, however, no question that Marx did see communist society as one in which political power would have been eliminated. For Marx, political power is the organised power of a class. Communism abolishes class by removing its economic basis, that is, the differential distribution of the means of production. Without class differences in social and economic life, the need for politics as the organised use of violence disappears and society will be based on free, cooperative association.

If Marx's thought was utopian, it was no more so than that of radical thinkers in the Enlightenment such as Rousseau or contemporaries such as Proudhon. Marx wrote little about how a future communist society was to be organised or about what kinds of constraints on 'pure' autonomy would have to be observed in such a society. Much of what is significant and valuable in Marx's work is overlooked if we concentrate only on this aspect of his thought. Of much greater importance in grasping the radicalism of Marx's thought is the recognition of his laying bare the interconnections between economic and political power in modern capitalist societies. More than any other thinker at this time, it was Marx who exposed these relations and in doing so formed a body of knowledge that was central for the trajectory of radical politics in the late nineteenth and twentieth centuries. Where, however, Marx's vision of a society beyond politics is important is in its effects on his thinking about political organisation in the present. Marx is an anti-political thinker to the extent that his belief in an economic and technological solution to the problems of capitalism comes to override considerations about the nature and transformation of political power in the present. It is in this respect that Marx, like earlier figures in this study, can be seen as adopting the ambivalent view of the political inherent in the radical attitude.

This ambivalence toward political power may be traced back to Marx's earliest work and in particular its relationship to Hegel's thought. It is often thought that around 1844 Marx's thought underwent a transition from philosophical to more distinctly political concerns. This transition is sometimes attributed to Marx's discovery of the ideas of socialism and communism and his rejection of the kind of Enlightenment thinking which had dominated the political and intellectual milieu of his youth.[37] Yet Marx's early engagement with philosophy was already a 'political' concern, in the sense that it was Hegel's philosophy of politics, the state and law that was the point of departure for his theoretical endeavours.[38] For Marx, Hegel's 'system' of philosophy was not simply a set of abstract theses but had an important bearing on the character of the state and politics in Germany at the time. Like many of the younger thinkers in Berlin who had studied Hegel's philosophy and been taught by Hegelian lecturers (Hegel died in 1830, just a decade before Marx came to study in Berlin), Marx interpreted Hegel as a conservative thinker whose philosophical identification of the rational with the actual was essentially a justification for contemporary social and political order.[39] After completing his doctoral thesis in philosophy in Berlin, and having already begun to write politically oriented articles, Marx spent the summer of 1843 composing a manuscript titled *Critique of Hegel's Philosophy of Right*. In this text we can already see an understanding of political power and its relationship to social life that was to be central to Marx's 'mature work', that is his critique of political economy and the development of his theory of history.

In the *Critique of Hegel's Philosophy of Right*, Marx set out by taking Hegel to task for his 'mystification' of the state. In *The Philosophy of*

Right, Hegel had claimed that only with the arrival of the modern state do we witness the conditions in which human freedom can be realised.[40] The state reconciles the egoistic individual who is a member of civil society, pursuing his needs through his relations with others, and the individual as part of a wider affective community, exemplified by the selfless relationships of family life. The state achieves this reconciliation by recognising individuals *qua* individuals as members of civil society, with their own rights and particular interests. At the same time, the state is seen by Hegel, contrary to the contractarian tradition in political thought, as more than an association for the pursuit of particular interests. Through the institutions of the monarchy, a rational bureaucracy and the representation of particular social interests in the Estates, the state provides the conditions in which the pursuit of particular interests is consonant with the achievement of the universal interests of man. These universal interests are, for Hegel, realised in the achievement of freedom. This 'freedom', however, is not freedom in the narrow sense of freedom from constraint, the liberty of the atomistic individual. Freedom is a state of self-determination that can only be realised within a particular kind of ethical community, one established in the state. Hegel's understanding of human freedom and of its realisation through the mediation of the state is intimately connected to his philosophy of history, in which world-history is the determination of Spirit (*Geist*) as it seeks to realise its own inherent freedom. The state is, therefore, ultimately a vehicle of Spirit or in other words the philosophical counterpart of the God of Protestant theology.

This is the sense in which Marx accused Hegel of 'mystifying' the state: the state as empirical reality is said to be a product of Spirit, which 'has no other than the logical aim, namely "to become infinite and actual spirit for itself". In this is contained the entire mystery of the Philosophy of Right and of Hegelian philosophy in general'.[41] Against this mystification of the state, Marx wished to stress 'that the activities and functions of the state are human activities' and that 'the activities etc. of the state are nothing but the modes of existence and operation of the social qualities of men'.[42] It is because Hegel conceived of the state as an abstract realisation of Spirit that he could resolve real distinctions by means of conceptual fiat. Thus, Marx argued, Hegel wanted to maintain that the sovereignty in the person of the monarch is at the same time popular sovereignty, an expression of the will of the people. But Marx wishes to deny this. In effect, sovereignty is held either by the monarch or the people (in a republican constitution); it cannot be held by both at the same time, other than in some abstract and mystical sense.

It was not Marx's intention in his critique of Hegel to champion republican over monarchical government. The relevant contrast Marx made was not between these two forms of constitutional government, but between both of them and what he describes as 'democracy'. Although he nowhere in his critique of Hegel outlined exactly what he meant by this term, it is clear that he was not using it to denote either classical republican democracy or modern representative democracy. Rather, by 'democracy' Marx means something like the very absence of political power, a condition in which each and all have full control over their conditions of existence and their relationships with others. Thus, in contrast to monarchy where 'the whole, the people, is subsumed under one of its modes of existence, the political constitution', in democracy 'the *constitution itself* appears as only *one* determination, and indeed as a self-determination of the people'.[43] Moreover:

> Just as it is not religion that creates man but man who creates religion, so it is not the constitution that creates the people but the people which creates the constitution ... Relative to democracy all other forms of state are its Old Testament. Man does not exist for the law but rather the law for the good of man; it is *human existence*, while in others man has only *legal existence*. That is the fundamental difference of democracy.

And:

> In democracy that state as a particular is *only* particular, and as universal is the actual universal, i.e. not a determinate thing in distinction from other content. The modern French have conceived it thus: in true democracy the *political state disappears* ... In democracy the constitution, the law, the state is itself only a self-determination of the people and a determinate content of the people, in so far as it is political constitution.[44]

Thus, for Marx, the problem of the state does not turn around its particular form, that is whether it takes on a monarchical or republican constitution. Rather, the problem is the notion of an abstract state form itself, of a political constitution that stands in abstraction from and 'above' society.

For Marx, this abstraction of the state and of a realm of political power was a modern phenomenon, made possible only with the emergence of a sphere of private life separated from the political hierarchy characteristic of feudalism. Under feudalism political and socio-economic roles were combined so that the state and society were not distinct. This form of political-cum-social order was a *'democracy of unfreedom'* in so far as the public and private realms were combined, but in order to protect the property in land of the aristocracy and to keep the producers in a state of bondage.[45] The distinction between state and society begins to disappear with the advent of the absolutist state and is the process completed in the French Revolution which, 'made the *estate-distinctions* of civil society into merely *social* distinctions, distinctions of private life, which are meaningless in political life'.[46] For Marx, one of Hegel's main errors was to have thought that the different Estates of Germany, based as they were on the feudal social order, could act as representatives of 'society'. The feudal order had been torn asunder by the development of commerce in civil society. This transformed the social into an undifferentiated sphere, doing away with feudal distinctions between ascriptive communities. Needs are no longer met through one's membership of these political-cum-social communities, but rather through one's activities as an individual member of civil society, engaged in transactions with others who are, formally to speak, one's equal. While Hegel had recognised the novelty of civil society as a system for the satisfaction of material needs, his mystification of the state meant he overlooked its real function in modern society: it was not a means of reconciling the material inequalities that existed in civil society, but rather it served to amplify and entrench them.

Marx's arguments against Hegel were very clearly influenced by the critique of Hegel's philosophy of religion developed by Ludwig Feuerbach and prominent within the intellectual circles that Marx moved in during the early 1840s. Marx adopted Feuerbach's 'transformative method' in the *Critique of Hegel's Philosophy of Right*.[47] For Feuerbach, Hegel's philosophy of history was fantastic, seeing existence as a predicate of thought. By 'inverting' Hegel, that is by seeing thought as a predicate of existence, we arrive at 'materialism', which for Feuerbach meant regarding man and his activities as the starting point for explaining his thought about the world rather than vice-versa. Religion from this perspective is to be explained from the point of view of man's material existence. This 'transformative method' of Feuerbach's can also be seen at work in an article that Marx wrote in late 1843, 'On the Jewish Question'. Marx's target in this piece was Bruno Bauer, a 'Young Hegelian', who like Marx was influenced by Feuerbach. Bauer had argued against Jewish calls for religious freedom in Germany because on his view genuine emancipation required a repudiation of absolutism and the establishment of secular civil rights for all within the context of a liberal state. For Marx, Bauer had confused political emancipation with what he called *'genuine human emancipation'*.[48] This required freedom not just from religion, but from the very conditions of religious life, namely the distinction between state and society. Invoking Feuerbach's critique of Hegel, Marx claimed that: 'The political state relates just as spiritually to civil society as heaven does to earth.'[49] Bauer had taken from Hegel the idea that the state is 'above' civil society, determining its character whereas the converse was true. As witness to this, Marx cited the case (via Tocqueville) of America, a country with the most liberal and secular of all political constitutions that nonetheless remained a deeply religious society. At the end of the essay Marx argued that: 'The *social* emancipation of the Jew is the *emancipation of society from Judaism*.'[50] While at first sight this might appear to be a piece of crude anti-semitism, what Marx was in fact arguing for was the emancipation of society from what was commonly identified (in a way that does indeed smack of anti-semitic caricature) as the social 'essence' of Judaism, namely commercial exchange. We can see in 'On the Jewish Question' the view that the distinction between the civil state and society is one that should be eradicated if 'genuine human emancipation' is to be achieved, and the view that such emancipation can only come about by a transformation of relations within civil society, that is, by the abolition of private property and exchange and its replacement with communal forms of property (communism).

There is a long and unresolved (and perhaps irresolvable) dispute about whether the 'early' Marx exemplified in these two texts was a 'humanist' who later, with the development of his 'scientific' theory of history, abandoned this position.[51] What cannot be in much doubt is that throughout his life Marx identified communism as a society in which the state and politics have been abolished. He remained faithful to the notion of 'true' democracy, in the sense that a communist society would be one where people had immediate control over their conditions of existence and their relations with others. Marx only hints in his later work at how such a society might be organised. What any such organisation presupposes, however, is a view of history and human interests that is worked out in earnest from 1844, firstly in the *Paris Notebooks* of that year, and in 1845 in *The German Ideology*, co-authored with Friedrich Engels.

From 1844 Marx turned his attention fully to political economy and its critique. This represents a shift away from the interest in juristic conceptions of private property that had occupied his earlier work, to an examination of the manner in which private property was generated and reproduced in what, from this time on, he identifies as capitalist society. In the first part of *The German Ideology*, Marx and Engels set out a general theory of history accounting for the rise of this form of society. This theory of history, or historical materialism, was later summed up somewhat programmatically by Marx in his famous 'Preface' to *A Contribution to the Critique of Political Economy* (1859). In the 'Preface', men's relations of production are said to correspond to 'a specific stage of development of their material productive forces'. The relations of production are 'the real basis from which arises a legal and political superstructure, and to which correspond specific forms of social consciousness'. Changes to the economic base of society occurs as a result of a 'contradiction' between the material forces of production and the relations of production 'or in what is merely a legal expression for this, with the property relations within which they had previously functioned'. The relations of production become 'fetters' on the forces of production rather than their means of development. As the economic structure undergoes revolution 'the whole colossal superstructure is more or less rapidly transformed'.[52]

Stated in this way and on the most plausible interpretation of the 'Preface',[53] historical materialism is a form of technological determinism where forms of society rise and fall according to the level of development of the productive forces. However, it is important to note that in the 'Preface' Marx says that this view of historical development only 'served as a guide for my studies',[54] and there are other places where his statement of historical materialism seems to give priority in historical change not to the productive forces but the relations of production or in other words to the relationship between different socio-economic classes. This is not a minor theoretical point: in the Marxist tradition the interpretation of historical materialism in terms of the primacy of either the forces or relations has had a significant impact on political practice.[55] Yet it was most likely not Marx's intention to assert the systematic primacy of productive forces over the relations or vice-versa. Forms of technology appear in a dialectical relationship to the organisation of the relations of production, so that they are at times compatible and at times contradictory. It is also evident, however, that Marx also saw this dialectical relationship as determined, at least at points in history, by the balance of political forces in any particular social formation. This is perhaps most clearly witnessed in the famous opening sentence of the first chapter of the *Manifesto of the Communist Party* (1848): 'The history of all society up to now is the history of class struggles.'[56]

This is a view that can also be found in Marx's critique of the French anarchist thinker, Pierre-Joseph Proudhon, the *Poverty of Philosophy* (1847). Marx accused Proudhon of a reliance on 'bourgeois' concepts such as justice and a failure to understand the mechanisms at work in exchange relations. Most importantly, what Proudhon lacked was an analysis of the capitalist mode of production in terms of socio-economic class. Accordingly, he failed to recognise that any future social revolution could only be carried out by the industrial proletariat as a class conscious of its position in relation to the bourgeoisie and not (as Proudhon claimed) by the self-interested smallholding peasantry, a class that had besides fallen into decline given the tendency of capitalism toward the centralisation and intensification of production. The kind of piecemeal 'revolution' that Proudhon advocated was for Marx impossible. It was only with a revolution of the proletariat that a genuinely classless and liberated society could be achieved: 'The condition of the emancipation of the working class is the abolition of every class.' This abolition will take place with the full development of the proletariat when 'the working class will substitute for the old civil society an association that will exclude classes and their antagonism, and there will no longer be political power properly so-called, because political power is precisely the official *resumé* of the antagonisms within civil society'.[57] The 'brutal' contradictions of capitalism will lead to a political revolution of the kind that Proudhon sought to avoid. Proudhon's mistake was to divorce the social and the political movement whereas 'there is never any political movement which is not at the same time social'.[58]

Proudhon's approach might be thought apolitical since he thought a society free from property and social inequality could be achieved outside political conflict between different social classes, that is, through the gradual development of a system of mutual, cooperative associations.[59] Marx disparaged Proudhon's apoliticism in this sense because it failed to take into account the links between interests and the exercise of power and in particular the bourgeoisie's control of the state. While modern societies operated on a distinction between the state and civil society, in effect the bourgeoisie was able to control state power in order to secure its interests within the latter realm. The state was a means of protecting private property, a central component of the machinery required by the bourgeoisie to reproduce the relations of production over time. In the *Manifesto*, Marx and Engels traced how this function of the state had developed with the rise of capitalism. The bourgeoisie's centralisation of production had as a necessary consequence the development of political centralisation: 'Provinces that were independent or scarcely even confederated, with different interests, laws, governments and taxes, were forced together into one nation, one government, one legal system, one class interest nationally, one customs zone.'[60] The state becomes an instrument of bourgeois rule: 'The power of the modern state is merely a device for administering the common affairs of the whole bourgeois class.'[61] Yet the success of the bourgeoisie presupposes the development of the proletariat as the producers of wealth and they will become the 'gravediggers' of capitalism:

> We have seen that the first step in the workers' revolution is the advancement of the proletariat to ruling class, victory for democracy ... The proletariat will use its political power to strip all capital from the bourgeoisie piece by piece, to centralise all instruments of production in the hands of the state, i.e. the proletariat organised as a ruling class, and to increase the total of productive forces as rapidly as possible.[62]

We see here, then, a programme for the post-revolutionary polity, with the state taking control of the means of economic administration in order to abolish private property, in other words, the basis of class relations. But this state centralisation appears as a temporary expedient since:

> When in the course of development class distinctions have disappeared, and all production is concentrated in the hands of associated individuals, then the public power loses its political character. Political power in its true sense is the organised power of one class for oppressing another.[63]

To summarise, Marx's theory of politics up until the *Manifesto* involved three main points. First, modern politics turns around the separation of the public from the private domains. The state or the political constitution, occupies the realm of the public whereas the needs of individuals are met within the private realm, i.e. that of civil society where atomised individuals exchange with one other. Second, the centralised or absolutist state evolves in early modern Europe as an instrument of the bourgeoisie. It is primarily an instrument of coercion (as opposed to ideology, which justifies bourgeois society by means of religious and moral belief) that the bourgeoisie manipulates in order to protect its property interests. Third, the working class will come to be in a position, as a result of the development of the capitalist system of production, which polarises class interests and provides the conditions for a growing class consciousness amongst the proletariat, where their engagement in political struggle will result in revolution. After the revolution, the state is manipulated by the proletariat as an instrument of class power in order to abolish bourgeois property and to defend the new society against bourgeois counter-revolution. However, because the state is an instrument of class power it will disappear alongside the abolition of classes. This will represent the victory of democracy, the triumph of free social association and co-operation over coercive political power.

While these different aspects of Marx's thought represent no more than a synthesis of early arguments articulated in the radical Enlightenment, what was genuinely original in his approach was his analysis of the anatomy of capitalism as both an abstract model or 'mode of production', and as a concrete reality that appeared in various kinds of social and political forms. After 1848 and the relative failure of the revolutions that had occurred across Europe in that year, Marx became more engrossed in working out the structural dynamics of capitalism, as both abstract model and concrete form, in order to try and divine its future development. This would result in his most famous work, *Capital*. While that book is often considered primarily as a text in abstract economic theory, there is no sense in which it can be separated from Marx's understanding of politics in capitalist societies. As Marx's analysis of capitalism becomes ever more intricate, in the places where he does directly consider the state and politics in capitalist societies after 1848 we tend to see a more complex and subtle approach being adopted.

This complexity is partly borne out of the character of Marx's later published political writings. Far from being abstract in nature, these mostly attended to specific political events and in particular those in France. In these writings we can see something of a development of Marx's theory of the state in capitalist society away from the instrumentalist view expressed most boldly in the *Manifesto*. Perhaps the most important event informing this modified conception of the state was the rise to power in France of Louis Bonaparte, first in the elections of 1848, when he became the President of the Second Republic and then in his coup d'état of 1851 after which he declared himself Emperor. Bonaparte was initially welcomed by some of the left in France, including Proudhon, because he seemed not to be representing the bourgeoisie but rather the smallholding peasantry. In his article, 'The Eighteenth Brumaire of Louis Bonaparte', Marx largely accepted this view of Bonaparte's social constituency, though for him it did not follow that socialists should back Bonaparte's regime. Bonaparte, at least originally, did indeed support the peasantry, though its more conservative rather than revolutionary elements. By appealing to the military, Bonaparte was able to exploit divisions in the bourgeoisie, in particular in its 'republican faction'.[64] After the revolution of 1848, which had toppled the bourgeois 'King of the French' Louis-Phillipe, the bourgeoisie was divided into republican and royalist factions, according to the extent to which their interests coincided with one or other form of political constitution. Moreover, there was a further division within the royalist bourgeoisie between 'legitimists', that is those who wanted to see the restoration of the Bourbon line, and Orléanists, who wished to see Louis-Phillipe's heir succeed to the throne. For Marx this was a significant split:

> Just as in private life one distinguishes between what a man thinks and says, and what he really is and does, so one must all the more in historical conflicts distinguish between the fine words and aspirations of the parties and their real organisation and their real interests, their image from their reality. Orléanists and legitimists found themselves side by side in the republic with the same demands. If each side wanted to carry out the *restoration* of its own royal house in opposition to the other, then this signified nothing but the desire of each of the *two great interests* into which the *bourgeoisie* has split landed property and capital – to restore its own supremacy and to subordinate the other. We are talking in terms of two interests within the bourgeoisie, for large landed property, in spite of its flirtations with feudalism and pride in its pedigree, has been thoroughly assimilated to the bourgeoisie by the development of modern society. Thus the Tories in England long fancied that they were in raptures about royalty, the church and the beauties of the ancient constitution, until a time of trial tore from them the confession that they were only in raptures about rent.[65]

The significance of this passage is that it indicates how the bourgeoisie may be divided in terms of material interest and the impact this division has on political action. Different parties, holding different ideas about the best kind of political constitution, come to represent these interests and by so doing make the state a ground of contestation rather than, as it appeared in the *Manifesto*, 'a device for administering the common affairs of the whole bourgeois class'. In the *Eighteenth Brumaire*, Marx allows that given these divisions a space open up that allows non-bourgeois interests to seize control of state power and use it in their own interests.

Bonaparte was able to gain the support of the army and the peasantry in order to abolish the parliamentary state of the bourgeoisie and create a military dictatorship. The presupposition of Bonapartism was, however, the bureaucracy of the centralised executive state that the bourgeoisie had created. This 'parasite', as Marx termed it, had grown to the extent that it 'restricts, controls, regulates, oversees and supervises civil life from its most all-encompassing expressions to its most insignificant stirrings, from its universal modes of existence to the private existence of individuals'. The bourgeoisie needed such an extensive state to support its material interests as 'it accommodates surplus population and makes up in the form of state maintenance what it cannot pocket in the form of profit, interest, rent and fees'. It also supported its political interests by repressing the revolutionary proletariat and peasantry: 'Thus the French bourgeoisie was compelled by its class position both to negate the conditions of existence for any parliamentary power, including its own, and to make the power of the executive, its adversary, irresistible.'[66] Once the bourgeoisie had lost parliamentary control of this powerful executive-cum-bureaucracy, the conditions existed for it to fall into the hands of non-bourgeois forces and to become a 'parasite' on society. While the French state had developed to such an extent under absolutism and Napoleon in order to prepare 'the class rule of the bourgeoisie', 'only under the second Bonaparte does the state seem to have achieved independence with respect to society and to have brought it into submission'.[67]

There are some striking similarities between this analysis and that of Tocqueville's in *The Old Regime and the French Revolution*. Marx is largely at one with Tocqueville in recognising that Bonaparte's *coup* was not a class revolt, but rather a parvenu's seizure of a centralised state bureaucratic apparatus that had become large autonomous of social and economic life. At the same time, Marx argued, it was indeed Bonaparte's function to try and maintain 'bourgeois order' even without the direct rule of the bourgeoisie. Marx sees the state under the younger Bonaparte as a body that is not directly controlled by the dominant economic class, but which nonetheless meets its interests. For Marx, the choice presented to the French bourgeoisie in 1851 was despotism or anarchy. Hence it supported Bonapartism because the alternative was a revolution that was likely to destroy its material interests. The Bonapartist state was in effect the only choice open to the bourgeoisie at the time. It is a point that Marx made more forcefully in *The Civil War in France* (1871) written on the occasion of the downfall of Bonaparte's Second

Empire at the hands of Prussia:

> In reality, it [Bonapartism] was the only form of government possible at a time when the bourgeoisie had already lost, and the working class had not yet acquired, the faculty of ruling the nation. It was acclaimed throughout the world as the saviour of society. Under its sway, bourgeois society, freed from political cares, attained a development unexpected even by itself. Its industry and commerce expanded to colossal dimensions; financial swindling celebrated cosmopolitan orgies; the misery of the masses was set off by a shameless display of gorgeous, meretricious and debased luxury. The state power, apparently soaring high above society, was at the same time itself the greatest scandal of that society and the very hot-bed of all its corruptions. Its own rottenness, and the rottenness of the society it had saved, were laid bare by the bayonet of Prussia.[68]

What Marx does in his analysis of Bonapartism is to recognise the power the state has come to have over society as a consequence of its historical development in relation to civil society. The organisation of political power and the contestation that takes place in its domain cannot be simply reduced or subordinated to the structure of socio-economic life. It is an approach fully in line with his political 'realism', in so far as it recognises the relative openness of the outcome of political contestation. Bonapartism was one possible response to a crisis faced by the French bourgeoisie in the mid-nineteenth century, but as the relative stability of the liberal and representative state in America and Britain indicated, the character of public power in capitalist societies was dependent on the particular features of the specific social formation in which it was contained.

Thus in the *Critique of the Gotha Programme* (1875), Marx wrote:

> 'Present day society' is capitalist society, which exists in all civilised countries, more or less free of admixtures of medievalism, more or less modified through the historical development of each country, more or less advanced. By contrast, the 'present day state' changes with each country's borders. It is different in the Prusso-German empire from the way it is in Switzerland, different in England from the way it is in the United States. '*The* present-day state' is thus a fiction.

However, this is followed by:

> The various different states of different civilized countries, in spite of their various differences have something in common, namely that

they are based on modern bourgeois society just that is only more or less capitalistically developed. Hence they also have certain essential characteristics in common. In this sense it is possible to talk of the 'present-day' type of state, but in the future by contrast, its current basis, present-day bourgeois society, will have died off.[69]

If we can say that Marx's understanding of the relationship between state and society does become more complex after 1848, so that the state can take on various forms in capitalist society and that the outcome of particular political struggles is relatively open, what is consistent throughout is his belief that whatever form the state in capitalism takes, it will ultimately disappear with the end of bourgeois society. Marx resolutely rejected the notion that his insistence on the disappearance of bourgeois society was a product of wishful thinking or utopianism. It would disappear because of the mechanics of capitalist production that were everywhere leading to class polarisation and the intensification of economic crises of capitalism. Revolution was not inevitable in the sense that it was provided for by providence or a speculative philosophy of history, but proletarian revolution in the not too distant future was highly likely given the increasing frequency with which the objective conditions for its realisation were appearing.

However, as Sheldon Wolin has argued, as Marx came to see the growing complexity and power of capitalism during the 1850s and 1860s (the period in which he was preparing and writing, *Capital*) the fate of capitalism increasingly seemed to lie less in the hands of the revolutionary proletariat and more in a process without a subject, namely the 'objective' development of the capitalist system of production.[70] In Marx's writing, the notion of 'crisis' looses the sense of immanent and irrevocable decision, instead becoming a more or less technical description of certain structural features of the economy at points in the trade cycle of capitalism. But the objective crisis need not result in a political revolution. Capitalism's resilience against itself is something of which Marx was increasingly aware. It had been able to avert revolution by adapting. But this adaptation had been carried out politically and ideologically, dampening down class conflict by providing material and spiritual comforts to the industrial working class that made the commitment to the revolution seem risky or even unnecessary and dangerous. Unlike many of Marx's immediate successors, Eduard Bernstein and Lenin, as we will see in the next chapter, understood the profound implications that this point had for the political organisation of the working class.

The Paris Commune had been broken up in blood by a state that was not prepared to tolerate the revolutionary threat it presented to the French bourgeoisie. The failure of the commune was evidence, as Marx realised, that the kind of popular insurrectionary revolution he had supported in 1848 was ever less likely to succeed in advanced industrial capitalist societies. The public power in these societies had become highly centralised and had at its disposal a large administrative-military apparatus that could be effectively deployed to crush any attempt at armed revolution. Marx's shrewd analysis of the relationship between economic and political power left little hope for revolution, at least in its old-fashioned sense. But rather than attempt a systematic reconceptualisation of the political grounds on which the transformation to socialism might become possible, Marx largely resorted to his formal model of capitalist economic development, insisting that the long term technical tendency to a falling rate of profit, and consequent class polarisation, would make revolution 'inevitable'. At the same time, capitalism bequeathed to the workers the technological means to build socialism.

It is, then, in this ultimate subordination of the political to the economic, rather than in any utopian musings over a society freed from political power, that we most clearly see Marx's anti-political tendencies. While Marx recognised the importance of the organisation of political power for the maintenance of social and economic relations under capitalism, he failed to grasp the extent to which challenging and transforming capitalism was also a problem of political power. On the question of politics, Marx left an ambiguous legacy to his followers.

6
Crisis and Decision: Lenin and Schmitt

The Enlightenment and the French Revolution witnessed the placing to the fore in political theory of the concept of crisis. Reinhart Koselleck has argued that the notion of crisis underwent a fundamental transformation from the late eighteenth century. It ceased to denote a set of circumstances or a condition in which a judgement or decision is unavoidable and rather served to represent a permanent state of conflict and civil war that could only be overcome through a radical and irreversible break with the past.[1] This understanding of crisis as an ongoing feature of social and political life, rather than a moment of decision, reflected the scepticism in important currents of Enlightenment thought and nineteenth-century radicalism not just about particular leaders or forms of government, but about the very conditions that made political decision possible. Anarchist thinkers like Pierre-Joseph Proudhon and Mikhail Bakunin argued that there was no form of compulsory political organisation that could be consistent with human freedom. But this rejection of or deep antipathy toward political organisation was not just confined to anarchism. Both liberalism and Marxism saw the ultimate crisis and solution to the problems of modernity lying not in the political, but the social and economic spheres. Liberals opposed the state in so far as it supported and forwarded the interests of the old regime: monarchy, landed aristocracy and the church. Marxists opposed the state in so far as it supported and forwarded the interests of the bourgeoisie. For liberals, emancipation meant the breaking free from the traditional bonds of pre-modern society, and the freedom of the individual to engage in open exchange, of opinions and commodities, in the public forum. On this view the specific political organisation of the state should be separate from civil society and subordinate to its demands; the state should represent the general will of civil society and function to promote its good. For Marxists, freedom meant proletarian freedom, the emancipation of the working class from the exploitation it suffered under its capitalist masters. The proletarian state that would come about after the socialist revolution would function to defend the working class against bourgeois counter-revolution, and act as the vehicle through which social and economic transformation would be brought about. The proletarian state would, however, 'wither away' once the revolution had been safeguarded and a socialist economy had been constructed. Politics would cease to have any meaning in a society where material inequality and need had been abolished.

At the turn of the twentieth century, however, both liberal and Marxist radicals were faced with a problem that had come into greater relief as the optimistic rationalism and progressivism of the Enlightenment receded ever further into the past. Radical social change could not come about other than through political organisation and the contestation of state power. The Enlightenment belief in the transformation of social life through education and moralisation was utopian. Any new society would have to be built through political power and the struggle with or reordering of states that were considerably more centralised and power-ful than they had been at the time of the French Revolution. But what was also apparent was that the transformation of large societies with a complex division of labour (and in some cases empires) would not come about spontaneously. The question of the political organisation of the state thus became central to both liberals and socialists, Marxist and non-Marxist alike, at this time.[2]

In this chapter, we will explore how this question of political power was treated by the most famous of all twentieth-century revolutionaries, V. I. Lenin. However, we will also turn to a very different thinker, one who at first glance looks to be diametrically opposed to Lenin's politics, the German authoritarian conservative, Carl Schmitt. In fact, Lenin and Schmitt held similar views of the character and importance of political power. Unlike Lenin, however, Schmitt understood the nature of 'the political' in a way that points to the flaws in the ultimately anti-political cast of Lenin's thought, and indeed in the anti-political nature of the radical attitude in general.

Lenin

V. I. Lenin (1870–1924) was first and foremost a revolutionary whose major political texts cannot be regarded in isolation from the context of Imperial Russia in the late 1800s and early 1900s. Throughout his adult life Lenin sought to formulate a strategy of revolution for the overthrow of the absolute Czarist state and the construction of a socialist society. Above all other considerations the question of how revolution in Russia could be achieved is at the heart of his texts. At the same time, however, we would fail to give an adequate account of Lenin's views if we did not locate them in the intellectual context of European Marxism at the turn of the twentieth century. Lenin's political education was strongly coloured by the Marxism of the Second International (1889–1914), the association of national socialist (or social democratic) parties that came together after Marx's death and which was to be strongly shaped by debates over the character of Marxist theory. The leading political party affiliated to the Second International, in terms of size and influence, was without question the German Social Democratic Party (SPD). In the 1880s and 1890s, its two leading theoretical lights were Karl Kautsky and Eduard Bernstein. Kautsky was to become the 'pope of socialism',[3] the leading defender of Marxist 'orthodoxy'. Bernstein, in contrast, was by 1900 the bête noire of 'orthodox' Marxists, the father of 'revisionism' and enemy of revolutionary socialism.

It is worth briefly exploring the main points of contention between Kautsky and Bernstein as the debate between Marxist orthodoxy and revisionism constitutes an important part of the background against which Lenin's considerations of political power were formed. Kautsky and Bernstein had been the main authors of the SPD's offical statement of its theory and goals, the Erfurt Programme of 1891. The first part of the Programme stated what both Kautsky and Bernstein took to be the essence of Marxism: the theory of the development and ultimate demise of the capitalist system of production as a result of its internal economic logic. Capitalism was subject to recurrent crises of production that intensified the class struggle between the bourgeoisie and proletariat. Capitalism moved relentlessly toward the replacement of agriculture with industry and the creation of a mass industrial working class. Capital became move concentrated in the hands of ever few members of the bourgeoisie as smaller capitalists were driven to the wall in the frequent and increasingly severe economic downturns. Consequently, the structural dynamics of the capitalist mode of production resulted in a stand off between the two main classes in society. The socio-economic circumstances arose in which the possibility of a revolutionary transformation of society became manifest, and this revolution was ultimately achieved by the working classes' seizure of political power and its employment to construct a socialist economy. The Programme is clear that the transformation of capitalism into socialism can only take place with the concerted political action of the working class as a whole and not simply through trade-union activity. The SPD exists for this reason: its task is 'to mould the struggle of the working class into a conscious, uniform progress and direct it toward its immutable goal'.[4]

By the end of the 1890s, however, Bernstein had moved away from this argument for the inevitability of socialist revolution. He had come to see socialism not as the goal of a single class, but rather as a system that established a 'higher and more perfect form of civilisation'.[5] The reasons for this 'revision' were systematically set out in his book, *The Preconditions of Socialism and the Tasks of Social Democracy* (1899). The central chapter challenges the 'orthodox' Marxist theory of the development of modern capitalism. The theory of the economic collapse of capitalism rests upon a model of production in which capitalists compete with one another on an open market. There is a contradiction inherent in this system: the fundamental driving force for each capitalist, the desire to increase his rate of profit, when taken in concert with that of all other capitalists leads to its downfall. However, if capitalists are able to extend their markets or engage in cooperative production, then this may reverse the effects predicted in the formal model of capitalist economic development. Indeed, Bernstein argued, this is exactly what had occurred. Imperialist expansion allowed the capitalist nations of Europe to exploit new world markets; trusts, cartels and new credit systems emerged to control the anarchic nature of production; and developments in transport and communications had allowed large capitalist corporations to better regulate trade and industrial output.[6]

Marx had recognised that these kinds of factors could prolong the life span of the capitalist system, but ultimately they merely delayed the final catastrophe. Bernstein now rejected this argument: while parts of Marx's economic theory were accurate – his accounts of the falling rate of profit and economic slump brought about by underconsumption – other aspects of it were inadequate in light of recent empirical developments. In short, the evidence for an imminent collapse of Western capitalism was not to be found. Indeed, the trends of capitalist economies indicated their continued vitality and insulation from crises of production. Bernstein marshalled empirical evidence to demonstrate that the capitalist class was not contracting; that there had been a major growth of joint-stock companies throughout capitalist countries in the second half of the nineteenth century, and thus a dispersion of the ownership of productive capital; that incomes were increasing across the board; that small and middle-sized industrial and agricultural concerns were multiplying rather than declining; and that the industrial working class as a whole was not experiencing immiseration: wages were increasing in all its sectors and there was no evidence of expansion in the size of the impoverished industrial reserve army of labour.[7]

Bernstein's questioning of Kautsky's orthodox Marxist account of capitalist economic development had a very clear political imperative. Like other reform-minded socialists of the same period, such as the British Fabians, Bernstein felt that the best opportunity for radical social change lay not in waiting for a social revolution determined by the internal contradictions of the economic system (which was not likely to occur), but rather the organisation of a working-class political movement that would participate (where it could) in parliamentary politics in order to gradually win greater rights for the workers. Capitalism would not be abolished in a revolution but gradually and peacefully reformed by an alliance of 'progressive' political forces, that is, working-class socialist parties cooperating with bourgeois liberal radicals and reformers.

In fact, much more has been made of the 'revisionist controversy' than the content of the dispute between Bernstein and Kautsky merits. As Gary Steenson points out, '[w]ith the exception of the exclusively proletarian character of the party, Bernstein and Kautsky disagreed on very few questions of [political] tactics'.[8] Both sought a form of socialism that would bring about radical social and economic change. Kautsky, however, believed that Bernstein's judgement about the possibility of reform through cooperation with the liberal bourgeoisie was inappropriate to Germany. It might have been an approach that British working-class organisations could have followed in the more democratic conditions of a parliamentary democracy with universal (male) suffrage, but this was not true in Germany where the bourgeoisie was largely reactionary and protected by the Kaiserist military-bureaucratic state, and where, although socialists could participate in elections, the three-class franchise system weighted votes in favour of the bourgeoisie and aristocracy.[9] Bernstein and Kautsky agreed on the main point that the primary function of social democracy was to politically organise the working class, but whereas the former saw this as a way in which socialism could be introduced through parliamentary democracy, Kautsky maintained that it could only be to gain position for the proletariat in the revolution which, according to his orthodox defence of Marxist economic theory, was imminent.

Before 1914, Lenin saw himself as a loyal supporter of Kautsky's orthodox position on virtually all questions of theoretical doctrine and political tactics. This commitment to orthodoxy stretched back to his first major published text, *The Development of Capitalism in Russia* (1899). One of Lenin's main targets in the book was the Narodniks (or populists), the Russian revolutionary group that emerged in the 1860s and 1870s. The Narodniks sought a revolution of the peasantry (around 80% of the Russian population at the time) against rich peasant land owners, the nobility and the monarchy. Importantly, the Narodniks believed that an economic revolution toward socialism in Russia could be achieved on the basis of the traditional Russian peasant agrarian commune. This thesis was a direct refutation of the orthodox Marxist argument that a socialist economy was only possible from a base of advanced industrial capitalism. In *The Development of Capitalism in Russia*, Lenin set out to defend this orthodox claim and to argue, against the Narodniks, that the Russian agricultural economy had already been subject to a process of capitalist industrialisation. In the agricultural sector, the social division of labour had proceeded apace and the economic system was geared primarily toward the production of commodities to be exchanged on markets: 'Thus, agriculture itself becomes industry (i.e., produces commodities), and the same process of specialisation [as in the wider capitalist economy] takes place in it.'[10] At the same time, Lenin affirms the Marxist account of the development of capitalism by arguing that the peasantry were being gradually proletarianised, i.e., that there was a movement of workers from the country to urban industrial centres.

Short of its criticisms of the Narodniks, *The Development of Capitalism in Russia* had little to say concerning questions of revolutionary political organisation and tactics. Lenin's next major work, *What is to be Done?* (1902), addresses these questions in a way that precipitated the 1903 split in the Marxist Russian Social-Democratic Labour Party between the Bolsheviks and Mensheviks.[11] In 1902 Lenin was in European exile, editor of the clandestine revolutionary journal *Iskra* and still a rather obscure character. *What is to be Done?* made him famous and set him up as an important figure in the RSDLP.[12] Orthodox Marxism had little to say about political organisation other than the idea that the Marxist party was in someway 'representative' of the proletariat, but that the working class 'as a whole' should be the agent of revolutionary transformation. What Lenin did, while claiming that he was still firmly in the orthodox camp, was to provide an unequivocal account of the way in which the revolutionary party should 'represent' the proletariat. He rejected the argument of the 'Economists' that the creation of a social democratic party in Russia was premature and that the working class was not advanced enough to lead a revolution. The 'Economists' 'are constantly straying from a social-democratic to the trade-unionist conception of politics'. This trade-unionist conception of politics involves 'the common striving of all workers to secure from the government measures which are aimed at alleviating the distress intrinsic to their condition, but which do not abolish that condition, i.e., which do not remove the subjection of labour to capital'.[13]

'Economism' and 'reformism', for Lenin, were simply accommodations with the bourgeoisie, ways of maintaining rather than abolishing the economic exploitation of the proletariat (or the peasantry-proletariat). In 1902 Lenin did not stray from orthodoxy in arguing that the proletarian revolution required the development of an advanced industrial capitalist economy (though, he argued, the Russian economy was closer to this than most tended to think), and that it would be secured only with the socialisation of the means of production and abolition of class distinctions. Where, contrary to his explicit denials, he did depart from the orthodoxy of a figure like Kautsky, was in his conception of the party as the 'vanguard' of the proletariat. On this view, as Georg Lukàcs put it, 'the party must prepare the revolution'.[14] For Lenin, the formation of a spontaneous revolutionary proletarian consciousness was impossible. It was the party who had to educate the working class into this consciousness. The social democrats had to 'go among all classes of the population' to spread the message of the imminence and necessity of revolutionary transformation. The party should consist of a relatively small number of professional revolutionaries who were trained Marxist propagandists and activists. It had to operate clandestinely and have the skills to combat and defeat the Czarist secret police.

What is to be Done?, then, recognises the importance of the problem of political organisation in a fashion that had eluded earlier Marxists. No doubt there was an element of pragmatism in Lenin's approach. Russia was not like England, nor even Germany, in the sense that the workers could not politically organise within the law. The Czarist state prohibited any such working-class organisations and ruthlessly employed its secret police to crack down on revolutionary activity. It was impossible in these circumstances to have a social democratic party, like the German SPD, which had a mass membership and open democratic procedures. Yet Lenin's emphasis on the necessity of political organisation and activity was not simply a reflection of the peculiarities of the Russian situation. Lenin recognised that both the overthrow of Czarism and the movement toward the construction of a socialist economy required a committed and specially trained political agency that was able to use force, in the last instance, in order to achieve its goals. This political realism contrasted with the quietism of many orthodox Marxists in the Second International who believed that the 'revolution' would come from below as a result of the proletariat coming to form a majority of society as determined by of the socio-economic development of capitalism. The pressure from below would lead to gradual democratic reforms (as it had in England) and the workers would use democracy to establish their rights and build socialism. The kind of political organisation that Lenin advocated was accordingly seen as unnecessary and dangerous and looked to his opponents, such as the Mensheviks, a great deal like Blanquism: an insurrectionary movement of professional revolutionaries striving to seize control of state power and to construct an authoritarian form of socialism.

The charge of Blanquism against Lenin is far from groundless.[15] Like Auguste Blanqui, Lenin held that the revolution had to come about through the violent seizure of power by professional revolutionaries. With respect to the socialist revolution, this is most clear in his works just prior to the October 1917 Revolution: the 'April Theses' and *State and Revolution*. But even at the beginning of the early 1900s, Lenin was clear that the revolutionary party would have to be in the vanguard of social revolution. His *Two Tactics of Social-Democracy in the Democratic Revolution*, written in the aftermath of the 1905 Russian Revolution, called for the creation of a 'revolutionary-democratic dictatorship of the proletariat and the peasantry'.[16] Again, Lenin claimed, this form of government was called for by orthodox Marxist theory, which stipulated that socialism had to proceed from a capitalist economic basis. The only way in which capitalism could advance in Russia, in light of Czarist despotism, was through a 'bourgeois revolution', i.e. the redistribution of land and property and the full development of a European type of capitalism, coupled with property and other civic rights established in a democratic republic. The more rapid this social transformation, the more rapid the advent of socialism as the inevitable outcome of capitalist economic development: 'The revolutionary path is one of rapid amputation, which is the least painful to the proletariat, the path of the immediate removal of what is putrescent, the path of least compliance with and consideration for the monarchy and the abominable, vile, rotten, and noxious institutions that go with it.'[17] The Russian bourgeoisie was, however, too weak and venal to oversee such a rapid transformation itself, and thus it fell to the social democrats to lead the democratic bourgeois revolution. In light of the fundamental disagreement over tactics within and general lack of popularity of the RSDLP in 1905, this all sounds hugely fanciful and, moreover, rests on an unquestioning faith in the veracity of the orthodox Marxist account of historical and social development. However, what Lenin's argument here again demonstrates is his early commitment to the notion of the importance of political organisation for social and economic change. His argument in *Two Tactics* in fact represents a significant departure from the orthodox Marxist idea that the state is little more than an instrument of the dominant economic class. If the peasantry-proletariat could use state power in order to oversee the introduction of the democratic republic, it follows that the state had to have significant autonomy from class relations and could be employed in order to transform them.

Lenin is often dismissed as little more than an opportunist who changed his views on political organisation and tactics depending on circumstances. Thus Lenin in 1905 appears to be saying that a proletarian revolution would not be possible until Russia had gone through a prolonged period of capitalist development. By 1917, however, with the collapse of the Czarist regime and the precarious position of the Provisional Government in the face of well armed revolutionaries who had made significant political inroads during the First World War, Lenin seemed to abandon this position, arguing that the time was now ripe for the socialist revolution. As Neil Harding argues, however, this change in Lenin's view was not simply a response to new political opportunities, but reflects a development of his theoretical stance preceding the shift in political tactics. More particularly, it was Lenin's understanding of the relationship between international capitalism and imperialism, developed from 1910 onwards, which transformed his view of the political tactics of social democracy.[18] Lenin's *Imperialism, The Highest Stage of Capitalism* (1916) is in many respects a highly derivative piece of work, borrowing freely from Marxist authors like Rudolf Hilferding, his fellow Bolshevik Nikolai Bukharin and the English liberal political theorist J. A. Hobson.[19] Nonetheless, it is an important text in that it signals a change in Lenin's understanding of the international capitalist system. The 1914 War was, for Lenin, a contest between imperial powers that had developed in the direction of 'monopoly capitalism'. The emergence of large industrial cartels meant that '[c]apitalism has been transformed into imperialism'.[20] The international economic system ceased to be based on competition between relatively small capitalist enterprises. Capitalist development on an international scale occurred unevenly: large industrial monopolies and finance capital first emerged only in a few countries such as England, France and Germany. These nations sought out new markets for commodities and financial capital, markets that were secured at the end of the nineteenth century through imperial territorial expansion. The rise of imperialism had two important consequences for social democratic political tactics. First, the rapid scramble for territories by the imperial powers from the 1880s was bound to bring them into conflict. The war of 1914 was an outcome of this imperialist struggle to carve out new markets in pre-capitalist parts of the world.[21] Second, European imperialism had the effect of encouraging the formation of national identities in colonised territories as a reaction to the oppression and exploitation of the colonising power. The European capitalist powers were thus contributing to their own downfall by equipping colonised people with the means to oppose imperialism and assert their own independence.[22]

As Harding claims, Lenin saw in imperialism the potential for an alliance between socialist parties in advanced industrial capitalist societies and national independence movements in colonised territories that would bring down the international capitalist system.[23] The 1914 war represented a moment of fatal weakness for the most powerful capitalist nations as they fought each other to a standstill. This instability could be exploited by a combination of the internal threat posed by socialist revolutionaries and the collapse of their empires at the hands of national liberation movements. It was in these circumstances that Lenin once again pointed to the overriding importance of the organisation of political power for the success of any revolutionary social and economic transformation of the capitalist system. Accordingly, the aim of revolution in Russia should be now not to introduce bourgeois democracy and encourage the development of a mature capitalist economic system, but rather to start off a chain of socialist revolutions in the more advanced capitalist powers of Europe that in turn would provide Russia with the international support it needed to rapidly develop a socialist economy. The opportunity for such a revolution arose with the February 1917 Revolution and the creation of a Provisional Government that struggled to establish its authority. It was in these circumstances that, in his famous 'April Theses', Lenin exhorted the Bolsheviks to overthrow the Provisional Government and introduce a 'dictatorship of the proletariat'.

Lenin's justification for the dictatorship of the proletariat as a form of government is to be found in his best-known theoretical text, *The State and Revolution*, published in August 1917 shortly before the Bolshevik Revolution. He repudiates both the liberal view of the state as a means of reconciling class interests and what he sees as a more subtle 'Kautskyite distortion of Marxism' (by this point Lenin had turned against his old mentor) in which the democratic or parliamentary state can be preserved in its current form and taken over by socialists in order to socialise the means of production.[24] Following Engels, he portrays the bourgeois state as a public force reliant on 'special bodies of armed men', its army, police and other means of coercion. This state as coercive apparatus is employed by capitalists in its own interests, either through the direct corruption of the officials or through what Engels described as 'an alliance of the government and the Stock Exchange'.[25] The Provisional Government had by both of these means become an instrument of the bourgeoisie. It could not simply be taken over in its present form as a representative parliamentary democracy. For Lenin, in existing parliamentary democracies 'the real business of the "state" is performed behind the scenes and is carried on by the departments, Chancelleries and General Staffs'.[26] It was here, rather than in the hands of elected parliamentarians, that the real power of the state lay, and this military-bureaucratic apparatus stood separately from society as an instrument of bourgeois class rule. It had to be dismantled and replaced with a different form of class rule: the dictatorship of the proletariat.

Under the dictatorship of the proletariat, the state becomes an 'organisation of violence for the suppression' of the bourgeoisie:

> The proletariat needs state power, a centralised organisation of force, an organisation of violence, both to crush the resistance of the exploiters and to *lead* the enormous mass of the population – the peasants, the petty bourgeoisie, and semi-proletarians – in the work of organising a socialist economy.

Echoing *What is to be Done?*, Lenin argues that Marxism:

> educates the vanguard of the proletariat, capable of assuming power and *leading the people to socialism*, of directing and organising the new system, of being the teacher, the guide, the leader of all the working and exploited people in organising their social life without the bourgeoisie and against the bourgeoisie.[27]

The revolution thus requires a political leadership possessed of the means of violence in order to quell bourgeois resistance and to oversee the construction of a socialist economy through the redistribution of land and the organisation of industrial production. Lenin could not, however, justify this as a dictatorship of the *proletariat*, rather than the party, unless some mechanism existed by which the working class could be effectively represented. The model Lenin took here was the Paris Commune of 1871 or rather the account of the Paris Commune provided by Marx in *The Civil War in France*. The Commune showed the way in which representative institutions could be transformed from 'talking shops to "working bodies" '. The Commune had abolished the distinction between legislature and deputies, with the elected delegates of the Parisian workers directly participating in the government of the city. For Lenin, this system provided the blueprint for a 'voluntary centralism', that is 'the voluntary amalgamation of the communes into a nation, of the voluntary fusion of the proletarian communes, for the purpose of destroying bourgeois rule and the bourgeois state machine'.[28] In 1917 the role of the Commune as such was to be taken up by the Soviets of workers, dominated by the Bolsheviks and left-wing members of the Mensheviks and Socialist-Revolutionaries.

Much of *The State and Revolution*, then, prosecutes Lenin's earlier concern with the organisation and deployment of public power as a vehicle for social and economic transformation. At the same time, however, the text is characterised by a central ambiguity. Lenin reverts quite openly to the orthodox Marxist notion that the state is simply an instrument of and subordinate to class power. But the dictatorship of the proletariat would then be the dictatorship of a minority, since the industrial working-class was still hugely outnumbered by the peasantry in Russia in 1917. How could such a dictatorship be justified? It was here that Lenin had to resort to his faith in the truth of the orthodox Marxist account of historical and social development, and in so doing he adopted an anti-political stance that vitiates his earlier analysis of the centrality of political power. The aim of the proletarian revolution is ultimately the 'withering away of the state'. Once bourgeois resistance had been defeated and a socialist economy constructed, the problem of social organisation would be overcome by a technological fix: the advent of communism as a system of material abundance that would eliminate the systemic grounds of social conflict:

> We set ourselves the ultimate aim of abolishing the state, i.e., all organised and systematic violence, all use of violence against people in general. We do not expect the advent of a society in which the principle of subordination of the minority to the majority will not be observed. In striving for socialism, however, we are convinced that it will develop into communism and, therefore, that the need for violence against people in general, for the *subordination* of one man to another, and of one section of the population to another, will vanish altogether since people will *become accustomed* to observing the elementary conditions of social life *without violence* and *without subordination*.[29]

The 'withering away' of the state is at the same time a 'withering away of democracy' as an organised political system, for 'freed from capitalist slavery, from the untold horrors, savagery, absurdities and infamies of capitalist exploitation, people will gradually *become accustomed* to observing the elementary rules of social intercourse that have been known for centuries and repeated for thousands of year in all copy-book maxims. They will become accustomed to observing them without force, without coercion, without subordination, *without the special apparatus* for coercion called the state'.[30]

Lenin is clear that the withering away of the state will accompany the withering away of the 'excesses' of 'individual persons' as a result of the end of the capitalist exploitation that is the 'fundamental social cause' of 'the violation of the rules of social intercourse'.[31] But this argument provides an economic solution to what is a political problem: the constitution of social order as the norms that govern the conduct of individuals and groups. The difficulty here is Lenin's subscription to a 'vulgar' Marxism that resolves the plurality of various different social interests and values to the material interests of individuals as members of classes defined in economic terms. One of the most common criticisms of this kind of Marxism is that it simply conjures away the specificity of social conflicts based on ideology, religious belief, nationality, ethnicity or gender. There is, however, a more important failure of Lenin's Marxism: its inability to recognise that economic or material interests are not in themselves 'given', but are a product of particular forms of political organisation and relations of power.[32] The kind of 'communist' society that Lenin envisaged – that is a society devoid of private ownership of productive property, where technology has advanced to a level that minimises the amount of socially necessary labour time – might indeed be possible. This kind of society, however, would still require mechanisms for maintaining social order, for regulating what work there was to do, for ordering the distribution of scarce resources and for the resolution of disputes between groups and individuals. In any society with complex social order, an advanced division of labour and a rapid rate of technological change, there is always the possibility that systematic and sustained conflicts will arise. Without the political – that which, as we will see presently, Carl Schmitt defines as the ability of any community to distinguish its friends from its enemies – such conflict is likely to escalate into civil war.

Despite his claim to the contrary,[33] Lenin's ultimate solution to the problem of public power in *The State and Revolution* is indeed utopian. It is this utopianism, the final goal of a society beyond politics and conflict, that at the same time justifies the dictatorship of the proletariat as the legitimate form of government. It was clear, however, that in this system it was not the working class as whole that was to govern. Nor could it. It was left to Karl Kautsky, in his withering critique of Lenin's political position in *The State and Revolution*, to point this out:

> A class can rule, but not govern, for a class is a formless mass, while only an organisation can govern. It is the political parties which govern in a democracy. A party is, however, not synonomous with a class, although it may, in the first place, represent a class interest. One and the same class interest can be represented in very different ways, by various tactical methods. According to their variety, the representatives of the same class interests are divided into different parties. Above all, the deciding factor is the position in relation to other classes and parties.[34]

Lenin and the Bolsheviks abolished parliamentarianism in Russia: the Constituent Assembly, elected in November of 1917 with a large majority of Socialist Revolutionary deputies, was convoked in January 1918 only to be quickly closed down by the Bolshevik government. The Bolsheviks claimed legitimacy through the All-Russia Congress of Soviets, delegates to which were appointed from the local and regional soviets. It was through this mechanism that the dictatorship of the proletariat was to appear as a form of government by the whole working class. But Kautsky was quite right to claim that it was no such thing. The government of Russia was the Bolshevik party, its rule based on its capacity to employ violence to protect its position and to oversee the radical transformation of social and economic life. Other parties in Russia, such as the Mensheviks and Socialist Revolutionaries, also claimed to represent the real interests of the working class. Ultimately their failure was the result not of their 'incorrect' understanding of the dynamics of class relations and the course of historical development, nor even of a lack of popular support, but largely of their inability to marshal enough trained men with guns to successfully oppose Lenin and the Bolsheviks.

Lenin's political thought and actions turned around the notion of crisis: first the crisis of the absolute state in Russia and then the crisis of international capitalism. Perhaps more than any other figure in the early twentieth century, he saw that the way out of this crisis was through political organisation. The revolution could not come about through gradual economic and social change; the motor of history, in this respect, was not economic or technological development, but the political actions of groups of human beings. It was for this reason that Antonio Gramsci famously described the Bolshevik Revolution as a 'revolution against *Capital*'.[35] This revolution was carried out through the device of the 'dictatorship of the proletariat' which, as we have seen, was for all intents and purposes the dictatorship of the Bolshevik party. This was a political dictatorship in an important sense of the term 'political': it involved the making of vital decisions about how Russia or the Soviet Union as it was to become, was to be shaped: for example, the dissolution of the Constituent Assembly, the signing of the Treaty of Brest-Litovsk, the conduct of the civil war, War Communism, the New Economic Policy and so on. Such decisions could only be made by a government that was able to successfully employ the means of violence to achieve its ends. It had to be 'political' in the sense that it required continued complex political organisation for the radical transformation of social and economic life. But at the same time, the political character of Bolshevik rule was based on the notion that it was justified as the only true representative of the interests of the whole working class. The result was a highly centralised form of dictatorship that set Russia on an authoritarian path, allowing for the emergence a military-bureaucratic state apparatus required first to defend the Bolshevik state against its enemies in the course of the civil war, and then to force the country, at great cost to human life, into rapid industrialisation.

Toward the end of his life in 1924, Lenin began to have grave doubts about the direction this military-bureaucratic state was taking. Thus, for example, in his final article in *Pravda*, 'Better Fewer but Better' (1923),[36] he recognised the need to curtail the size of the central bureaucracy and curb the excesses of bureaucratic party members. But his solution to the problems of the bureaucratic centre was to create another centralised administrative body, the Workers' and Peasants' Inspection, a small group of 'irreproachable Communists' who could cut through the bureaucratic tangle. As Lenin's most astute intellectual biographer notes: 'Here at the end, in the last pamphlets he wrote in this his political testament, Lenin became a Jacobin.'[37] The solution Lenin here offers to the problems of centralised bureaucracy is a small group of individual 'experts'. Ultimately, then, Lenin even bypassed the party as the instrument of the people and left then in the hands of a few 'virtuous' communists. Whatever the historical legacy of this policy, its anti-political sentiment is clear. The huge problems that were confronted by Russia in the early 1920s were resolved into technical or administrative difficulties. Thus it was that the most politically radical of all early twentieth-century political theorists showed his colours as a deeply anti-political thinker.

Schmitt

Carl Schmitt (1888–1985) was a conservative and authoritarian thinker who embraced the Nazi regime in Germany after 1933, explicitly striving to become its 'crown jurist'. On the face of it his work would seem to have no place in a study dedicated to examining some of the main moments in the history of modern radical political thought. Yet Schmitt's writings in the period of the Weimar Republic in Germany are thoroughly radical. Schmitt challenged the central features of liberal political theory as it had developed since the French Revolution from a conservative position. He denounced the liberal and parliamentary politics of Weimar Germany because he believed that they had lent themselves to the destabilisation of the state in relation to society and had created the conditions in which a Bolshevik-style revolution might succeed. There can be no question that while Schmitt is most famous for his critique of liberalism, for him the greatest enemy to confront in Germany in the 1920s was revolutionary socialism and communism. However, Schmitt's dissatisfaction with liberalism and parliamentarianism was not motivated by a reactionary mindset. He must certainly be counted as a critic of political modernity, but it is far from clear that Schmitt sought out anything like a 'return' to absolutism. In this regard, his conservatism is as complex and as radical as that of Edmund Burke, a figure with whom he closely identified.[38]

Partly because of his Nazi past,[39] aside from a number of German intellectuals few political theorists engaged with Schmitt's texts after 1945. Since the 1980s, however, there has been a significant re-evaluation of his work both in continental Europe and in the English-speaking world. Surprisingly, much of the renewed interest in Schmitt has emanated from left-leaning scholars.[40] One possible reason for this is a fairly widespread belief on the modern left that in the last part of the twentieth century Marxism failed to provide any new or penetrating insights into the character of the liberal capitalist state. Since the 1970s Marxism has by-and-large become associated with disciplines such a literary and cultural studies, geography, and, in the guise of 'analytical Marxism', the philosophy of social explanation. For many on the left interested in Marxism as a distinct theory of the state, since the work of Gramsci little has emerged from Marxist authors that provides any strong basis for theoretical and practical challenges to liberal capitalism.

While Schmitt is a thinker on the right, his attraction lies in his incisive criticisms of the kind of legal and political order that today exists in the most powerful states in the world. Weimar Germany consisted of a liberal democratic state with a capitalist economy, albeit one that was subject to severe and, as it turned out, inexorable crises. Nonetheless, Schmitt's criticisms of this political system, even if they could only have originated in the peculiar conditions of the Weimar Republic, may be taken as having continued relevance today. Indeed, since the collapse of communism as an alternative political and economic system to liberal capitalism, and the liberal democratisation and marketisation of societies outside the West during the 1980s and 1990s, Schmitt's critique may seem more pertinent than ever.

But the strength of Schmitt's work lies not just in its perceptive analysis of the condition of the state, sovereignty and politics in modern liberal-constitutional regimes. In the course of his writing in the 1920s and early 1930s Schmitt also managed to diagnose and to trace the development of the peculiar condition characteristic of Western political thought in modernity, that is the kind of theoretical ambiguity present in authors of both the 'left' and 'right', both 'radical' and 'conservative', that we have taken to be definitive of the radical attitude. In short, Schmitt is one of the few authors in the history of modern Western political thought to recognise that this history is constituted, on the one hand, by a recognition of the centrality of power to the character of human social life, and in particular power organised into definite institutions and practices that are autonomous of other social institutions and practices (or 'the political'), and on the other hand the desire to tame or even abolish power through the liberation of a moral content inherent in human nature that has been suppressed by the manifestations of power in specific political forms. For Schmitt, this meant that at least since the French Revolution radical and revolutionary groups, informed by a belief in the subordination of state to society, politics to morality, strove to gain and wield the power of the modern state without constraint since, in a way reminiscent of the theological conflicts of the Reformation, they were driven by an unassailable belief in the higher justice of their actions. Paradoxically, the desire to abolish power had led to its unfettered growth and the possibility of a permanent 'tyranny of values'. Schmitt believed that the only way to avert this tyranny of values was by a reassertion of the power of the state as the protector of society. Like Hobbes, he believed that the protection-obedience relationship between the state and its subjects was necessary if social peace was to be maintained alongside individual freedom.

While many of those today influenced by Schmitt's writings do not advocate his authoritarian statist solution, they argue that the prospects for democratic social and political change in the present cannot be carried by any substantive theory of the good or formal theory of the right. Rather, radical change requires a confrontation with the character of public power and an account of the possible ways in which it can be challenged and deployed to meet particular political goals. In this respect, at least, Lenin and Schmitt can be taken to have operated on similar conceptual and political grounds.

Schmitt trained as a lawyer in Berlin and Munich prior to (and partly during) the First World War. The events of the immediate post-war period in Germany – the abdication of the Kaiser in the wake of defeat, the widespread social disorder and attempted communist revolution and finally the punitive measures imposed on Germany by the Treaty of Versailles – had a profound impact on a generation of Germans who, like Schmitt, sought civil peace and national renewal. For Schmitt, as for others, an important consequence of the widespread social tumult was personal politicisation; some would take the path charted out by revolutionary socialism and communism; for many members of the liberal bourgeoisie the solution lay in the creation of a constitutional state that could effectively combine the representation of various social interests with order; others on the reactionary right sought a return to the absolutist state, 'above' society, and capable of rebuilding German military might in order to reassert its national interests against imperial rivals. Schmitt's politicisation would, before 1932, by-and-large involve an acceptance of the constitutional order that was established at Weimar in 1919, with an awareness of the weakness of parliamentary government in the face of popular political movements (of both left and right) that sought to subvert it and its potential to become little more than a battleground between particular social interests. Schmitt, a Catholic by birth, would in these years hold a political position close to that of the Catholic Centre Party. As Balakrishnan points out, many German Catholics felt no great emotional tie to the old Wilhelmine regime, implicated as it was with the repression of Catholics during Bismarck's *Kulturkampf* of the 1870s, and were pragmatically disposed toward the new Republic.[41] After the relative stability enjoyed in Weimar Germany between 1923–29,[42] however, Schmitt would increasingly move toward a rejection of parliamentary government and argue for an ever starker form of authoritarianism.

Schmitt's politicisation took place not so much as an identification with a particular location on the political spectrum, but rather as a move away from his traditional juristic training on matters of the state and politics. This had encouraged abstract reflection and a disengagement from practical politics, not least because of the authoritarian atmosphere of Wilhelmine Germany where radical intellectuals, particularly those on the left, were likely to find their careers blocked (if not befalling a worse fate).[43] The intellectual and political freedom of immediate post-war Germany presented a space in which discourses of the state, politics and law could now flourish. It was an opportunity taken up eagerly by intellectuals, such as Max Weber who played an important role in the drafting of the Weimar constitution in 1919. Throughout the 1920s, intellectuals on the left such as Otto Kirchheimer and Franz Neumann, liberals such as Hans Kelsen and conservatives like Schmitt, would stake out important positions in the fields of political and legal thought that continue to play a central role in political theory in the early twenty-first century.

One of the most significant of Schmitt's texts in the early Weimar period was *Political Romanticism* (1919). The book is ostensibly a critique of the aesthetic romanticism of nineteenth-century German authors, most notably Friedrich Schlegel and Adam Müller. The vantage point from which Schmitt criticises these authors is, however, political rather than aesthetic. Nineteenth-century romanticism was primarily an anti-political movement in the sense that its contemplations of the world proceeded from a 'subjectified occasionalism', the belief that the world is best understood from the viewpoint of the privatised individual who choses when (the 'occasion') to engage with the world in order to explore the quality of his aesthetic experiences and his 'inner nature'.[44] Political events represented such an occasion, one with which the romantic engaged while maintaining a distance from and a distaste for committed political activity. Accordingly, it was impossible to recognise in romantic writings anything that resembled a coherent political position. Rather, romantics aestheticised and poeticised politics, switching freely from revolutionary to conservative positions in so far as they could be worked into their detached and occasional perspectives on the political world. It was a great mistake, then, to view romantic authors as political thinkers, and for Schmitt it was particularly important not to confuse the romantic reaction against the modern world with the distinctly political position taken up by 'conservative' thinkers such as Burke, de Maistre, and Bonald. These 'founders of the counterrevolutionary theory ... were active politicians, each with his own responsibility. For years, they maintained a tenacious and energetic opposition against their governments. They were always filled with the sense that they were not elevated above the political struggle, but were instead obligated to decide in favour of what they regarded as right'.[45]

What makes the romantic attitude toward modernity possible is modernity itself: it provides the conditions for a privatised subjectivity and a detachment from the kind of ascriptive communities characteristic of pre-modern Europe. Schmitt was thus pointing to a connection between the apolitical and anti-political attitude of the romantic reaction to the Enlightenment and the liberalism of the privatised, bourgeois liberal subject.[46] Despite Schmitt's favourable citing of Burke, de Maistre and Bonald, it is not precisely clear where the book stands on the left-right divide. However, as Balakrishnan points out, Schmitt's next work, *Die Diktatur* (1921), is unambiguously on the right.[47] Schmitt here makes a distinction between 'commissarial' and 'sovereign' dictatorship. The former is a temporary form of dictatorship expressly provided for by a constitution in periods of exceptional emergency and designed to replace the normal institutions of government in order to protect public safety. This kind of constitutional dictatorship was first announced in the Roman public office of the dictator, an extraordinary magistrate who would voluntarily surrender his post within a period of months or at the end of a successful military campaign. In contrast, sovereign dictatorship 'sees in the total existing order the condition, which it wishes to eliminate through its actions. It does not merely suspend an existing constitution but ... attempts to create a condition in which it can establish a constitution which it views as the true constitution. It appeals not to an existing, but rather to a newly arising constitution'.[48] What Schmitt principally has here in mind as a sovereign dictatorship is the Bolshevik regime, something that he regarded as dangerous because of the unfettered expression it gave to popular sovereignty or 'the dictatorship of the proletariat'. In this respect, Schmitt claimed that a democracy based on the Rousseauian conception of the sovereign general will was essentially incompatible with sustained social order. In such a democracy: 'Out of its endless, elusive, groundless power emerges ever new forms, which it can at any time shatter, never limiting itself.'[49] Popular sovereignty thus needs to be constrained by a constitution, as it has been in liberal-constitutional states, that restricts the capacity of the people (or a majority of the people) to freely alter the shape of the political form of the state. In *Die Diktatur* Schmitt thus demonstrated a tension between democracy and liberal constitutionalism that would be a central term of analysis in his later critique of liberalism.

Another of the important texts that Schmitt published in early Weimar was *Roman Catholicism and Political Form* (1923).[50] In this book

Schmitt portrayed the Catholic Church as a specifically political institution that possessed a distinct political rationality. Historically, the Catholic Church had played a crucial role in forging a Europe of separate national entities that existed in a state of relative peace. Catholicism was central to the development of a *jus publicum Europaeum*. The Catholic Church was a *complexio oppositorum* that had performed a central unifying function in European history and not, as it had been portrayed in the Protestant Reformation, the property of a self-interested and other-worldy sacerdotal order. In *Roman Catholicism and Political Form*, Schmitt holds out the hope that the Church could act as a counterpoint to liberalism and socialism as anti-political doctrines that gave primacy to economic interests, and that it could thereby act as the potential saviour of European civilisation. While in the ensuing years Schmitt came to see that actually existing political Catholicism was concerned with protecting its own special interests,[51] he nonetheless retained the belief in the importance of a unifying European force of a distinctly political character. While Schmitt was a German 'nationalist', this focus on the importance of European political unity rendered his nationalism far more complex than that of the traditional reactionary right or of modern ultra-nationalists and fascists.

Schmitt's take on Roman Catholicism involves a view of the importance of 'political theology' that is more fully set out in a book bearing this title, first published in 1922. However, the book starts off not with a discussion of the concept of political theology, but rather with Schmitt's famous definition of sovereignty: 'Sovereign is he who decides on the exception'.[52] Schmitt's 'decisionism' is most succinctly captured in this single sentence. The sovereign is to be identified as that person or body who has the power to decide on the exception in at least two senses: the decision that the situation addressed is an exceptional one; and the decision about how to respond to the exceptional situation so conceived.[53] For Schmitt, the exception 'can be best characterised as a case of extreme peril, a danger to the existence of the state, or the like. But it cannot be circumscribed factually and made to conform to a preformed law'.[54] He thus wishes to emphasise that the essence of sovereignty is not the determination or application of the norm, rule or law, but rather the determination or application of the exception to the norm, rule or law. The concept of a supreme authority must involve the idea that it has the power to alter the rules on which it operates and in reality it is only men who possess such power. Abstract legal sovereignty is entirely formal: it makes sense only insofar as the sovereign power conforms to the rules that legally and constitutionally define it and stipulate its sphere of competence. But it makes no sense to say that the legal sovereign is sovereign either if it does not have the power to depart from the legal-constitutional rules or if it operates under the sufferance of another entity that is not bound by these legal-constitutional rules. It is the ideas of sovereignty as indivisible and of the sovereign as the *legibus solutus* and uncommanded commander, to be found in the texts of early modern theorists of sovereignty such as Bodin and Hobbes, that Schmitt wishes to re-establish. Unlike these earlier thinkers, however, for Schmitt the sovereign is sovereign not simply because it makes the laws within an established procedure, or because it is itself not subject to those laws, but rather since it has the power to determine when the whole procedure that is used for determining the laws should be departed from, suspended, or even abolished.

There is then, for Schmitt, a distinction to be made in the concept of a legal order between the norm and the decision: 'Like every other order, the legal order rests on a decision and not on a norm.' Even in the 'normal' situation, 'he is sovereign who definitely decides whether this normal situation actually exists'.[55] Accordingly, the very existence of a normal situation in which the established norms, rules or laws operate depends on the possibility of a decision to depart from it. It follows that:

> The exception is more interesting than the rule. The rule proves nothing; the exception proves everything: It confirms not only the rule but also its existence, which derives only from the exception. In the exception the power of real life breaks through the crust of a mechanism that has become torpid by repetition.[56]

What is important with respect to the concrete operation of sovereignty is the way in which the actual power to decide on the exception is connected to the formally supreme legal authority in the state. Schmitt here argues against the tradition of 'legal positivism' in German jurisprudence as that was most prominently represented by Hans Kelsen's 'pure theory of law'. For Kelsen, the state was to be identified with the legal order. Law is based on norms, positive principles on which particular legal rules should be constructed and which should be studied independently of all other political, social or ideological considerations. All laws should emanate from a fundamental or founding norm, the *Ursprungsnorm*, which is manifested in the constitution of the state.[57] 'The state, meaning the legal order, is a system of ascriptions to a last point of ascription and a last basic norm.' But: 'Kelsen solved the problem of the concept of sovereignty by negating it.'[58] In other words, Kelsen merely identifies the state with the legal order without demonstrating what power it has independently of the legal norms with which it is identified, to constitute the legal order and to determine in what circumstances the legal-constitutional norm does not apply.

Kelsen's liberal legalism fails, for Schmitt, to provide any answer to the question of what to do in the face of radical social conflict and turmoil; it strives to neutralise and depoliticise the state, restricting it to the adjudication of private disputes according to given constitutional norms. It cannot, however, show the way to deal with the emergency situation as a public and political crisis. In a way that meshes with his work on Catholicism, Schmitt asserts that we can only begin to see a way out of this crisis by recognising the properly theological character of politics. At the start of chapter 3 of *Political Theology* he claims that: 'All significant concepts of the modern theory of the state are secularised theological concepts not only because of their historical development ... but also because of their systematic structure, the recognition of which is necessary for a sociological consideration of these concepts'. The concept that Schmitt most clearly has in mind here is sovereignty itself. The modern concept of sovereignty is a secularised version of the theological notion of an omnipotent lawgiver. Related to this the 'exception in jurisprudence is analogous to the miracle in theology'.[59] The emergency situation is like the miracle in the sense that the latter constitutes a departure from the divine order of things. For Schmitt, secularisation as a sociological process of modernity has involved a dual challenge: not just to the theological concepts of the divine law-giver and miracles, but to their secular manifestation in the form of the concepts of sovereignty and the exception. Modern secular liberalism thus seeks to neutralise not only the consequences of religious belief – an act that is already performed by the Protestant assertion of inner-faith and the demystification of earthly life – but to depoliticise society by the relegation of sovereignty and decision to a legal order embodied in a constitution that stands above and apart from political power, conceived of in terms of the relationship between individuals with plural, socially or economically given interests.

By 1923 Schmitt had come to a view of the connective strands that ran through modern political thought and the way that the main elements of such thinking were both reflected in and perpetuated by the existing legal and political order in liberal-constitutional, capitalist states. Romanticism and liberalism shared in common a foundation in the privatising subjectivity that had accompanied the decline of pre-modern European political and religious order; both liberal-constitutional and more radical forms of thought, such as revolutionary socialism and communism, were products of the secularised Enlightenment movement toward the neutralisation and depoliticisation of the state. What was at issue between modern liberalism and socialism was the relevant character of freedom in the economic sphere of life. Socialism claimed that inequality in the ownership of productive property was the fundamental source of the lack of freedom experienced by the proletariat in capitalist societies; for liberals such inequalities in property could be justified in so far as they were a necessary concomitant of a legal order that guaranteed an individual liberty consistent with social order. While revolutionary socialists and communists sought to overturn economic inequality by dismantling not just the legal and political order but the very character of social relations, their aim was ultimately the same as that of liberals: the elimination of political conflict. Communist men may face problems of allocation, that is problems associated with 'the administration of things', but these could be fixed by science and technology. For liberals, there was a similar desire to substitute the administration of things for politics, though not through a revolution. The problems that resulted from the existence of inequality in property holding, plural interests and values could, for liberals, be resolved through discussion and the principle site of discussion in the liberal-constitutional state was parliament.

Schmitt's *The Crisis of Parliamentary Democracy* (1923) is a coruscating critique of the principle of parliamentarianism and the depoliticising logic it represents. In the Preface to the second edition of the book, written in 1926, Schmitt writes:

> Parliamentarianism exists today as a method of government and a political system. Just as everything else that exists and functions tolerably, it is useful – no more and no less. It counts for a great deal that even today it functions better than other untried methods, and that a minimum of order that is today actually at hand would be endangered by frivolous experiments. Every reasonable person would concede such arguments. But they do not carry weight in an argument about principles. Certainly no one would be so undemanding that he regarded an intellectual foundation or a moral truth as proven by the question, What else?[60]

Certainly, nothing in this passage indicates Schmitt's outright opposition to parliamentarianism as 'a method of government'. Nonetheless, Schmitt wished to explore the paradoxes of the doctrine of parliamentary government and by so doing to outline his view of what was necessary in order to ensure that such a system did not lead to the dissolution of social and political order. Schmitt's answer to this problem is an authoritarian one: to provide for the *Reichspräsident* extraordinary emergency powers to dissolve parliament and legislate without its consent (which Schmitt believed to be already provided for by Article 48 of the Weimar constitution). More generally, however, Schmitt sees the fundamental flaw of parliamentarianism, as an intellectual principle, in its subscription to the liberal concept of the derivation of 'truth' from discussion.

There is an important distinction to draw, Schmitt argues, between the notions of deliberation and discussion. Deliberation is a universal feature of human history. It takes place wherever people wish (as in most instances) to avoid conflict through negotiation and compromise. Such a form of deliberation, however, 'is not the principle of a specific kind of state or form of government'.[61] In contrast, parliamentarianism, as a liberal doctrine, sees discussion as taking place from a perspective of disinterestedness. Parliamentary representatives do not represent the naked interests of the groups that elect them to parliament, but rather the good of the whole national community. What measures best support the interests and welfare of that community can be determined through discussion in the parliamentary forum. From the late eighteenth century, it was this liberal view of representation, evident in the work of thinkers such as Edmund Burke, the Federalists and Benjamin Constant, that informed the creation and transformation of parliamentary government. The constitution of the liberal parliamentary state is geared around this general liberal principle: 'That the truth can be found through an unrestrained clash of opinion and that competition will produce harmony. The intellectual core of this thought resides finally in its specific relationship to truth, which becomes a mere function of the eternal competition of opinion.'[62] Parliament is an open forum of discussion where opinion is freely exchanged; the doctrine of the balance of powers ensures that such diverse opinions can be openly and effectively put forward without any particular interest coming to monopolise the 'truth'; and in a liberal-constitutional state or *Rechsstaat*, as in Kelsen's jurisprudence, it is the law as the impersonal embodiment of the truth that stands as the sovereign power, not some named individual or assembly.[63]

The liberal principle of discussion emerged and served to inform the political struggles of the eighteenth and nineteenth centuries against princely absolutism, a system of government that was effectively liberalism's intellectual opposite based as it was on secrecy, the fusion of legislative, judicial and executive branches of government in the hands of the prince and the personal character of the sovereign power. The liberation of parliaments from the personal authority of the prince provided an open forum in which truth and justice could be secured. For Schmitt, whether or not this desire for parliamentary government in the nineteenth century was based on the real possibility of securing a disinterested representative legislature, it was clear that by the early years of the twentieth century the emergence of organised social and economic interests and mass political parties had turned the parliamentary plenum into a façade behind which partisan interests vied for power. At best parliaments had become a bargaining forum and pool from which ministers, as representatives of particular interest groups, were selected. At worse, 'in a few states, parliamentarianism has already produced a situation in which all public business has become an object of spoils and compromise for the parties and their followers, and politics, far from being the concern of an elite, has become the despised business of a rather dubious class of persons'.[64]

Obviously, Schmitt's primary concern here was the parliamentary regime of the Weimar Republic, which between 1919–23 existed alongside the kind of widespread social and political conflict that had seen an attempted left-wing revolution and an attempted right-wing *putsch*. The new Republic had meekly acceded to the payment of reparations in the Treaty of Versailles, leaving the German economy reeling. Parliament had become a battleground between left and right, with 'moderates' increasingly squeezed between them. Important as this context is for understanding Schmitt's *The Crisis of Parliamentary Democracy*, it was still a text concerned with criticising the theoretical basis of parliamentarianism rather than any of its specific empirical manifestations.[65] For Schmitt a central paradox of modern liberal parliamentarianism is the combination of the principle of discussion with the principle of democratic sovereignty. Modern democracy for Schmitt means the creation of homogenous national groups (though not necessarily homogenous in terms of culture, ethnicity or race), the 'people', based 'on the principle that not only are equals equal but unequals will not be treated equally'.[66] National democracies are the creation of politics in a very specific sense: they require the delineation of friends from enemies and the exclusion of the latter. The criterion of 'the political' for Schmitt is this distinction between friend and enemy.[67] Liberal parliamentarianism, however, strives for a 'democracy of mankind' in which '[e]very adult person, simply as a person, should *eo ipso* be politically equal to every other person'.[68] In this respect, the intellectual foundation of liberal parliaments is simply at odds with the concept and practice of modern democracy. Democracy requires the forging of the *demos* as a political act within a specific national territory. Democracy is not a universal concept in the sense that 'the people' consists of all human beings. Moreover, Schmitt claimed that modern democracy is for all practical purposes a question of who has the power 'over the means with which the will of the people is to be constructed: military and political force, propaganda, control of public opinion through the press, party organisations, assemblies, popular education, and schools. In particular only political power, which should come from the people's will, can form the people's will in the first place'.[69]

Liberal parliamentarianism is anti-political in the sense that it seeks to overcome the friend-enemy distinction by aspiring to represent the universal interests of man in general as bearers of a human nature, human rights and so on. For Schmitt, this aspiration is entirely incompatible with the character of modern democracy as the political expression of the 'will of the people': that is the formation of the people in relation to its opposite, the public enemy that constantly poses a threat to the security of the political community. The principle of discussion had thus given way, in Weimar Germany and in other parliaments, to a legislature that was the battleground between different interests, or in other words, enemies who all sought to establish what constituted the 'will of the people'. In what is perhaps Schmitt's most famous book, *The Concept of the Political* (first published in 1927), he claims that the current crisis of parliamentary democracy could only be overcome by re-establishing the political, that is, the power to distinguish between the friend and enemy of the national community in the domain of the state over and above society. With the rise of mass democracy, the nineteenth and early twentieth centuries had seen the erosion of the distinction between the state and society. The state becomes involved in the 'ostensibly neutral domains' of religion, culture, education and the economy, while at the same time society comes to take on the political functions of the state. For Schmitt: 'This results in the identity of state and society. In such a state, therefore, everything is at least potentially political, and in referring to the state it is no longer possible to assert for it a specifically political character.'[70]

For Schmitt, this is the 'total state': it marks the demise of liberalism in so far as state and society cease to be distinct domains, with the state legislating for and administering wide-ranging areas of social and private life. At the same time, the total state in a parliamentary regime becomes a hostage to whatever coalitions of parties and interest groups can muster a legislative majority. The reality of the situation is that parliamentary representation is the representation of divergent and perhaps irreconcilable social interests and values. Simultaneously, the dominant position ascribed in liberal democracies to the legislative body, as the expression of the true will of the people, over the executive power means that the state becomes a vehicle for the prosecution of sectional interests and values. The state is effectively depoliticised; in other words its function of distinguishing between friend and enemy as the foundation of the protection-obedience relationship disappears and the result is the constant threat of civil disorder and war.

The modern liberal theory of parliamentary representation received one of its highest expressions in the Abbé Sieyes' *What is the Third Estate?*, written at the point of the creation of the French National Assembly in the 1789 Revolution.[71] Sieyes saw the nation as the rightful constituent power, that is the legitimating source from which the constitution was derived. As Duncan Kelly demonstrates, Schmitt's own view of representation is strongly coloured by Sieyes' understanding of the character of the constituent power and its relation to the state.[72] Sieyes claimed that the National Assembly represented the popular constituent power; for Schmitt, such representation of the constituent power was possible and desirable in modern sovereign nation-states. However, where he departed from Sieyes and Enlightenment liberalism more generally was in his claim that this constituent power could not be achieved through a representative parliamentary body. Such a body does not represent the 'political unity of the people' but only various sectional interests and values. It was for this reason that Schmitt turned (as had Hobbes) to the notion of a representative sovereign (and political) power that could effectively embody the national will and protect it by exercising a monopoly of state power: in Weimar Germany this was the *Reichspräsident*.[73]

Schmitt's work of the Weimar period might, then, be seen as 'conservative' and 'authoritarian' in a particular sense. Schmitt's conservatism lay in his belief that the central task of political action was the securing of the protection-obedience relationship between sovereign and subjects in order to preserve social order and civil peace. His authoritarianism is shown in his argument that a political leader at the helm of the state should have the power to override a democratically elected legislature in order to fulfil the necessary political function of sovereign power: that is, the distinction of friend from enemy, the protection of peace and order from public enemies. While modern radical democratic thinkers may balk at such conservatism and authoritarianism, a number of them have nonetheless taken Schmitt's ideas very seriously. One of the most powerful aspects of Schmitt's work is that he recognises that the alliance of a non-political liberalism and mass democracy has effectively rendered parliamentary 'discussion' otiose. Parliament acts as a façade behind which the bureaucratic agencies of the modern state operate without being held to democratic account.[74] Schmitt's critique of liberal-constitutional parliamentarianism is thus of continuing relevance, particularly in contemporary circumstances: the prolonged period of political stability in Western democracies since 1945 that has allowed parliamentary government to proceed largely unchallenged; and the move away from authoritarian to liberal-democratic and parliamentary regimes in South America, Central and Eastern Europe and other parts of the world over the last 20 to 30 years. While Schmitt's solution is not acceptable to radical democratic thinkers, his diagnosis of the deficiencies of liberal parliamentarianism is important for exploring what alternative forms of democratic government, direct or representative, may successfully hold the powerful bureaucratic-cum-technological forces of the state to popular account.

Accordingly, Schmitt's work should be considered as an important moment in the history of radical political thought: it was radical in its context and continues to have radical implications in the present. But Schmitt's critique of liberalism and of 'Enlightenment' thought more generally has an important bearing on our understanding of the modern radical attitude. What Schmitt recognises in the history of modern political theory is the articulation of two incompatible principles: the principle of the existential reality of power in its specific manifestations as the primary precondition of and medium through which the world can be transformed according to common goals; and the uninterrupted desire inherent in modernity to overcome power and social conflict by means of the substitution of a moral for the political order. As Leo Strauss perceptively saw, Schmitt's work is itself subject to the criticism that it prioritises a moral order – the order of warlike morals suggested by his definition of the political – in the organisation of human social conduct.[75] Schmitt's work thus sheds light on the ambiguous character of the radical attitude in modern political theory and may itself be seen as an illustration of that ambiguity.

Conclusion: The Radical Attitude and Utopia

It is sometimes said that we can divide radicalism into Utopian and non-Utopian varieties. Utopian radicalism looks to an ideal state of human freedom and peaceful co-existence in which power and conflict have been abolished. This kind of radicalism tells us little about how such a society might be possible, and tends to fall back on stories of human progress as the outcome of immutable laws of development, whether divine, natural, moral, economic, technological, scientific or whatever. In contrast, non-Utopian radicalism accepts the presence and permanence of political power in complex forms of human society and looks to how it might be organised in order to meet specific goals.

I hope this book has made clear that these two forms of radicalism are not mutually exclusive. Indeed, if we look at some of the most prominent texts in the history of Western political thought, we see them co-existing in what I have called the 'radical attitude'. To draw attention to the ambivalent character of this attitude is not to dismiss it as a 'mistake'; it is not to praise non-Utopian radicalism while damning the Utopian. Utopianism is a powerful current of thought in the Western tradition and some of the most important texts we have – from More to Swift to Orwell – could not have been written without it. But works like More's *Utopia*, Swift's *Gulliver's Travels* and Orwell's *Nineteen Eighty-Four* (strictly speaking a dystopian novel) are so powerful (and radical) not because they bring into question the order of the Utopias that they construct, but the order of what these Utopias model: the world as its exists in the here and now.

Perhaps the best kind of Utopian radicalism points to the fact that we already live in Utopia. This does not sound such a fanciful idea when we reflect that ideas about the 'end of history' have recurred frequently in recent years and have been greeted with the utmost seriousness. The end of the Cold War and the emergence of 'globalisation' were meant to have brought to a close the age of ideologies, the clash between great Utopian visions of the future. That they have not done so is, given the character of the radical attitude in modern political theory, singularly unsurprising. Critical counter-Utopianism can reveal the configuration of political power in the present and unearth resources that can be used to contest it. The challenge for radical political theory today is, then, not to reject Utopian thinking out of hand. But it is the question of the organisation of political power that must be its primary concern.

Notes

Introduction

1. On the structure of political ideologies, see M. Freeden, *Ideologies and Political Theory* (Oxford: Oxford University Press, 1996).
2. See J. G. A. Pocock, *Politics, Language and Time* (Chicago, IL: University of Chicago Press, 1989), ch. 1; Q. Skinner, *The Foundations of Modern Political Thought*, vol. 1 (Cambridge: Cambridge University Press, 1978), pp. x–xiv.
3. See H. Spruyt, *The Sovereign State and Its Competitors: An Analysis of Systems Change* (Princeton, NJ: Princeton University Press, 1994).

Chapter 1   The Reformation and the Radical Attitude: Luther, Müntzer and Calvin

1. Q. Skinner, *The Foundations of Modern Political Thought*, vol. 2 (Cambridge: Cambridge University Press, 1978), pp. 3–12.
2. *Ibid.*, pp. 23–4.
3. M. Luther, 'On the Freedom of a Christian', in *Luther's Works*, vol. 31 (Philadelphia, PA: Fortress Press, 1957).
4. *Ibid.*, p. 345.
5. *Ibid.*, p. 346.
6. *Ibid.*, pp. 349–50.
7. Luther, 'On the Freedom of a Christian', pp. 358–9.
8. *Ibid.*, p. 366.
9. *Ibid.*, p. 369.
10. M. Luther, 'Treatise on Good Works', in *Luther's Works*, vol. 44 (1966).
11. *Ibid.*, p. 80.
12. *Ibid.*, pp. 90–1.
13. *Ibid.*, pp. 92, 93, 100.
14. M. Luther, 'To the Christian Nobility of the German Nation', in *Luther's Works*, vol. 44 (1966), p. 129.
15. *Ibid.*, p. 131.
16. M. Luther, 'Temporal Authority: To What Extent it Should be Obeyed', in *Luther's Works*, vol. 45 (1962), p. 89.
17. *Ibid.*, p. 90.
18. *Ibid.*, p. 91.
19. *Ibid.*, p. 95.
20. *Ibid.*, pp. 111, 107.
21. *Ibid.*, p. 112.
22. *Ibid.*
23. M. Luther, 'Admonition to Peace, A Reply to the Twelve Articles of the Peasants in Swabia', in *Luther's Works*, vol. 46 (1967).

24. M. Luther, 'Against the Robbing and Murdering Hordes of Peasants', in *Luther's Works*, vol. 46 (1967), pp. 51–2.
25. M. Luther, 'Whether Soldiers Too Can Be Saved', in *Luther's Works*, vol. 46 (1967), p. 96.
26. H. Höpfl, Introduction to *Luther and Calvin On Secular Authority* (Cambridge: Cambridge University Press, 1991), p. x.
27. Luther, 'On Temporal Authority', p. 89.
28. W. A. Mueller, *Church and State in Luther and Calvin: A Comparative Study* (New York: Anchor Books, 1954), ch. 3.
29. The older Luther was intolerant of other faiths, most notably Judaism and Islam. His notoriously anti-semitic 'On The Jews and their Lies' recommends the burning of synagogues, the razing of Jewish houses and, ultimately, the expulsion of Jews from German lands. M. Luther, 'On the Jews and their Lies', in *Luther's Works*, vol. 47 (1971).
30. G. H. Williams, *The Radical Reformation* (Philadelphia, PA: The Westminster Press, 1965).
31. *Ibid.*, ch. 13.
32. The former group tended to reject overtures toward violent resistance and had a greater impact on the formation of Anabaptism, a doctrine that was largely pacific in outlook. See Skinner, *The Foundations of Modern Political Thought*, vol. 2, pp. 74–5.
33. See F. Engels, *The Peasant War in Germany* (London: George Allen and Unwin, 1926).
34. H. Loewen, *Luther and the Radicals* (Waterloo, Ontario: Wilfrid Laurier University, 1974), p. 51.
35. *Ibid.*, p. 53.
36. T. Müntzer, 'The Prague Protest', in M. G. Baylor ed., *The Radical Reformation* (Cambridge: Cambridge University Press, 1991), p. 10.
37. The audience consisted of Frederick of Saxony's brother, Duke John, and several other important Saxon nobles.
38. T. Müntzer, 'Sermon to the Princes', in Baylor ed., *The Radical Reformation*, pp. 25, 30.
39. T. Müntzer, 'A Highly Provoked Defence', in Baylor ed., *The Radical Reformation*, p. 80.
40. *Ibid.*, p. 81.
41. 'To the Assembly of the Common Peasantry', in Baylor ed., *The Radical Reformation*, p. 101.
42. *Ibid.*, p. 105.
43. *Ibid.*, p. 111.
44. *Ibid.*, pp. 114–15.
45. *Ibid.*, p. 119.
46. *Ibid.*, p. 121.
47. H.-J. Goertz, *Thomas Müntzer: Apocalyptic Mystic and Revolutionary*, trans. Jocelyn Jaquiery (Edinburgh: T & T Clark, 1993), p. 206.
48. M. Luther, 'Dr. Martin Luther's Warning to His Dear German People', in *Luther's Works*, vol. 47 (1971), p. 30.
49. *Ibid.*, p. 55.
50. See R. S. Wallace, *Calvin, Geneva and the Reformation* (Edinburgh: Scottish Academic Press, 1990).

51. S. Wolin, *Politics and Vision: Continuity and Innovation in Western Political Thought* (Princeton, NJ: Princeton University Press, 2004), p. 150.
52. A. E. McGrath, *A Life of John Calvin: A Study in the Shaping of Western Culture* (Oxford: Basil Blackwell, 1990), pp. 85–6.
53. *Ibid.*, pp. 95–6.
54. *Ibid.*, pp. 98–9.
55. *Ibid.*, pp. 109–10.
56. Wolin, *Politics and Vision*, p. 157.
57. *Ibid.*, p. 170.
58. *Ibid.*, pp. 112–13.
59. M. Walzer, *The Revolution of the Saints* (London: Weidenfeld & Nicolson, 1966).
60. Skinner, *The Foundations of Modern Political Thought*, vol. 2, p. 323. Walzer also reduces Calvinism to 'ideology' in the sense of a psychological means of justifying the interests of its believers. This overlooks the importance of Calvinism as a belief system in shaping the interests of its believers according to its theological content. See R. C. Hancock, *Calvin and the Foundations of Modern Politics* (Ithaca, New York: Cornell University Press, 1989), p. 13.
61. J. Calvin, 'Civil Government', in *Institutes of the Christian Religion*, vol. II, ch. XX (*Library of Christian Classics*, vol. XXI), trans. F. L. Battles (Philadelphia, PA: Westminster Press, 1960), pp. 1485–6.
62. *Ibid.*, p. 1486.
63. *Ibid.*, p. 1487.
64. *Ibid.*, p. 1488.
65. *Ibid.*, pp. 1489–90.
66. *Ibid.*, p. 1511.
67. *Ibid.*, p. 1512.
68. *Ibid.*, p. 1517.
69. *Ibid.*, p. 1521.
70. *Ibid.*, p. 1519.
71. Skinner, *The Foundations of Modern Political Thought*, vol. 2, p. 192.
72. M. Weber, *The Protestant Ethic and the Spirit of Capitalism*, trans. T. Parsons (London: Routledge, 1992).

Chapter 2   The Politicisation of Man in the Seventeenth Century: The Levellers and Hobbes

1. See P. Gregg, *Free Born John: A Biography of John Lilburne* (London: Phoenix Press, 1961).
2. D. Wootton, 'The Levellers', in J. Dunn ed., *Democracy: The Unfinished Journey* (Cambridge: Cambridge University Press, 1992), p. 71.
3. P. Zagorin, *A History of Political Thought in the English Revolution* (London: Routledge and Kegan Paul, 1954).
4. R. A. Gleissner, 'The Levellers and Natural Law: The Putney Debates of 1647', *The Journal of British Studies*, 20, 1 (1980), 64–89.
5. C. B. Macpherson, *The Political Theory of Possessive Individualism: Hobbes to Locke* (Oxford: Oxford University Press, 1962).

6. G. E. Aylmer ed., Introduction to *The Levellers and The English Revolution* (London: Thames & Hudson, 1975), pp. 13–14.
7. For Lilburne's biography, see Gregg, *Free-Born John*; H. N. Brailsford, *The Levellers in the Enlgish Revolution* (Stanford, CA: Stanford University Press, 1961), ch. VI. For Overton see Brailsford, *The Levellers*, ch. IV. For Walwyn, see Brailsford, *The Levellers*, ch. V.
8. W. Walwyn, 'Toleration Justified and Persecution Condemned', in A. Sharp ed., *The English Levellers* (Cambridge: Cambridge University Press, 1991).
9. The Westminster Assembly of Divines had been set up by the Long Parliament in 1643 in order to investigate how the Church of England was to be reformed. By the Solemn League and Covenant of the same year, in return for the Scots coming to the military aid of the English Parliament, which was at the time losing the war against Charles I, Parliament had given its assent to the preservation of the Church of Scotland and the reform of the Church of England 'according to the word of God and the example of the best reformed Churches'. For the Presbyterians in Parliament, this effectively meant that the English Church must be reformed along the same lines as the Church of Scotland, whereas the Independents, who received Leveller support, argued that this did not necessarily represent the 'best reformed' church. See Sharp, Introduction to *The English Levellers*, p. 13.
10. Walwyn, 'Toleration Justified', p. 15.
11. *Ibid.*, pp. 15–16.
12. *Ibid.*, pp. 17, 20.
13. *Ibid.*, p. 26.
14. J. Lilburne, 'The Freeman's Freedom Vindicated', in Sharp ed., *The English Levellers*, p. 31.
15. Wootton, 'The Levellers', p. 76.
16. *Ibid.*, p. 77.
17. Brailsford, *The Levellers*, pp. 117–18.
18. J. C. Davis, 'The Levellers and Christianity', in B. Manning ed., *Politics, Religion and the English Civil War* (Oxford: Clarendon Press, 1973), p. 227.
19. R. Overton and W. Walwyn, 'A Remonstrance of Many Thousand Citizens', in Sharp ed., *The English Levellers*, pp. 33–4.
20. Macpherson, *The Political Theory of Possessive Individualism*, p. 136.
21. *Ibid.*, p. 191.
22. D. Wootton, 'Leveller Democracy and the Puritan Revolution', in J. H. Burns ed., *The Cambridge History of Political Thought, 1450–1700* (Cambridge: Cambridge University Press, 1991), pp. 430–1.
23. *Ibid.*, p. 432; I. Hampsher-Monk, 'The Political Theory of the Levellers: Putney, Property, and Professor Macpherson', *Political Studies*, 24 (1976), 397–422.
24. R. Hanson, 'Democracy' in T. Ball, J. Farr and R. L. Hanson eds, *Political Innovation and Conceptual Change* (Cambridge: Cambridge University Press, 1989), pp. 74–5.
25. *Ibid.*
26. Macpherson, *The Political Theory of Possessive Individualism*, p. 158.
27. J. Locke, *Two Treatises of Government* (Cambridge: Cambridge University Press, 1988).

28. R. Overton, 'An Arrow Against All Tyrants', in Sharp ed., *The English Levellers*, p. 55.
29. *Ibid.*, pp. 55, 57.
30. See C. Hill, *Puritanism and Revolution: Studies in Interpretation of the English Revolution of the 17th Century* (London: Pimlico, 1972), p. 99.
31. See D. W. Petegorsky, *Left-Wing Democracy in the English Civil War: A Study of the Social Philosophy of Gerrard Winstanley* (New York: Haskell House, 1972).
32. J. Harrington, *The Commonwealth of Oceana and A System of Politics* (Cambridge: Cambridge University Press, 1992); J. G. A. Pocock, *The Ancient Constitution and the Feudal Law: A Study in English Historical Thought* (Bath: Cedric Chivers, 1957), ch. VI.
33. 'The Case of the Armie' in W. Haller and G. Davies eds, *The Leveller Tracts, 1647–1653* (Gloucester, Mass.: Peter Smith, 1964), p. 78. This text seems to have been written by John Wildman, an important Leveller agitator in the New Model Army.
34. J. Bodin, *On Sovereignty*, trans. J. H. Franklin (Cambridge: Cambridge University Press, 1992).
35. H. Grotius, *The Rights of War and Peace* (Indianapolis, IN: The Liberty Fund, 2005).
36. R. Overton and W. Walwyn, 'A Remonstrance of Many Thousand Citizens', in Sharpe ed., *The English Levellers*, pp. 44–5.
37. Pocock, *The Ancient Constitution*, p. 127.
38. R. B. Seaberg, 'The Norman Conquest and the Common Law: The Levellers and the Argument from Continuity', *The Historical Journal*, 24, 4 (1981), 791–806.
39. See Hill, *Puritanism and Revolution*, ch. 3.
40. A. C. Houston, ' "A Way of Settlement": The Levellers, Monopolies and the Public Interest', *History of Political Thought*, XIV, 3 (1993): 381–420, p. 385.
41. Sharp ed., *The English Levellers*, pp. 136–7.
42. Though as Sharp points out, article 18 was designed more than anything to defend the Levellers against the charge that they supported the levelling of property and estates. *Ibid.*, p. 137, n. 14.
43. *Ibid.*, p. 136.
44. *Ibid.*, p. 138.
45. Houston, ' "A Way of Settlement" ', p. 399.
46. *Ibid.*, p. 391.
47. Q. Skinner, *Visions of Politics, Volume III: Hobbes and Civil Science* (Cambridge: Cambridge University Press, 2002), pp. 267–70.
48. Though the precise status of the relationship between natural and civil science in Hobbes's texts is ambiguous. See N. Malcolm, *Aspects of Hobbes* (Oxford: Clarendon Press, 2002), ch. 5.
49. For biographies of Hobbes see A. P. Martinich, *Hobbes: A Biography* (Cambridge: Cambridge University Press,1999) and R. Tuck, *Hobbes* (Oxford: Oxford University Press, 1989).
50. Tuck, *Hobbes*, pp. 3–8.
51. R. Descartes, *Discourse on Method*, trans. D. A. Cress (Indianapolis, IN: Hackett, 1980).
52. Tuck, *Hobbes*, p. 18.
53. Skinner, *Visions of Politics, Volume III* , pp. 6–8.
54. T. Hobbes, *Man and Citizen* (Indianapolis, IN: Hackett, 1991).

55. T. Hobbes, *The Elements of Law, Natural and Politic* (London: Frank Cass & Co., 1969).
56. T. Hobbes, *Leviathan: The Matter, Forme and Power of a Common-Wealth, Ecclesiastical and Civill* (Cambridge: Cambridge University Press, 1996), p. 28.
57. *Ibid.*, pp. 32–3.
58. Skinner, *Visions of Politics, Volume III*, ch. 10; Martinich, *Hobbes*, ch. 8.
59. Skinner, *Visions of Politics, Volume III*, p. 288.
60. Martinich, *Hobbes*, pp. 161–2.
61. *Ibid.*, pp. 214–5.
62. Hobbes, *Leviathan*, pp. 479–80.
63. *Ibid.*, pp. 77–9.
64. *Ibid.*, pp. 79, 82–3.
65. *Ibid.*, p. 83.
66. A. P. Martinich, *The Two Gods of 'Leviathan': Thomas Hobbes on Religion and Politics* (Cambridge: Cambridge University Press, 1992).
67. Pocock, *Politics, Language and Time*, p. 201.
68. Hobbes, *Leviathan*, p. 480.
69. Pocock, *Politics, Language and Time*, p. 177.
70. Hobbes, *Leviathan*, p. 403.
71. *Ibid.*, pp. 343, 407
72. *Ibid.*, p. 404.
73. *Ibid.*, pp. 313–14.
74. *Ibid.*, pp. 267–8.
75. *Ibid.*, pp. 280, 283, 284.
76. *Ibid.*, pp. 37–8.
77. Malcolm, *Aspects of Hobbes*, pp. 30–1.
78. Hobbes, *Leviathan*, pp. 40–1.
79. *Ibid.*, p. 86.
80. *Ibid.*, pp. 88–9.
81. *Ibid.*, p. 90.
82. *Ibid.*, p. 91.
83. *Ibid.*, pp. 91, 93–4.
84. *Ibid.* p. 114.
85. *Ibid.*, p. 120.
86. *Ibid.*, p. 122.
87. Wolin, *Politics and Vision*, p. 255.
88. *Ibid.*, p. 256.
89. Skinner, *Visions of Politics, Volume III*, p. 233.
90. Hobbes, *Leviathan*, pp. 224–5. Macpherson claimed in *The Political Theory of Possessive Individualism* that much like Locke and the Levellers, Hobbes can be seen as a representative of the emerging bourgeoisie in seventeenth century England: the Leviathan state was intended to provide the conditions in which free market exchange could occur. Yet what Hobbes says in this passage and in several other places clearly repudiates this view. And as Keith Thomas shows, while Hobbes's thought certainly contains notions that might be thought 'bourgeois' in social character, these are interwoven with aristocratic and popular themes (K. Thomas, 'The Social Origin of Hobbes's Political Thought', in K. C. Brown ed., *Hobbes Studies* (Oxford: Basil Blackwell, 1965)).

91. Hobbes, *Leviathan*, p. 119.
92. M. Foucault, *The Order of Things: An Archaeology of the Human Sciences*, trans. A. M. Sheridan Smith (London: Routledge, 2002).

Chapter 3   Enlightenment, Law and Nature: Montesquieu and Rousseau

1. T. L. Pangle, *Montesquieu's Philosophy of Liberalism: A Commentary on the Spirit of the Laws* (Chicago, IL: University of Chicago Press, 1973).
2. F. L. Ford, *Robe and Sword: The Regrouping of the French Aristocracy after Louis XIV* (New York: Harper & Row, 1965).
3. L. Althusser, *Montesquieu, Rousseau and Marx: Politics and History*, trans. Ben Brewster (London: Verso, 1982).
4. E. Durkheim, *Montesquieu and Rousseau: Forerunners of Sociology*, trans. R. Manheim (Ann Arbor, MI: University of Michigan Press, 1965); R. Aron, *Main Currents of Sociological Thought*, vol. 1, trans. Richard Howard and Helen Weaver (London: Weidenfeld and Nicolson, 1965).
5. E. Cassirer, *The Philosophy of the Enlightenment* (Boston, MA: Beacon Press, 1955), p. 210; Aron, *Main Currents*, vol. 1, p. 14.
6. For Montesquieu's biography see R. Shackleton, *Montesquieu: A Critical Biography* (Oxford: Oxford University Press, 1961).
7. The *parlements* in medieval and early modern France had ostensibly judicial functions and most of their offices were held by members of the *noblesse de robe*. From the fifteenth century, they were often able to exercise effective legislative powers, though such rights had been increasingly curtailed by the monarch in the seventeenth century, particularly under the 'absolutist' reign of Louis XIV. Each *parlement* had an elected president and below him a small number of *présidents à mortier*, offices which were proprietary and held exclusively by members of the nobility.
8. J. N. Shklar, *Montesquieu* (Oxford: Oxford Univeristy Press, 1987), p. 8.
9. Montesquieu, *Persian Letters*, trans. C. J. Betts (London: Penguin, 1993), pp. 91–2.
10. *Ibid.*, p. 165.
11. Montesquieu, *The Spirit of the Laws*, trans. A. M. Cohler, B. C. Miller and H. S. Stone (Cambridge: Cambridge University Press, 1989), pp. 460–1; R. C. Bartlett, 'On the Politics of Faith and Reason: The Project of Enlightenment in Pierre Bayle and Montesquieu', *The Journal of Politics*, 63, 1 (2001), 1–28.
12. Montesquieu, *Persian Letters*, p. 53.
13. *Ibid.*, pp. 53–6.
14. *Ibid.*, pp. 56–8.
15. *Ibid.*, pp. 58–60.
16. *Ibid.*, pp. 60–1.
17. N. O. Keohane, *Philosophy and the State in France: The Renaissance to the Enlightenment* (Princeton, NJ: Princeton University Press, 1980), p. 419.
18. M. Richter ed., Introduction to *The Political Theory of Montesquieu* (Cambridge: Cambridge University Press, 1997), p. 41.
19. Shklar, *Montesquieu*, pp. 49, 50–1.

20. See D. Carrithers, 'Montesquieu's Philosophy of History', *Journal of the History of Ideas*, 47, 1 (1986), 61–80.
21. Montesquieu, *Considerations on the Causes of the Romans' Greatness and Decline*, in Richter, *The Political Theory of Montesquieu*, p. 164.
22. *Ibid.*, p. 160.
23. *Ibid.*, p. 161.
24. Althusser, *Montesquieu*, p. 20.
25. Montesquieu, *The Spirit of the Laws*, p. 6.
26. *Ibid.*, p. 9.
27. *Ibid.*, pp. 6–7.
28. *Ibid.*, p. 7.
29. *Ibid.*, p. 10.
30. *Ibid.*, p. 21.
31. *Ibid.*, p. 24.
32. *Ibid.*, p. 26.
33. *Ibid.*, p. 29.
34. *Ibid.*, pp. 155–6.
35. *Ibid.*, p. 57.
36. Shklar, *Montesquieu*, p. 82.
37. Montesquieu, *The Spirit of the Laws*, p. 36.
38. J. G. A. Pocock, *Virtue, Commerce and History* (Cambridge: Cambridge University Press, 1985), ch. 1.
39. Pangle, *Montesquieu's Philosophy of Liberalism*, p. 5.
40. Richter, Introduction to *The Political Theory of Montesquieu*, p. 85.
41. Aron, *Main Currents*, vol. 1, p. 29.
42. *Ibid.*, p. 13.
43. A. MacIntyre, *A Short History of Ethics* (London: Routledge, 2002), p. 174.; see also J. Plamenatz, *Man and Society*, vol. 1 (London: Longman, 1963), pp. 264, 282; Richter, Introduction to *The Political Theory of Montesquieu*, p. 32.
44. Althusser, *Montesquieu*, p. 40.
45. Aron, *Main Currents*, p. 50.
46. *Ibid.*, p. 51.
47. *Ibid.*, p. 52.
48. C. Pateman, *Participation and Democratic Theory* (Cambridge: Cambridge University Press, 1970).
49. J. Miller, *Rousseau: Dreamer of Democracy* (New Haven, CT: Yale University Press, 1984).
50. J. W. Chapman, *Rousseau: Totalitarian or Liberal?* (New York: AMS Press, 1968).
51. G. Della Volpe, *Rousseau and Marx and Other Writings*, trans. J. Fraser (London: Lawrence & Wishart, 1978); L. Colletti, *From Rousseau to Lenin*, trans. J. Merrington and J. White (London: Verso, 1972), pp. 143–93; A. Levine, *The General Will: Rousseau, Marx and Communism* (Cambridge: Cambridge University Press, 1993).
52. J. L. Talmon, *The Origins of Totalitarian Democracy* (London: Mercury Books, 1961), part 1, chapter 3; L. G. Crocker, *Rousseau's Social Contract: An Interpretive Essay* (Cleveland, OH: Case Western Reserve Press, 1968).
53. B. de Jouvenel, 'Rousseau's Theory of the Forms of Government' in M. Cranston and R. S. Peters eds, *Hobbes and Rousseau: A Collection of Critical*

Essays (New York: Anchor Books, 1972); J. N. Shklar, *Men and Citizens: A Study of Rousseau's Social Theory* (Cambridge: Cambridge University Press, 1969).

54. J. Starobinski, *Jean-Jacques Rousseau: La transparence et l'obstacle* (Paris: Éditions Gallimard, 1971); R. Fralin, *Rousseau and Representation: A Study of the Development of His Concept of Political Institutions* (New York: Columbia University Press, 1978).

55. For Rousseau's biography see Maurice Cranston's three volumes: *Jean Jacques: The Early Life and Work of Jean-Jacques Rousseau, 1712–54* (Chicago, IL: University of Chicago Press, 1991); *The Noble Savage: Jean-Jacques Rousseau, 1754–62* (London: Allen Lane, 1991); *The Solitary Self: Jean-Jacques Rousseau in Exile and Adversity* (London: Allen Lane, 1997).

56. Cranston, *Jean-Jacques*, p. 15.

57. *Ibid.*, pp. 63–4.

58. J.-J. Rousseau, *Discourse on the Sciences and Arts* (*First Discourse*) in V. Gourevitch ed. and trans., *The Discourses and Other Early Political Writings* (Cambridge: Cambridge University Press, 1997), p. 6.

59. *Ibid.*, pp. 11–12.

60. *Ibid.*, p. 16.

61. *Ibid.*, p. 27.

62. Shklar, *Men and Citizens*, p. 3.

63. L. Strauss, 'The Intention of Rousseau', in Cranston and Peters eds, *Hobbes and Rousseau*, p. 269.

64. J.-J. Rousseau, *Julie: or the New Heloise, Collected Writings of Rousseau*, vol. 6 (Hanover, New Hampshire: University Press of New England, 1997); *Emile*, trans. B. Foxley (London: Dent, 1974).

65. J.-J. Rousseau, *The Confessions* (London: Wordsworth, 1996), p. 378.

66. J.-J. Rousseau, *Discourse on the Origins and Foundations of Inequality Among Men* (*Second Discourse*), in Gourevitch ed., *The Discourses*, p. 132.

67. R. Derathé, *Jean-Jacques Rousseau et la science politique de son temps* (Paris: Presses Universitaires de France, 1950).

68. Rousseau, *Second Discourse*, p. 127.

69. *Ibid.*, pp. 138, 146.

70. *Ibid.*, p. 154.

71. *Ibid.*, p. 159.

72. *Ibid.*, p. 161.

73. *Ibid.*, pp. 173–5.

74. *Ibid.*, pp. 115–16.

75. J.-J. Rousseau, *Of the Social Contract*, in V. Gourevitch, ed. and trans., *The Social Contract and Other Later Political Writings* (Cambridge: Cambridge University Press, 1997), p. 50.

76. *Ibid.*, p. 53.

77. J.-J. Rousseau, *Considerations on the Government of Poland*, in Gourevitch ed., *The Social Contract*, p. 194.

78. Rousseau, *Of the Social Contract*, p. 114.

79. *Ibid.*, pp. 118–20.

80. *Ibid.*, pp. 68–72.

81. *Ibid.*, p. 93.

82. *Ibid.*, p. 150.
83. E. Cassirer, *The Question of Jean-Jacques Rousseau*, trans. P. Gay (New Haven, CT: Yale University Press, 1989).
84. J. Rawls, *A Theory of Justice* (Oxford: Oxford University Press, 1971).
85. R. Koselleck, *Critique and Crisis: Enlightenment and the Pathogenesis of Modern Society* (Cambridge, MA: The MIT Press, 1988).

Chapter 4   Conservatism and Radicalism: Burke and Paine

1. See A. Cobban, *Edmund Burke and the Revolt against the Eighteenth Century: A Study of the Political and Social Thinking of Burke, Wordsworth, Coleridge and Southey* (London: Allen and Unwin, 1960); M. Freeman, *Edmund Burke and the Critique of Political Radicalism* (Oxford: Basil Blackwell, 1980).
2. On Burke's 'ambivalent' conservatism, see I. Kramnick, *The Rage of Edmund Burke: Portrait of an Ambivalent Conservative* (New York: Basic Books, 1977).
3. J. Locke, *An Essay Concerning Human Understanding* (London: Penguin, 1997); D. Hume, *A Treatise of Human Nature* (London: Penguin, 1985).
4. E. Burke, *A Philosophical Enquiry into the Origin of our Ideas of the Sublime and Beautiful* (London: Routledge and Kegan Paul, 1958), pp. 39, 51.
5. Kramnick, *The Rage of Edmund Burke*, p. 34.
6. S. K. White, *Edmund Burke: Modernity, Politics, and Aesthetics* (Thousand Oaks, CA: Sage 1994), p. 5.
7. F. P. Lock, *Edmund Burke, Volume 1, 1730–1784* (Oxford: Clarendon Press, 1998), p. 122.
8. C. B. Macpherson, *Burke* (Oxford: Oxford University Press, 1980).
9. K. Marx, *Capital*, vol. 1 (London: Penguin,1990), pp. 925–6.
10. See L. Strauss, *Natural Right and History* (Chicago, IL: University of Chicago Press, 1953), ch. VI; P. Stanlis, *Edmund Burke and the Natural Law* (Ann Arbor, MI: University of Michigan Press, 1958).
11. E. Burke, 'Speech on American Taxation', in P. Langford ed., *The Writings and Speeches of Edmund Burke, Volume II: Party, Parliament and the American Crisis* (Oxford: Clarendon Press, 1981), p. 458.
12. See D. P. Fidler and J. M. Welsh eds, Introduction to *Empire and Community: Edmund Burke's Writings and Speeches on International Relations* (Boulder, CO: Westview Press, 1999).
13. Lock, *Edmund Burke*, p. 415.
14. Fidler and Welsh, Introduction to *Empire and Community*, p. 22.
15. *Ibid.*, pp. 18–29.
16. The trial would prove ultimately unsuccessful: Hastings was acquitted on all counts in 1795 against the background of increasing national and imperial chauvinism in the wake of the French Revolution.
17. E. Burke, 'Speech on Opening of Impeachment', in Fidler and Welsh eds, *Empire and Community*, pp. 206, 207.
18. *Ibid.*, pp. 221–2.
19. *Ibid.*, p. 225. Burke here includes the 'Grand Seignior' – the Sultan of the Ottoman Empire – in the order of European sovereigns.
20. *Ibid.*, p. 227.

21. *Ibid.*, pp. 223–4.
22. Stanlis, *Edmund Burke and the Natural Law*, p. 7.
23. *Ibid.*, p. xi.
24. Pocock, *Politics, Language and Time*, ch. 5.
25. See C. P. Courtney, *Montesquieu and Burke* (Oxford: Basil Blackwell, 1963).
26. D. Cameron, *The Social Thought of Rousseau and Burke: A Comparative Study* (London: Weidenfeld & Nicolson, 1973), p. 117.
27. Quoted in C. C. O'Brien, Introduction to E. Burke, *Reflections on the Revolution in France and on the Proceedings in Certain Societies in London Relative to that Event* (Harmondsworth: Penguin, 1986), p. 13.
28. Quoted in R. R. Fennessy, *Burke, Paine and the Rights of Man: A Difference of Political Opinion* (The Hague: Martinus Nijhoff, 1963), p. 100.
29. Burke, *Reflections*, p. 113.
30. *Ibid.*, p. 116.
31. *Ibid.*, pp. 119, 120.
32. *Ibid.*, pp. 194–5.
33. *Ibid.*, p. 151.
34. Kramnick, *The Rage of Edmund Burke*, p. 30.
35. Lock, *Edmund Burke*, p. 469.
36. W. Godwin, *An Enquiry Concerning Political Justice and Its Influence on Modern Morals and Happiness* (Harmondsworth: Penguin, 1976).
37. Strauss, *Natural Right and History*, p. 302.
38. E. Burke, 'First Letter on a Regicide Peace', in Fidler and Welsh eds, *Empire and Community*, pp. 315–6.
39. Strauss, *Natural Right and History*, p. 315.
40. *Ibid.*, p. 319.
41. Cameron, *The Social Thought of Rousseau and Burke*, p. 169.
42. J. Cheetham, *The Life of Thomas Paine* (New York: Southwick & Pelsue, 1809).
43. I. Kramnick, *Republicanism and Bourgeois Radicalism: Political Ideology in Eighteenth Century England and America* (Ithaca, NY: Cornell University Press, 1990).
44. G. Kates, 'From Liberalism to Radicalism: Tom Paine's *Rights of Man*', *Journal of the History of Ideas*, 50 (1989), 569–87.
45. E. Foner, *Tom Paine and Revolutionary America* (Oxford: Oxford University Press, 1976), pp. 6–7; J. Keane, *Tom Paine: A Political Life* (Boston, MA: Little Brown & Co., 1996), p. 43.
46. *Ibid.*, p. 61.
47. *Ibid.*, pp. 267–82.
48. Foner, *Tom Paine and Revolutionary America*, pp. 14–15; Keane, *Tom Paine*, pp. 73–5.
49. See B. Bailyn, *The Ideological Origins of the American Revolution* (Cambridge, MA: Harvard University Press, 1992), p. 132; S. Lynd, *Intellectual Origins of American Radicalism* (Cambridge, MA: Harvard University Press, 1982), pp. 25–6.
50. T. Paine, *The Rights of Man*, in B. Kuklick ed., *Thomas Paine: Political Writings* (Cambridge: Cambridge University Press, 2000), p. 164.
51. T. Paine, *Common Sense*, in Kuklick ed., *Thomas Paine: Political Writings*, p. 2.
52. *Ibid.*, p. 3.

53. Paine, *Common Sense*, pp. 4–5.
54. Keane, *Tom Paine*, p. 118.
55. Paine, *Common Sense*, p. 87.
56. *Ibid.*, p. 7.
57. Paine, *Common Sense*, pp. 9–11.
58. *Ibid.*, p. 13.
59. A. J. Ayer, *Thomas Paine* (Chicago: University of Chicago Press, 1988), p. 10.
60. Paine, *Common Sense*, p. 28.
61. Bailyn, *The Ideological Origins of the American Revolution*.
62. T. Paine, *The Crisis*, in Kuklick ed., *Thomas Paine: Political Writings*, p. 49.
63. See I. Rachum, *'Revolution': The Entrance of a New Word Into Western Political Discourse* (Lanham, MD.: University Press of America, 1999), p. 202.
64. J. Dunn, 'Revolution', in Ball et al. eds, *Political Innovation and Conceptual Change*, p. 337.
65. See Keane, *Tom Paine*, pp.168–80.
66. Paine, *The Rights of Man*, p. 66.
67. *Ibid.*, p. 62.
68. *Ibid.*, p. 63.
69. *Ibid.*, p. 86.
70. *Ibid.*, p. 165.
71. *Ibid.*, p. 167.
72. G. Claeys, *Thomas Paine: Social and Political Thought* (Boston, MA: Unwin Hyman, 1989), pp. 96–101.
73. Paine, *The Rights of Man*, pp. 232–49; 'Agrarian Justice', in Kuklick ed., *Thomas Paine: Political Writings*, pp. 320–38.
74. Paine, *The Rights of Man*, p. 239.
75. J. Mill, *Essay on Government*, in T. Ball ed., *James Mill: Political Writings* (Cambridge: Cambridge University Press, 1992).
76. Paine, *The Rights of Man*, p. 184.
77. T. Paine, *The Age of Reason*, in Kuklick ed., *Thomas Paine: Political Writings*, p. 317.
78. *Ibid*, pp. 302–3.
79. Keane, *Tom Paine*, pp. 368–9.
80. For example, he encouraged the French to invade England, depose George III, and make way for an English Republic. See Claeys, *Thomas Paine*, p. 33.
81. Paine, *The Age of Reason*, p. 336.
82. Fennessy, *Burke, Paine and the Rights of Man*, p. vii.

Chapter 5   Democracy and Revolution: Tocqueville and Marx

1. See A. Jardin, *Tocqueville: A Biography*, trans. L. Davis (Baltimore, Maryland: Johns Hopkins University Press, 1988), chs 1–3.
2. Quoted in L. Siedentop, *Tocqueville* (Oxford: Oxford University Press, 1994), p. 4.
3. *Ibid.*
4. *Ibid.*, pp. 22–3.

5. F. Furet, 'The Intellectual Origins of Tocqueville's Thought', *Tocqueville Review*, 7 (1986), 117–29, quote on pp. 121–2.

6. *Ibid.*, pp. 122–3.

7. A. Tocqueville, *Democracy in America* (vols. 1 and 2), trans. G. E. Bevan (London: Penguin, 2003), pp. 15–16, 23–4.

8. *Ibid.*, p. 41; for Tocqueville's views on slavery see S. Gershman, 'Alexis de Tocqueville and Slavery', *French Historical Studies*, 9, 3 (1976), 467–83.

9. Tocqueville, *Democracy in America*, p. 43.

10. Tocqueville recognised that there were important social differences between the south and the north that explained both the desire to retain slavery in the north and abolish it in the south, and more general tensions between these parts of the Union. Such differences were likely to result in conflict and threaten the survival of America as a united nation. See *ibid.*, pp. 440–4.

11. *Ibid.*, pp. 48–9.

12. *Ibid.*, pp. 50–4.

13. *Ibid.*, p. 55.

14. A. Tessitore, 'Alexis de Tocqueville on the Natural State of Religion in the Age of Democracy', *The Journal of Politics*, 64, 4: 1137–1152, (2002) p. 1114.

15. S. Wolin, *Tocqueville Between Two Worlds: The Making of a Political and Theoretical Life* (Princeton, NJ: Princeton University Press, 2001), p. 324.

16. Tocqueville, *Democracy in America*, p. 103.

17. *Ibid.*, pp. 185–9.

18. J. Madison, J. Jay and T. Hamilton, *The Federalist Papers* (Harmondsworth: Penguin, 1987), ch. 10.

19. Tocqueville, *Democracy in America*, p. 55.

20. *Ibid.*, pp. 645–8.

21. On the role of political associations, see *ibid.*, 219–27; the discussion of civil associations occurs in volume 2, *ibid.*, pp. 595–609.

22. *Ibid.*, p. 23.

23. *Ibid.*, p. 297.

24. *Ibid.*, p. 336.

25. *Ibid.*, p. 357.

26. *Ibid.*, pp. 365, 369.

27. *Ibid.*, p. 612.

28. Aron, *Main Currents of Sociological Thought*, p. 231.

29. Wolin, *Tocqueville Between Two Worlds*, p. 5.

30. Siedentop, *Tocqueville*, p. 112.

31. A. Tocqueville, *The Old Regime and the French Revolution*, trans. A. S. Kahan (Chicago, IL: University of Chicago Press, 1998), p. 88.

32. *Ibid.*, p. 106.

33. F. Furet and F. Mélonio, Introduction to Tocqueville, *The Old Regime*, p. 24.

34. Tocqueville, *The Old Regime*, p. 101.

35. *Ibid.*, p. 216.

36. The first kind of criticism can be found in the work of 'elite theorists' such as Vilfredo Pareto (V. Pareto, *The Mind and Society: A Treatise in General Sociology* (London: Jonathan Cape, 1935)). The second is mainly associated with authors in the Frankfurt School sympathetic to Marx's aspiration for human emancipation but profoundly disturbed by suggestions that it could be achieved by means of science and technology. See T. Adorno and

M. Horkheimer, *Dialectic of Enlightenment*, trans. J. Cumming (London: Verso, 1997).

37. Marx's father was much influenced by the most prominent of the Enlightenment philosophers such as Voltaire and Rousseau, and was part of the liberal movement in the Rhineland, perhaps the most 'enlightened' part of Germany in the early nineteenth century. But there were also important romantic and idealist influences on the young Marx. See D. McLellan, *Karl Marx: His Life and Thought* (London: Macmillan, 1973), ch. 1.

38. S. Avineri, *The Social and Political Thought of Karl Marx* (Cambridge: Cambridge University Press, 1968), p. 13.

39. In fact, this is a questionable interpretation of Hegel, who in a number of places, including the *Philosophy of Right*, appears as a liberal thinker urging reform of the monarchy and bureaucracy in line with a conception of popular sovereignty drawn from Kant and Rousseau. See S. Avineri, *Hegel's Theory of the Modern State* (Cambridge: Cambridge University Press, 1972).

40. G. W. F. Hegel, *Elements of the Philosophy of Right*, trans. H. B. Nisbet, (Cambridge: Cambridge University Press, 1991).

41. K. Marx, *Critique of Hegel's Philosophy of Right*, in J. O'Malley ed. and trans., *Karl Marx: Early Political Writings* (Cambridge: Cambridge University Press, 1994), p. 3.

42. *Ibid.*, p. 4.

43. Marx, *Critique of Hegel's Philosophy of Right*, p. 8.

44. *Ibid.*, pp. 9–10.

45. *Ibid.*, p. 11.

46. *Ibid.*, p. 16.

47. Avineri, *The Social and Political Thought of Karl Marx*, pp. 11, 14.

48. K. Marx, 'On the Jewish Question', in O' Malley, *Karl Marx: Early Political Writings*, p. 32.

49. *Ibid.*, p. 36.

50. *Ibid.*, p. 56.

51. The most persuasive advocate of the latter argument is L. Althusser, *For Marx*, trans. B. Brewster (London: Verso, 1990), chs 2 and 3.

52. K. Marx, 'Preface' to *A Contribution to the Critique of Political Economy*, in T. Carver ed. and trans., *Karl Marx: Later Political Writings* (Cambridge: Cambridge University Press, 1996), p. 160.

53. See G. A. Cohen, *Karl Marx's Theory of History: A Defence* (Oxford: Oxford University Press, 1978).

54. Marx, 'Preface', p. 159.

55. There is, however, no determinate relation between these interpretations and particular kinds of political practice. A form of technological determinism was accepted by social democratic theorists such as Karl Kautsky and Eduard Bernstein. This strain of Marxism would lead, more or less logically, to reformist parliamentary socialism in Western Europe. On the other hand, the Stalinist interpretation of Marxism as dialectical materialism (Diamat) also invoked a strong technological determinism. More radical forms of Marxism, such as those of Lenin and Mao, tended to emphasise the priority of the relations of production.

56. K. Marx and F. Engels, *Manifesto of the Communist Party*, in Carver ed., *Karl Marx: Later Political Writings*, p. 1.

57. K. Marx, *The Poverty of Philosophy* in O'Malley ed., *Karl Marx: Early Political Writings*, p. 183.
58. *Ibid.*, p. 184.
59. See K. S. Vincent, *Pierre-Joseph Proudhon and the Rise of Republican Socialism* (Oxford: Oxford University Press, 1984), chs 4–6.
60. Marx and Engels, *Manifesto*, p. 5.
61. *Ibid.*, p. 3.
62. *Ibid.*, pp. 19–20.
63. *Ibid.*, p. 20.
64. K. Marx, 'The Eighteenth Brumaire of Louis Bonaparte' in Carver ed., *Karl Marx: Later Political Writings*, p. 140.
65. *Ibid.*, pp. 56–7.
66. *Ibid.*, p. 67.
67. *Ibid.*, p. 116.
68. K. Marx, 'The Civil War in France', in Carver ed., *Karl Marx: Later Political Writings*, p. 183.
69. *Ibid.*, pp. 221–2.
70. S. Wolin, 'Reading Marx Politically', in J. R. Pennock and J. W. Chapman eds, *Marxism, Nomos XXVI* (New York: New York University Press, 1983).

Chapter 6   Crisis and Decision: Lenin and Schmitt

1. Koselleck, *Critique and Crisis*.
2. This was the case for the 'New Liberals' in Britain such as T. H. Green and J. A. Hobson (see M. Freeden, *The New Liberalism: An Ideology of Social Reform* (Oxford: Clarendon, 1978)). The English political pluralists in the early twentieth century, such as J. N. Figgis and Harold Laski sought out alternative forms of political organisation in the doctrine of associationalism (see P. Hirst ed., *The Pluralist Theory of the State: Selected Writings of G. D. H. Cole, J. N. Figgis and H. J. Laski* (London: Routledge, 1993)); non-Marxist socialists also sought out non-state forms of political organisation, for example G. D. H. Cole's guild socialism (G. D. H. Cole, *Guild Socialism Restated* (London: Parsons,1920)) and the revolutionary syndicalism of the French CGT (see J. Jennings, *Syndicalism in France: A Study of Ideas* (London: Macmillan,1990)).
3. J. Joll, *The Second International 1889–1914* (London: Routledge and Kegan Paul, 1975), p. 91.
4. S. Miller and H. Potthoff, *A History of German Social Democracy from 1848 to the Present*, trans. J. A. Underwood (Leamington Spa: Berg, 1986), pp. 240–2.
5. H. Tudor and J. M. Tudor eds, *Marxism and Social Democracy: The Revisionist Debate 1896–8* (Cambridge: Cambridge University Press, 1988), p. 14.
6. E. Bernstein, *The Preconditions of Socialism and the Tasks of Social Democracy*, trans. H. Tudor (Cambridge: Cambridge University Press, 1993), p. 84.
7. *Ibid.*, pp. 56–97.
8. G. Steenson, *Karl Kautsky, 1854–1938: Marxism in the Classical Years* (Pittsburgh, PA: University of Pittsburgh Press, 1991), p. 118.
9. *Ibid.*
10. V. I. Lenin, *The Development of Capitalism in Russia: Collected Works, Volume 3*, (Moscow: Progress Publishers, 1972), p. 67.

11. The RDSLP was founded in 1898 as a Marxist opposition to the Narodniks.
12. R. Service, *Lenin: A Biography* (London: Pan Macmillan, 2000), pp. 137–8.
13. V. I. Lenin, *What is to be Done?*, trans. J. Fineberg and G. Hanna (London: Penguin, 1988), pp. 120; 110.
14. G. Lukàcs, *Lenin: A Study in the Unity of his Thought* (London: New Left Books, 1977), p. 32.
15. See G. Lichtheim, *Marxism: An Historical and Critical Study* (London: Routledge & Kegan Paul, 1964), p. 337.
16. V. I. Lenin, *Two Tactics of Social-Democracy in the Democratic Revolution* in *Selected Works* (London: Lawrence & Wishart: 1969), p. 125.
17. *Ibid.*, p. 78.
18. N. Harding, *Lenin's Political Thought, Volume 2: Theory and Practice in the Socialist Revolution* (London: Macmillan, 1981), pp. 1–5, 41.
19. R. Hilferding, *Finance Capital*, trans. M. Watnick and S. Gordon (London: Routledge & Kegan Paul, 1981); N. Bukharin, *Imperialism and World Economy* (London: Merlin, 1972); J. A. Hobson , *Imperialism: A Study* (Ann Arbor, MI: University of Michigan Press, 1965).
20. V. I. Lenin, *Imperialism: The Highest Stage of Capitalism* in *Selected Works*, p. 181.
21. Harding, *Lenin's Political Thought*, pp. 60–3.
22. Lenin, *Imperialism*, pp. 257–8.
23. Harding, *Lenin's Political Thought*, pp. 63–4.
24. V. I. Lenin, *The State and Revolution* in *Selected Works*, p. 268.
25. *Ibid.*, p. 272.
26. *Ibid.*, p. 296.
27. *Ibid.*, pp. 280–1.
28. *Ibid.*, p. 301.
29. *Ibid.*, p. 322.
30. *Ibid.*, p. 328.
31. *Ibid.*, p. 329.
32. See P. Hirst, *Law, Socialism and Democracy* (London: Allen & Unwin, 1986), pp. 28–30.
33. Lenin, *The State and Revolution*, p. 329.
34. K. Kautsky, *The Dictatorship of the Proletariat* (Ann Arbor, MI: The University of Michigan Press, 1964), p. 31.
35. A. Gramsci, 'The Revolution Against *Capital*', in *Selections from Political Writings (1910–1920)*, trans. J. Matthews (London: Lawrence & Wishart, 1977).
36. V. I. Lenin, 'Better Fewer but Better' in *Selected Works*, pp. 700–12.
37. Harding, *Lenin's Political Thought*, p. 307.
38. As Jan-Werner Müller has claimed, Schmitt's writings also resemble Burke's in that they both wrote primarily as partisans, adopting an aesthetic style designed to 'persuade and even mobilize' rather than a scholarly one aimed toward the 'truth'. See J.-W. Müller, *A Dangerous Mind: Carl Schmitt in Post-War European Thought* (New Haven, CT: Yale University Press, 2003), p. 9.
39. Schmitt joined the Nazi party in 1933 and in November of that year, under the patronage of Herman Göring, became President of the Union of National Socialist Jurists. Schmitt justified (in retrospect) the Nazi's Enabling Act, applauded Hitler's actions on the Night of the Long Knives when Ernst Röhm and other leaders of the SA were executed extra-judicially, and began to pepper

his writings with anti-semitic sentiments, something that had been absent in his earlier works (indeed, Schmitt had a number of Jewish students and friends prior to 1933). In 1936 Schmitt was denounced in the SS publication, *Das Schwarze Korps*, for not advocating scientific racism and because of his pre-1933 Jewish contacts. After this Schmitt withdrew, apparently out of fear, from Nazi political organisations. In 1945 he was captured by the Allies, interned and interrogated ahead of the Nuremburg trials, but was not indicted. He was banned from teaching for life, though continued to publish on legal theory in West Germany up until his death. While after 1945 Schmitt made several, though somewhat cryptic, attempts to explain away his Nazi affiliations as a product of necessity and fear, like Martin Heidegger he at no point repudiated them or published any explicit condemnation of Nazi rule. For accounts of Schmitt's Nazi associations see J. W. Bendersky, *Carl Schmitt: Theorist for the Reich* (Princeton, NJ: Princeton University Press, 1983), part IV; G. Balakrishnan, *The Enemy: An Intellectual Portrait of Carl Schmitt* (London: Verso, 2000), pp. 177–208.

40. See J. L. Cohen and A. Arato, *Civil Society and Political Theory* (Cambridge, MA: The MIT Press, 1992), ch. 5; C. Mouffe, *The Return of the Political* (London: Verso, 1993); and the collection of essays in C. Mouffe ed., *The Challenge of Carl Schmitt* (London: Verso, 1999).
41. Balakrishnan, *The Enemy*, p. 28 and ch. 4.
42. The Catholic Centre Party participated in Weimar governments throughout this period.
43. Bendersky, *Carl Schmitt*, pp. 21–2.
44. C. Schmitt, *Political Romanticism*, trans. G. Oakes (Cambridge, MA: The MIT Press, 1986), p. 18–19.
45. *Ibid.*, p. 116.
46. G. Oakes, Translator's Introduction to Schmitt, *Political Romanticism*, p. xxxi.
47. Balakrishnan, *The Enemy*, p. 32; C. Schmitt, *Die Diktatur* (Duncker & Humblot: Berlin, 1994).
48. Quoted in Bendersky, *Carl Schmitt*, p. 32.
49. Quoted in Balakrishnan, *The Enemy*, p. 37.
50. C. Schmitt, *Roman Catholicism and Political Form*, trans. G. L. Ulmen (Westport, CT: Greenwood, 1996).
51. Bendersky, *Carl Schmitt*, p. 49.
52. C. Schmitt, *Political Theology: Four Chapters on the Concept of Sovereignty*, trans. G. Schwab (Chicago, IL: University of Chicago Press, 1985), p. 5.
53. T. B. Strong, Introduction to Schmitt, *Political Theology*, p. xii.
54. Schmitt, *Political Theology*, p. 6.
55. *Ibid.*, pp. 10, 13.
56. *Ibid.*, p. 15.
57. C. Thornhill, *Political Theory in Modern Germany: An Introduction* (Cambridge: Polity, 2000), p. 62.
58. Schmitt, *Political Theology*, pp. 19, 21.
59. *Ibid.*, p. 35.
60. C. Schmitt, *The Crisis of Parliamentary Democracy*, trans. E. Kennedy (Cambridge, MA: The MIT Press), p. 3.
61. *Ibid.*, pp. 5–6.
62. *Ibid.*, p. 35.

63. *Ibid.*, pp. 33–44.
64. *Ibid.*, p. 4.
65. This much can be gleaned from the text's original German title: *Die Geistesgeschichtliche Lage des heutigen Parlamentarismus*, which can be roughly translated as 'The Intellectual-Historical Position of Contemporary Parliamentarianism'. See Ellen Kennedy's Note on the Translation to *The Crisis of Parliamentary Democracy*, p. viii.
66. *Ibid.*, p. 9.
67. C. Schmitt, *The Concept of the Political*, trans. G. Schwab (Chicago, IL: University of Chicago Press, 1996).
68. Schmitt, *The Crisis of Parliamentary Democracy*, p. 11.
69. *Ibid.*, p. 29.
70. Schmitt, *The Concept of the Political*, p. 22.
71. E. Sieyes, *Qu'est-ce que le Tiers état?* (Geneva: Droz, 1970).
72. D. Kelly, 'Carl Schmitt's Political Theory of Representation', *Journal of the History of Ideas*, 65, 1 (2004), 113–34.
73. *Ibid.*, pp. 132–3.
74. Cohen and Arato, *Civil Society and Political Theory*, p. 232; P. Hirst, 'Carl Schmitt's Decisionism' in Mouffe ed., *The Challenge of Carl Schmitt*, p. 16.
75. L. Strauss, 'Notes on Carl Schmitt, *The Concept of the Political*', trans. J. H. Lomax in Schmitt, *The Concept of the Political*, p. 97.

Index

208 *Index*